THE

# SOCIAL CONDITION

AND

# EDUCATION OF THE PEOPLE

IN

# ENGLAND.

BY JOSEPH KAY, ESQ., M.A.,

OF TRINITY COLLEGE, CAMBRIDGE; BARRISTER AT LAW; AND LATE TRAVELLING BACHELOR OF THE UNIVERSITY OF CAMBRIDGE.

"The best way to help the Poor is to enable them to help themselves."
"The object of all Government should be the happiness of the *majority* of the people."

NEW YORK:
HARPER & BROTHERS, PUBLISHERS,
FRANKLIN SQUARE.
1864.

# PREFACE TO THE AMERICAN EDITION.

Some eighteen months passed in England, Scotland, and Ireland, during which time I visited all the great working centres, as well as many of the principal agricultural counties, convinced me that the great culture, refinement, and education of the higher classes of society were purchased at the cost of utter degradation and brutality of the lower orders. Having collected full evidence from official documents, from reports of various societies, and from the daily press, monthly and quarterly reviews, that my personal convictions were correct; I was prepared to lay before general American readers a picture of English life sufficiently revolting, to persuade the most skeptical among us, that our political institutions, notwithstanding all their faults, should be guarded as invaluable, if estimated by comparison with the result of the past thirty years' workings of Great Britain's internal policy.

Arriving in New York during the summer of 1861, I was staggered at assurances from my friends that our own cities had of late years gone from bad to worse, and that the same research here would teach me we had no superiority to boast of in comparison with London, Glasgow, Manchester, and Birmingham, and I confess that the surface of things appeared to confirm their statements. Meanwhile, however, two years have proved to my own satisfaction that the mass of the brutality in our sea-board cities is an imported article, and while we cannot hope to land our immigrants pure and undefiled, when we know the source whence they are derived, we can and do raise their children from the mire, and we know that our country is now rich in respectable citizens whose parents were part and parcel of Great Britain's brutality—citizens who would have been born to a dead weight of hopeless lifelong degradation had those parents never come to America.

The lesson would be valuable and instructive to us Americans now, but the bitter feeling that has grown up between the two nations, would colour American recitals of British sins, and the reader could not divest himself of the impression that they were prejudiced statements. It has appeared to me that a double value would follow the work if it was done by an English hand, and accordingly I republish some chapters of a book by Joseph Kay, Esq., as well known for his integrity as for the thorough character of his study of the subject in hand. Mr. Kay was commissioned by the Senate of Cambridge University, England, to travel through Western Europe, to examine the comparative social condition of the poorer classes of the different countries. His book was published in London in 1850, entitled "The Social Condition and Education of the People of Europe," but the chapters on England alone are sufficient for the lesson that we are seeking. They are a warning for us and hence useful, although abounding in facts that are not agreeable, and of a description that need be read only by men who have duties at the polls, and those few women who take an active part in raising or guarding our various institutions.

The result of Mr. Kay's labours is best stated in his own words. Summing up his estimate of the position of England's population, he says on the last page of this volume, "*The poor of England are more depressed, more pauperized, more numerous in comparison to the other classes, more irreligious, and very much worse educated than the poor of any other European nation, solely excepting Russia, Turkey, South Italy, Portugal, and Spain.* About 1850 there was some spasmodic attempt at correcting part of the horrors detailed by Mr. Kay, but the flood has increased immensely since, and we see how impossible it is to stop it under the present system of British Government. In 1861, before the cotton famine commenced, and with no war on their hands, England and Ireland's paupers had increased about five per cent. yearly since 1851; with three millions more population *less* land was under cultivation than in 1851, and one third of her people were fed from foreign sources; the expenses of the government of Great Britain, exclusive of India and the Colonies, amounted to a million and a quarter of our present currency per day (72 millions sterling for the year); while her thirty millions populations consumed yearly thirty-one million gallons of spirits, besides rivers of wine and oceans of beer!—So much for the anticipation of Mr. Kay when he wrote ten years before!

Most Republics educate all classes, it being universally assented to as the vital element of their existence. A despotic sovereign often finds his safety in a careful exercise of power as an arbitrator between labour and capital, securing education for the representatives of the former while he protects those of the latter in the possession of their wealth; but in a government founded on the *power of a class* we find results described by Mr. Kay. The English point at us Americans as the disciples of the God Dollar, but how is it in England? I assert that no man, *with or without title*, in our day, exercises great political influence in England without being a personal representative of *money-power* direct or indirect. The result of that system is now before the reader. Among the lower orders the grandfather, the father, and son, alike wallow in the mud, and will continue so to do as long as they see no path to wealth, and that path will never open to the masses of Great Britain during the maintenance of her present laws of primogeniture, of land-tenure and transfer, for the protection of the church, and finally that franchise permitting only one million of votes in her thirty millions population. Change these laws that are now maintained to sustain the power of the wealthy, awaken the ambition of the lower orders with hope of bettering their condition, and we shall soon see the people in England marching on in their rightful orders of merit as they do with us. The thirst for education quickly follows the parent's acquisition of a respectable share of worldly goods.

But, meanwhile, all this future of England does not concern us so materially as her present. She has done and is doing all she can to sustain her system and to destroy the merit that exists in our own. No stone has been left unturned by the ruling classes of England, during the past two years, to degrade the people of America in the estimation of European populations, and to secure the failure of our form of representative government. I know not which side, the North or the South, has more cause to complain of England since our war commenced. Yet I should suppose Mr. Kay's picture sufficiently coloured, to be distasteful to the mechanics and farmers of the Southern-States, when they are pondering over the feasibility of again becoming British Colonists; while we in the North may receive his writings as descriptions of dangers to be avoided in future when we again hear those calls from the other side of the Atlantic, "Brothers, Cousins, come and trade with us."*

I have an object in reprinting Mr. Kay's chapters. I believe he describes the results of a form of government directly opposed to the principles of our own. I hope these results will induce my countrymen to value our institutions, and persuade all men among us to perform their part in sustaining them in their integrity until the favorable moment arrives for such changes as it may be desirable to make.

Finally, I will not place these chapters before the Ameri-

* Those among us too young to remember how lamb-like the British Lion has become, at past points of our history, when their *trade* with us had been placed in jeopardy by his previous roarings, may find an example of her usual policy in her relations to-day with Brazil. The Brazilian Minister has retired from London in consequence of a most disgraceful outrage perpetrated by the British Government against his country. His departure was entirely unexpected by the London Cabinet, and the change of tone in Parliament and the British Press, on Brazilian affairs, the following twenty-four hours, was a strong reminder to us that Brazil was one of the best customers for English manufactures.

can reader, without a tribute to the healthy, vigorous tone of refinement and cultivation, of the larger portion of those very classes that rule Great Britain, and would rule all other countries if permitted. They are probably superior in those virtues to the corresponding classes here. We thought too, until two years ago, that their *honesty* was in the same category. They read to us so many lessons on Repudiation, slavery, and general moral degradation, that we accepted clever Sydney Smith as our proper Mentor. *We are wiser now than we were then!*

Must we accept the events of the past fortnight in New York as refutation of the foregoing remarks? No! They confirm my assertions in the most unmistakable manner. They prove the comparative virtue of our populations.

The Government attempted the most severe ordeal that individual liberty can be called on to sustain, without taking the slightest precaution against the probable opposition of the dregs of the population of our largest city and very centre of foreign immigration. How has the uprising of the scum of New York affected us? From one end of the country to the other we find a manifest condemnation of what occurred, and positive determination now to carry out the conscription in its integrity as a rebuke to the suspicion that mob-law is to rule us. Other disturbances, in other towns, may doubtless occur, but if there is one intention expressed in the Northern States at this period, it is to secure the final supremacy of law and order at all hazards.

S.——

NEWPORT, R. I., July 24, 1863.

THE SOCIAL CONDITION AND EDUCATION

OF THE

# PEOPLE IN ENGLAND.

## CHAPTER I.

### THE CONDITION OF THE POOR IN ENGLAND.

General survey of the social condition of the poor in the towns and in the country districts.—Channing's opinion.—Chateaubriand's opinion. The amount of pauperism in England and Wales.—The amount of crime in England and Wales, and the connection between ignorance and crime.—The comparative amount of crime in the manufacturing and in the rural districts.—The condition of the children in our towns.—The city mission.—The English Church, in its relation to the poor.—The necessity for more clergy, and for a different order of clergy, for our towns.—The alarming increase in the number of vagrants during the last four years.—The character and habits of vagrants.—The lodging-houses for vagrants in the towns.—The frightful scenes to be witnessed in these places.—The burial-clubs and the practice of infanticide.—The cellar-houses to be found in our towns —The condition of the houses of the poor in our towns and in our villages.—The causes of this miserable condition of our poor: 1. The neglect of the intellectual training of the poor—2. The neglect of their religious education—3. The Game Laws—4. The system of laws which affect land—5. The gin-palaces. —6. The want of classification in our prisons.

I SHALL endeavour to show, from reports published by the Government, and by individuals of the highest authority on such questions, what is the present social condition of the poorer classes in our towns and in our country districts; and I shall endeavour, as briefly as possible, to point out the causes of the condition disclosed by these reports.

The laws, to which the poorer classes of our country are subjected, are so singularly different to those, to which the poorer classes of foreign countries are subjected, that it is most interesting to inquire, what the results of the two systems up to this period have been.

Throughout the greater part of Western Europe and North America, *all* the children of the poorest classes are educated, *gratuitously*, much better than the children of our shopkeepers; in England and Wales more than half the poor cannot read and write, while the majority of the remainder know nothing of science, history, geography, music, or drawing, and very little of the Scripture history. Throughout the greater part of Western Europe and North America the *habits* of the children are most carefully disciplined from their sixth to their fourteenth year; in England and Wales, little or no attention is paid to this most important national duty. Throughout the greater part of Western Europe and North America there is free trade in land, and the peasants can always, by exercising industry, self-denial, and prudence, make themselves proprietors; in England and Wales it is impossible for a peasant to purchase a piece of land, and it is becoming more and more difficult every day for a peasant even to obtain the uncertain tenure of a farm. Throughout the greater part of Western Europe and North America the governments provide admirable and exceedingly cheap schools and colleges for the sons of the shopkeepers; in England and Wales the schools for the shopkeepers' children are generally very expensive and miserably poor. Throughout the greater part of Western Europe and North America all the men, who are above twenty-one years of age, have a voice in the election of their representatives; in England and Wales the vast majority of the poorer classes are not allowed to take any part in the election of the members of Parliament. Throughout Western Europe and North America the churches are very democratic in their constitution, and are suited to the religious necessities of the *poor;* in England and Wales the English Church is aristocratic in its constitution, and the people of many districts are suffering from the want of a class of religious ministers, who could sympathise better with their wants, and who could better understand the peculiar necessities of their position in life, than many of our clergy, educated in the habits of, and selected from, the richer classes of society, can do.

If then the poorer classes of our people are much less happy, prudent, and prosperous than the poorer classes of a great part of Western Europe, we surely ought not to marvel.

The great French Revolution of 1789, by uprooting the feudal system in the greater part of Europe, and by making it possible for any member of the poorer classes of society in that part of Europe, by the exercise of industry and temporary self-denial, to acquire land,—by introducing the system of peasant proprietors into nearly the whole of Western Europe—a system never before tried, as far as history informs us,—and by first originating the idea of educating *all* the children of the poorest classes of society,—has begun a work, which will change the whole face of society, by lessening the present disparity between the different ranks, by civilising the poorer classes, by stimulating their providence and industry, and by greatly diminishing the amount of pauperism, crime, and suffering. This great and new experiment has not had nearly time enough as yet, to show all that it is capable of effecting. That its results, so far, have been very good, I have shown in the previous chapter; but what its effects will be, when the schools and the system of education have been perfected, and when two or three successive generations have been successively subjected, to the combined influence of the division of property and of an efficient education, it is impossible to foretel.

But what is the actual social condition of our poorer classes? Let us first consider the social POSITION of the poor, and afterwards their condition, as resulting from the former.

In the great mercantile and manufacturing towns of our country, it is quite true that the poor man, if he be only intelligent enough to defer his marriage, and to avoid burdening himself during his youth with the expenses of a family, may improve his condition in life, and raise himself in the social scale. But we have done as little as we could possibly help doing to give him the necessary intelligence, and it is impossible for the poor to obtain it for themselves. It is impossible for the poor themselves to bear the expenses of educating their children efficiently, even if they were intelligent enough to understand the value of a sound education for their children; and it is necessary to give them intelligence, before we can make them willing to bear any part of the expense. It is impossible for the voluntary efforts of the benevolent part of a nation ever to suffice for the immense and expensive work of educating the nation; and it is monstrous to burden them alone with a tax, which ought to affect the careless and selfish, at least as much as the others. We have not one half as many schools as we require for the children of our towns; and of those we have established, a great number are either managed by teachers, who are utterly unequal to the proper discharge of their duties, or are so wretchedly arranged, furnished, and ventilated, or so miserably conducted and supported, as to make it certain, that in many cases, they are doing very great harm to the children who frequent them. Of these schools, many are nothing but poor "dame schools," conducted often in cellars or garrets by poor women, who know how to read, but who often know nothing else, who labour to eke out a miserable livelihood, by undertaking the daily management of the children of their neighbours, and who endeavour with a birch or a cane to frighten the children into learning by rote verses of the Scriptures. Are the doctrines so taught, likely to be remembered afterwards with pleasure, or are they likely to exercise any great influence upon those, who connect them with so many unhappy remembrances and associations? Thus, even in the towns, where a poor man might hope to better his condition in society, if he were only intelligent enough to desire to do so, and to know how to realise his desires, we have hitherto refused to grant him that education, without which, except in solitary cases of remarkable natural genius, he cannot even commence the enterprise.

But unsatisfactory as the *position* of our town labourers is, that of our peasants is still worse. Unless the farm labourer—the English peasant—will consent to tear himself from his relations, friends, and early associations, and either transplant himself into a town or into a distant colony, he has no chance of improving his condition in the world: as "The Times" newspaper has often urged with great force, and especially in some articles published in 1844, "*once a peasant in England, and the man must remain a peasant for ever.*"

Few in number and inefficient in character as the schools for our town labourers are, still fewer and still more inefficient are the schools for our peasants. Even of those, which are established, the greater part are managed by half-educated women; and even where men are employed as teachers, they are generally persons of little or no education, who, being fit for no occupation requiring skill or hard labour, were engaged or set up as schoolmasters, as if instructing youth were an employment requiring less skill and earnest application than any other. Hence it results—and I speak it with sorrow and with shame, but with not less confidence in the assertion—that our peasantry are more ignorant, more demoralised, less capable of helping themselves, and more pauperised, than those of any other country in Europe, if we except Russia, Turkey, South Italy, and some parts of the Austrian empire. I speak this with deliberation, and refer my readers to the account of the condition of the peasants in Europe which I have already given.

But even if this were an exaggeration, and if the peasantry were not so ignorant and neglected, as I have represented them to be, they would be still utterly unable, in the majority of cases, to improve their condition, owing to the thoroughly depressing social system to which we have subjected them; a system, which was first established in the feudal times, which has long since been abolished in Norway, Sweden, France, Prussia, Saxony, Bavaria, Nassau, Wirtemburg, Baden, Switzerland, Belgium, Holland, Denmark, Italy, and America, but which survives here, to keep in our remembrance the unjust, but cunningly devised institution, of which it formed one of the main supports—I mean the system of laws regulating the descent, entailing, conveyance, purchase, and settlement of landed property.

The peasant is deprived by these laws of all inducement to exercise present self-denial, to defer his marriage, to live within his income, or to lay by his savings, even if he were intelligent enough, to understand the benefit, he might derive from such a course of conduct under a well-devised social system. For what benefit would he derive from such a course? He could not purchase with his savings a plot of ground, for land very seldom sells in small quantities except for building purposes; and even if it did, the difficulty and expense of obtaining the necessary legal conveyances present an almost insurmountable barrier. He has but little chance of getting a farm. They are, in these days, generally so large, that they would require more capital than he could ever hope to save; and even could he save enough, the competition for them among the sons of farmers is so great when one does fall vacant, that a peasant generally stands no chance of success, even if he were to make an application.

What advantage, then, would the English peasant gain if he were to exercise self-denial, to defer his marriage, and to lay by his earnings? Excepting that he would have a fund in hand to use in case of unforeseen misfortune, his economy would be of no good to him, unless he either left his country life, associations, and friends, to enter a town and embark in commercial enterprise, for which his early associations, habits, and education totally unfit him, or unless he tore himself from home to seek a livelihood in some distant land. The English peasant is thus deprived of almost every motive to practise economy, and self-denial, beyond what suffices to provide his family with food and clothing. Once a peasant in England, and a man cannot hope that he, himself, or his children will ever be anything better, than a mere labourer for weekly hire.

This unhappy feature of an English peasant's life was most powerfully, and only too justly, depicted in those articles of "The Times" to which I have referred above. It was there shown that during the last half-century, everything has been done to deprive the peasant of any interest in the preservation of public order; of any wish to maintain the existing constitution of society; of all hope of raising himself in the world, or of improving his condition in life; of all attachment to his country; of all feelings of there really existing any community of interest between himself and the higher ranks of society; and of all consciousness that he has anything to lose by political changes; and that everything has been done to render him dissatisfied with his condition, envious of the richer classes, and discontented with the existing order of things.

The labourer has no longer any connection with the land which he cultivates; he has no stake in the country; he has nothing to lose, nothing to defend, and nothing to hope for. The word "cottage" has ceased to mean what it once meant—a small house surrounded by its little plot of land, which the inmate might cultivate as he pleased, for the support and gratification of his family and himself. The small freeholds have been long since bought up and merged in the great estates. Copyholds have become almost extinct, or have been purchased by the great landowners. The commons, upon which the villagers once had the right of pasturing cattle for their own use, and on which, too, the games and pastimes of the villages were held, have followed the same course: they are enclosed, and now form part of the possessions of the great landowners. Small holdings of every kind have, in like manner, almost entirely disappeared. Farms have gradually become larger and larger, and are now, in most parts of the country, far out of the peasant's reach, on account of their size, and of the amount of capital requisite to cultivate them. The gulf between the peasant and the next step in the social scale—the farmer—is widening and increasing day by day. The labourer is thus left without any chance of improving his condition. His position is one of hopeless and irremedial dependence. The workhouse stands near him, pointing out his dismal fate if he falls one step lower, and, like a grim scarecrow, warning him to betake himself to some more hospitable region, where he will find no middle-age institutions opposing his industrious efforts.

It is no answer to all this, to tell me, that in Ireland the peasants have small plots of land, and that their state is still worse than that of our own people. The poor Irish have no certainty of tenure, and may be turned out of their little plots, even into the bleak and inhospitable night, without a remedy. They feel no interest in good farming, or in the improvement of their little lands; nor dare they expend capital upon them, even when they have any to expend; for they know not when they may be turned adrift, or when they may be deprived of their plot and their improvements. Fifty years ago it was so, in all parts of Denmark, Germany, Switzerland, and France: the peasants were mere tenants-at-will, and cared as little about their plots as tenants-at-will always have done; and their state in those days was just as miserable, and they were just as discontented, as the peasants of Ireland now are. The governments of those countries were forced to enable the tenants to purchase their plots; and since then, the condition and character of the peasants, and of the little proprietors, have been immeasurably improved; and now, the most prudent, economical, and conservative members of those countries, are the peasants and proprietors of the soil.

To become the proprietor of a small portion of land, is the next step in the social scale, by which alone a peasant can hope to rise: to add gradually to the first acquired portion, are the after steps. But we, and we alone, of all the well governed European nations, have deprived our peasants of all possibility of climbing the first of these steps, and of ever raising himself above the peasant class.

The social position of the peasants of England and Wales has considerably deteriorated in the last half-century.

Fifty years ago, the farms were very much smaller, and much more numerous, than at present. They did not require nearly so much capital to work them. They were not, therefore, removed, nearly so far, out of the reach of the peasants as at present. Any peasant, who was industrious and careful enough to lay by sufficient to stock a small farm, might reasonably hope to become a tenant of one.

Besides this, there were many small farms in every county of England and Wales, which were either freeholds or copyholds, and which belonged to the farmers themselves. These small proprietors were the survivors of the old English yeomanry; men who felt that they had a stake in the country, and who were filled with that old English feeling of sturdy independence and honest self-reliance, which always distinguishes a class of small proprietors, and which peculiarly distinguished our old yeomanry. The small proprietors and farmers formed a class, to which the tenant farmers and the peasantry themselves looked up with feelings of interest and pride; knowing that the freehold farmers had sprung, in many cases, from the ranks of the peasantry themselves, and knowing, that if they exerted themselves with equal industry, prudence, and economy, they, too, might possibly rise to the same positions in the social scale.

But all this class of yeomanry farmers have disappeared; the small tenant farmers are likewise rapidly disappearing; the smaller farms are gradually being united, so as to form large ones; and the chasm between the peasant and the next step in the social scale is every day becoming wider.

A short time since, I was travelling among the farmers of the middle of Wales. One of them, an old man, with whom I spent some time at Aberystwith, speaking to me of the state of the country fifty years ago, said, "Times are greatly changed, sir, since I was a young man. In those days, Wales was very little visited by the English. In many parts, which are now the resorts of travellers, there were then no roads at all. Many people now living can remember, when the high roads through their villages were made, and when the first coach was started upon them.

"In those days, there were, all over the centre and north of Wales, great numbers of freehold farmers, who owned their own farms and cultivated them themselves. I can remember, that Aberystwith was in those days the summer resort and bathing-place of these yeomanry farmers. Great numbers used to come up to Aberystwith in the summer, each of them bringing his horse with him. I can show you the fields, where their horses used to be turned out to grass in the evenings. Many of the farmers used to spend a few weeks every year in this manner, in order to meet one another and to converse together.

"But since that time, all this class of yeomanry farmers has entirely disappeared. Owing to different causes, the larger landed proprietors have, on all hands, diligently bought up all the smaller farms, have united them to their great estates, and have included them in their settlements.

"All the farmers at the present day hold their farms, at the will of their landlords, or rather at the will of the agents of their landlords, for it is very seldom, that a farmer is allowed to treat directly with his landlord. There are often, as many as three and four subagents, with one of the latter of whom the farmer is often obliged to treat, and on whose will the farmer depends for the continuance of his possession.

"The agents are almost absolute; for they know that nothing is easier, than to let a farm, when it falls vacant. There are always plenty of applicants, who will bid against one another, until one wonders, how the last bidder can expect to make a profit from his bargain. Indeed, the agents are often obliged to choose a lower bidder, rather than one of the higher; because they know that the highest bidder could not make it pay, and would soon be in the workhouse, after having, most probably, defrauded his landlord of part of his rental.

"You may imagine, what the powers of an agent in this country are, and what the extortion, they sometimes practise, is, and how helpless the farmers are, when I assure you, that I know, that a gentleman, who owns a great estate near Aberystwith, and who has always been an excellent landlord, and has managed his estates himself, was only a short time since offered, for the agency and direction of his estates, 2000*l.* a-year, and guarantees, in addition, for the receipt of as great a rental as his present one!

"The farmers are the creatures of the agents, are at their mercy absolutely, seldom transact directly with the landlords, and have very seldom any security of tenure."

This account was corroborated by other Welsh farmers, with whom I conversed. One told me, that he knew a case, where the landlord had a steward, A, who had a subagent, B, who had a subagent, C, and that the farmers on the part of the estate, which was managed by C, were entirely at his beck, and subjected absolutely to his management.

Another told me, that the competition for vacant farms was disastrous and ridiculous in the extreme. He said, that whenever one fell vacant, the peasants, feeling that it was their only chance of rising in the world, and that they could not be much worse off than at present, were willing to offer any rent for it, so that they might but try to farm it.

Such is the system, for which they have exchanged the old one of small farms and yeomanry farmers.

In Westmoreland and Cumberland there have been, from ancient times to within the last few years, a great number of small estates, varying in size from five to forty acres, and belonging to peasants and small farmers. These little estates and the houses upon them have always been distinguished by their neatness, good cultivation, and general prosperity. The peasantry of these parts of our island have always been remarkable for their intelligence, their sobriety, their activity, and their contentment.

I was in Westmoreland for some time, during the autumn of 1849, and I took great pains to discover the present condition of the last survivors of these small proprietors. I cannot describe it better, than by giving the words of a gentleman of great intelligence and of Conservative principles, who is engaged in the management of some of the largest estates in Westmoreland and Cumberland. He resides in that part of the country, and is interested in opposing the system of peasant proprietors. There are obvious reasons, why I cannot mention this gentleman's name. He said to me:—

"The greater proprietors in this part of the country are buying up all the land they can get hold of, and including it in their settlements. Whenever one of the small estates is put up for sale, the great proprietors outbid the peasants, and purchase it at all costs. The consequence is, that for some time past, the number of the small estates held by the peasants, has been rapidly diminishing in all parts of the country. In a short time, none of them will remain, but all will be merged in the great estates. While this has been going on, the great landowners have been also increasing very considerably the size of the farms. The smaller farms have been united, in order to form great farms out of them. So that, not only is it becoming more and more difficult every day for a peasant to *buy* land in this part of the country, but it is also gradually becoming impossible for him to obtain even a leasehold farm. The consequence is, that the peasant's position, instead of being what it once was, one of hope, is gradually becoming one of despair. Unless a peasant emigrates, there is now no chance for him. It is impossible for him to rise above the peasant class.

"All this I believe to be a great evil. I have lived all my life among these people, and I believe, that the old system of small estates was one, which did the greatest possible good to the peasants. It stimulated them to exertion, self-denial, and sobriety, by affording them a chance of obtaining a farm of their own; and when they had obtained one, it made them interested in the careful cultivation of the soil, in the preservation of public order, and in the general prosperity of the country.

"Besides all this, the situation and duties of a small landowner were in themselves an excellent education to the small proprietor. He had many things to do and think of, with reference to county rates, poor-rates, police, markets, agriculture, the effects of national proceedings on prices and on taxation, and the seasons. All this was as interesting to the peasants, and as improving to them, as it is to our country gentlemen, and it made up, in great measure, for the want of good schools and good instruction. But all the effect of this education of circumstance is now being done away. The situation of the peasant is becoming one void of hope, and of all improving influences whatever."

The rapidity with which the small freeholds have been merged in the larger throughout the country, is very singular, and is a very decisive proof of the deterioration of the social position of the farmers and peasants, especially when it is borne in mind, that, whilst the numbers of the small freeholds and farms have so much diminished, the numbers of the population have much more than doubled. In order that the peasant class should be in even as good a social condition now, as they were in some seventy years ago, the numbers of small freeholds, which were within their reach in those days, ought to have doubled, as the number of the peasants has done. But what has been the course of events?

In the year 1770, there were, it is said, in England alone, 250,000 freehold estates in the hands of 250,000 different families. In the year 1815, at the close of the revolutionary war, the whole of the lands of England were concentrated in the hands of only 32,000 proprietors.* So that, in fact, since 1770, the numbers of the freeholds have been diminishing, at a much greater ratio, than that at which the numbers of the population have been during the same time increasing.

As the Rev. Henry Worsley says, "the labourer's hope of rising in the world is a forlorn one. There is no graduated ascent up which the hardy aspirant may toil step by step with patient drudgery. Several rounds in the ladder are broken away and gone. A farm of some hundred acres, requiring for their due cultivation a large capital, would be a day-dream too gaudy ever to mix itself with the visions of the most ambitious labourer, earning, on an average, probably less than nine shillings a-week. The agricultural workman's horizon is bounded by the high red-brick walls of the union house: his virtual marriage settlement can only point to such a refuge if troubles arise: his old age may there have to seek its last shelter."†

And yet, notwithstanding that the peasants are deprived of any chance of obtaining land or a leasehold farm, it appears, from the statistics given by Mr. Porter, that in 1827, there were about 15,000,000 of statute

* The Rev. H. Worsley's Essay on Juvenile Depravity, p. 53.

† Essay on Juvenile Depravity, p. 54.

acres of land in the British islands, which were capable of being cultivated, but which were lying uncultivated.

In 1847 it appears, according to the same well known writer, that there were still remaining about 11,300,000 acres wholly uncultivated, all of which were capable of cultivation. Now, when we consider this fact in conjunction with the wretched state of our peasantry, it does appear somewhat unreasonable, that such a system should be suffered to exist.

What is the effect of all this? Why, that the millions in England and Wales fancy that they have nothing to lose and everything to gain by political changes, and that, instead of our institutions being based upon the conservatism of the masses, they are only based upon the conservatism of the few. So that we have really much more reason than any other country to dread the growth of democracy.

Besides the depressing and demoralising effect of our system of monopoly of land upon the peasants; another great evil which results from our English system of great and few farms, and great and few estates, is, that it drives vast numbers of the young peasants, and of the younger sons of farmers, into the manufacturing towns, and by overstocking their labour markets, renders it more and more difficult every year, for the small shopkeepers and labourers of these towns, to make a livelihood amid the ever-increasing competition around them.

Let us look this evil more fully in the face. An active and enterprising son of a farmer or peasant sees, that there is no chance of his ever getting a farm in his native parish, or of his ever purchasing or even renting a small plot of land, or of his ever rising above the rank of a farm labourer earning eight or nine shillings a-week. The only opening left for such a young man, if he would climb above the lowest rank in the social scale—the peasant's position—is, either to go and seek his fortune in one of our colonies, or in one of our towns. There are many such young men, who cannot persuade themselves to break off the ties of home and kindred, and to leave their native country, but who feel compelled to leave their native villages. All such crowd to the great manufacturing towns of England. The peasants go, to seek labour as operatives or artisans; the sons of the farmers go, to endeavour to establish shops or taverns. What is the result? The labour market in the manufacturing towns is constantly overstocked; the labourers and shopkeepers find new and eager competitors constantly added to the list; competition in the towns is rendered unnaturally intense, profits and wages are both unnaturally reduced; the town workhouses and the town gaols are crowded with inmates; the inhabitants are overburdened with rates, and the towns swarm with paupers and misery.

I know not what others may think, but to me it is a sad and grievous spectacle, to see the enormous amount of vice and degraded misery which our towns exhibit, and then to think, that we are doing all we can to foster and stimulate the growth and extension of this state of things, by that system of laws, which drives so many of the peasants of both England and Ireland to the towns, and increases the already vast mass of misery by so doing.

I speak with deliberation when I say, that I know no spectacle so degraded, and if I may be allowed to use a strong word, so horrible, as the back streets and suburbs of English and Irish towns, with their filthy inhabitants; with their crowds of half-clad, filthy, and degraded children, playing in the dirty kennels; with their numerous gin-palaces, filled with people, whose hands and faces show how their flesh is, so to speak, impregnated with spirituous liquors—the only solaces, poor creatures, that they have!—and with poor young girls, whom a want of religious training in their infancy, and misery, has driven to the most degraded and pitiful of all pursuits.

Go to London, reader, or to Manchester, or Liverpool, or Preston, or Norwich, or Nottingham, or York, or Chester, or to any other of our large and increasing manufacturing or commercial towns, and see if my description is exaggerated. An hour's walk in any one will suffice to convince you of its sad truth. And are you then willing to aid in stimulating this system?

Greater evils never threatened civilisation and religion, than the great cities which have been springing into existence within the last one hundred years. If we would save civilisation, religion, and the morality and happiness of our people, we must reform our towns. And one great step towards that end will be to do away with those causes, which drive so many of our agricultural population into them.

Dr. Channing, in his "Duty of Free States," says:—

"To a man who looks with sympathy and brotherly regard on the mass of the people, who is chiefly interested in the 'lower classes,' England must present much that is repulsive. . . . . The condition of the lower classes at the present moment is a mournful comment on English institutions and civilisation. The multitude are depressed in that country to a degree of ignorance, want, and misery, which must touch every heart not made of stone. In the civilised world there are few sadder spectacles than the present contrast in Great Britain of unbounded wealth and luxury, with the starvation of thousands and tens of thousands, crowded into cellars and dens, without ventilation or light, compared with which the wigwam of the Indian is a palace. Misery, famine, brutal degradation, in the neighbourhood and presence of stately mansions, which ring with gaiety, and dazzle with pomp and unbounded profusion, shock us as no other wretchedness does. . . . . It is a striking fact, that the private charity of England, though almost incredible, makes little impression on this mass of misery; thus teaching the rich and titled, 'to be just before they are generous,' and not to look to private munificence as a remedy for the evils of selfish institutions."

Listen to what the great French writer, the Viscount Chateaubriand, says in his "Essays on English Literature," Paris, 1838. "Society such as it now is in England will not continue to endure. According as education makes its way among the people, the cancerous sore which has gnawed social order since the beginning of the world, a sore that causes all the suffering and popular discontent that we see, will be detected. The too great inequality of ranks and fortunes was borne with so long as it was concealed, on the one hand by ignorance, and, on the other, by the factitious organisation of large towns; but, so soon as that inequality becomes generally apparent, it will receive its death-blow. Reconstruct if you can aristocratic fictions. Try to persuade the poor man, when he shall be able to read—him to whom knowledge is daily supplied by the press, scattering its lights in every town and village, —try to persuade the individual possessing the same information and intelligence as yourselves, that he ought to submit to all sorts of privations, while some one, his neighbour, enjoys, without labour, all the superfluities of life, and your efforts will be fruitless. Do not expect from the masses, virtues, which are beyond the force of humanity."

But let us examine the statistics and facts which show the condition of our poor.

First, with regard to their *pauperism.*

Before the enactment of the new poor law, we were expending *annually* between 6,000,000*l.* and 7,000,000*l.* for the relief of abject pauperism in England and Wales alone. Since the enacting of the new poor law, we have been expending in the same cause between 4,000,000*l.* and 5,000,000*l.* per annum; and, from Lady-Day, 1835, to Lady-Day, 1848—or, in 17 years—we expended on the same object, 87,505,826*l.*, without reckoning the vast sums, which have been sunk in the administration of the poor law in the different unions, or the immense sums, which have been given away annually by charitable individuals and charitable societies. All this, be it remembered, has been required to alleviate the miserable condition of our labouring population, and to keep crowds from actual starvation. Their independence is destroyed: they cannot live unless they depend upon the charity of the higher classes.

The enormous sums which—exclusive of all charitable donations—have been annually expended by the union boards, in alleviating the sufferings of our labourers since 1832, are given in the accompanying table.

Amount expended in the Relief and Maintenance of the Poor in England and Wales, exclusive of all the immense Expenditure of Poor Law Administration in the Unions and Parishes.

| Years. | £ |
|---|---|
| 1832 | 7,036,969 |

| Years. | £ |
|---|---|
| 1833 | 6,790,800 |
| 1834 | 6,317,255 |
| 1835 | 5,526,418 |
| 1836 | 4,717,630 |
| 1837 | 4,044,741 |
| 1838 | 4,123,604 |
| 1839 | 4,406,907 |
| 1840 | 4,576,965 |
| 1841 | 4,760,929 |
| 1842 | 4,911,498 |
| 1843 | 5,208,027 |
| 1844 | 4,976,093 |
| 1845 | 5,039,703 |
| 1846 | 4,954,204 |
| 1847 | 4,678,110 |
| 1848 | 5,435,973 |

Now, without proceeding further, it surely cannot, and will not be contended, that a labouring population, which requires such an expenditure as this—and that, too, in addition to the vast amount of charitable donations devoted annually to the same purpose—to keep part of it from actual starvation, can be in a very happy, prosperous, or satisfactory condition! What country is there in Europe, or in the world, where such an expenditure is found to be necessary to save the labourers from starvation? What other country in Europe, or in the world, is obliged to keep up such a poor-law system, and for such a purpose? What other country in the world is there, where private individuals are obliged to dole out so many charitable donations for the same unhappy purpose? Why should not our peasants be at least as well able to depend on their own exertions for subsistence, as the peasants of Germany, Switzerland, Italy, or the provinces of France? Why should not our peasants be as well able to dispense with charitable donations, and as much above receiving them, as our middle classes?

Why is it that the Prussian, Saxon, Swiss, and French peasantry do not require nearly so much public relief like this? Because they have been taught and enabled to help themselves, and because they are assisted, and not hindered, by legislation in their efforts to work out their own independence.

In 1848, in addition to the hundreds of thousands assisted by charitable individuals, 1,876,541 paupers were relieved by boards of guardians, or about one person out of every EIGHT of the population was a pauper in 1848. Let every one consider the astounding nature of this fact, and let him remember, that nothing like it exists in Germany, Switzerland, or France.

The numbers of paupers relieved each year since 1840, by the boards of guardians, in England and Wales, have been as follows:—

| Years. | Number of Paupers relieved in England and Wales. |
|---|---|
| 1840 | 1,199,529 |
| 1841 | 1,299,048 |
| 1842 | 1,427,187 |
| 1843 | 1,539,490 |
| 1844 | 1,477,561 |
| 1845 | 1,470,970 |
| 1846 | 1,332,089 |
| 1847 | 1,721,350 |
| 1848 | 1,876,541 |

In each of the above years there have been the above-mentioned vast numbers of paupers, who, *exclusive of all those assisted by charitable individuals*, have been unable to exist in England and Wales, without begging assistance from the guardians. And to these have to be added also, all the beggars and vagrants, who crowd our streets and roads, and of whom I shall say more hereafter, and all those, who are in the receipt of alms from their richer neighbours, but who do not like to apply to boards of guardians for relief.

More than 2,000,000 of people were kept from starvation in England and Wales in the year 1848 by relief doled out to them from public or from private sources; so vast is the amount of misery and social degradation among the poor of England and Wales, and so great the destitution to which they are reduced!

Look, too, at the statistics, which show the frightfully low moral condition of our labouring classes, and the connexion which is found to exist between the ignorance of the labourers and their criminality.

The following table shows the number and the character of the education of all those, who were committed for crime in England and Wales, from 1836 to 1847.

| Years. | Total No. of Persons committed for Crime. | No. who could neither read nor write. | | No. who could read only, or read and write imperfectly. | | No. who could read and write well. | | No. who had received superior Education. | | No. whose Instruction was not ascertained. | |
|---|---|---|---|---|---|---|---|---|---|---|---|
| | | Males. | Fem. | Males. | Fem. | Males. | Fem. | Males. | Fem. | Males. | Fem |
| 1836 | 20,984 | 5598 | 1435 | 8,968 | 2015 | 2016 | 199 | 176 | 15 | 490 | 72 |
| 1837 | 23,672 | 6684 | 1780 | 10,147 | 2151 | 2057 | 177 | 98 | 3 | 421 | 94 |
| 1838 | 23,094 | 6342 | 1601 | 10,008 | 2326 | 2051 | 206 | 74 | 5 | 430 | 51 |
| 1839 | 24,443 | 6487 | 1709 | 10,523 | 2548 | 2201 | 261 | 74 | 4 | 546 | 90 |
| 1840 | 27,187 | 7145 | 1918 | 12,151 | 2958 | 2038 | 215 | 100 | 1 | 541 | 125 |
| 1841 | 27,760 | 7312 | 1908 | 12,742 | 2990 | 1839 | 214 | 126 | 0 | 541 | 88 |
| 1842 | 31,309 | 8162 | 1959 | 14,983 | 3277 | 1890 | 231 | 65 | 4 | 633 | 98 |
| 1843 | 29,591 | 7344 | 1829 | 13,892 | 3158 | 2127 | 244 | 134 | 6 | 754 | 108 |
| 1844 | 26,542 | 6266 | 1635 | 12,745 | 2990 | 1892 | 264 | 109 | 2 | 537 | 102 |
| 1845 | 24,303 | 5698 | 1740 | 11,215 | 2964 | 1859 | 178 | 86 | 3 | 483 | 77 |
| *1846 | 25,107 | 7698 | | 14,941 | | 1936 | | 85 | | 446 | |
| *1847 | 28,833 | 95[illegible] | | 16,980 | | 2246 | | 81 | | 475 | |
| 1848 | 30,349 | 7530 | 2161 | 13,950 | 3161 | 2634 | 350 | 76 | 5 | 396 | 86 |

It shows how fearfully crime is increasing among our

poor, and how clear and undeniable it is, THAT THE GREATEST PART OF THEIR IMMORALITY IS THE DIRECT AND IMMEDIATE EFFECT OF THE UTTER NEGLECT OF THEIR EDUCATION.

Mr. Porter, from whose admirable work, "The Progress of the Nation," I have extracted this table, in commenting upon it, says :—

"The most cursory glance at these figures must carry conviction to every mind, that instruction has power to restrain men from the commission of crimes—of such a nature, at least, as will bring them before a bar of justice. If we class together those, who can neither read nor write, and those, who have acquired only an imperfect acquaintance with those elementary branches of knowledge—the scaffolding merely for the erection of the moral edifice—we find, that in the ten years comprised in the returns, there were, out of 252,544 persons committed, and whose degrees of instruction were ascertained, the great proportion of 229,300, or more than 90 in 100, *uninstructed* persons; while *only* 1085 *persons had enjoyed the advantages of instruction beyond the elementary degree*, and only 22,159 had mastered, without advancing beyond, the acts of reading and writing.

"These numbers embrace both males and females. If we examine the returns, with the view of determining the moral influence of instruction upon females, we find that among the 252,544 persons above described, there were 47,113 females, 18·65 per cent. of the whole; but when we inquire, in what proportions females are divided among the different classes as respects instruction, we see, that among the 220,300 uninstructed persons, there

* I have not by me the full analysis of the returns of these two years.

were 44,881 females, or 19·57 per cent.; while among 22,159 who could read and write well, there were but 2,189 females, or 9·88 per cent.; and among the better instructed 1085 persons, there were only 43 females, or 3·96 per cent. The proportions in each 10,000 persons accused that were furnished by the males and females of the social classes, were as follows:—

"In each 10,000 persons committed for crime there were—

| | Males. | Females. | Total. |
|---|---|---|---|
| Of— | | | |
| Those wholly uninstructed, and those who could read only, or read and write imperfectly - | 7303 | 1776 | 9079 |
| Those who could read and write well - - - - - | 791 | 86 | 877 |
| Those superiorly instructed - | 42 | 2 | 44 |
| | 8136 | 1864 | 10,000 |

"Of the 43 instructed females accused of crimes throughout England and Wales in ten years, the large proportion of 15 belong to the first year of the series. Of these, 12 were accused of simple larceny, 1 for receiving stolen goods, 1 for fraud, and 1 for perjury. *There were, consequently, in nine years, only twenty-eight educated females brought to the bar of criminal justice;* viz. 3 in 1837, 5 in 1838, 4 in 1839, only 1 in 1840, and in 1841 not one educated female was committed for trial among 7,673,633 females then living in that part of the United Kingdom. In the remaining four years the numbers were; in 1842, 4; 1843, 6; 1844, 2; and in 1845, 3.

"How much the internal peace of the country may be affected, by the prevalence of ignorance or the spread of knowledge, may be reasonably inferred from the state of instruction of persons tried at the special commission in October, 1842, arising out of the then recent rising in the manufacturing districts. This is shown by the following table:—

| | Cheshire. | Lancashire. | Staffordshire. | Total | Centesimal Proportion. |
|---|---|---|---|---|---|
| Neither read nor write - - | 26 | 47 | 81 | 154 | 27·16 |
| Read only - - | 30 | 26 | 99 | 155 | 27·34 |
| Read and write imperfectly - - | 28 | 97 | 59 | 184 | 32·45 |
| Read and write well | 9 | 28 | 36 | 73 | 12·87 |
| Superior Instruction | - - | - - | 1 | 1 | 0·18 |
| | 93 | 198 | 276 | 567 | 100·00 |

"In 1840, there were 100 males and 1 female who had received instruction beyond reading and writing, committed for trial in the various counties of England and Wales. Of this number, only 59 (58 males and *one* female) were convicted, being under 59 per cent. of the number accused, while the *convictions* generally in that year exceeded 73 per cent. of the *accused*.

"In twenty counties of England and Wales, with a population of 8,724,338 persons, there were convicted *fifty-nine* instructed persons, or 1 to every 147,870 inhabitants; while the remaining thirty-two counties, with a population of 7,182,491, *had not furnished one convict who had received more than the earliest elements of instruction.* It is even more worthy of remark, that Middlesex, the metropolitan county, with its 1,576,616 inhabitants, among whom the proportion of instructed persons is at least equal to that in any other county, *did not furnish one educated convict*, a fact which, considering the diversity, conditions, and occupations, and the amount of temptations that assail its inhabitants, would be most difficult to believe upon any testimony less certain than that of official returns.

"In 1841, in fifteen English counties, with a population of 9,569,064, there were convicted 74 instructed persons, or 1 to every 129,311 inhabitants; while the twenty-five remaining counties of England, and the whole of Wales, with a population of 6,342,661, *did not among them furnish one conviction of a person who had received more than the mere elements of education.* It will be remembered, as a most interesting fact, one which speaks irresistibly in favour of a general system of education, *that not one of the* 100 *was a female!*"

One remarkable fact, which singularly illustrates the evil effects of our rural system, is, that notwithstanding the extraordinary numbers of workmen crowded together in the manufacturing towns of Lancashire, and notwithstanding the moral injury, which those towns suffer from the continual influx of wretched beings driven thither by want from our rural districts and from Ireland, *the annual proportion of criminals to population is very considerably less in the manufacturing towns of Lancashire, than in many of our agricultural counties!*

The supposition that the proportion of crime to population is greater in the manufacturing than in the rural districts, is one which has been taken for granted by many writers, but which is totally unfounded. The reverse of this proposition is the truth. The error has arisen from calculating the annual amount of crime in Liverpool, as forming part of the crime committed in the *manufacturing* districts; forgetting that Liverpool is not a manufacturing town, but a *sea-port;* that it is the nearest English *sea-port* to Ireland; and that the greatest amount of the crime annually committed in Liverpool, is committed, either by vagrant Irish, by the constantly changing sailor population, or by the labourers in the docks, who are demoralised by association with the sailors.*

Let us shortly examine the extraordinary criminality of Liverpool.

It appears that in the eleven months ending 30th November, 1849, 6194 persons were brought before the magistrates of Liverpool charged with felony, *of whom only* 1489 *were natives of Liverpool; all the remainder*, viz. 4705, *were strangers!*

As Mr. Clay says, in his report for 1849:—"It is the GREAT SEA-PORT of the southern division, which throws its own dark aspect over the moral reputation of the entire county; and I now beg to submit evidence to demonstrate, how much the COMBINED criminality of Manchester, Salford, Bolton, and Preston—the great 'manufacturing centres'—falls below that of Liverpool alone, which scarcely, if at all, subjects to the action of machinery a single fibre of all the cotton landed from its magnificent docks. Having been obligingly furnished by Captain Willis, Mr. Dowling, Mr. Neale, Mr. Harris, and Mr. Banister with their respective reports on the state of crime in the several towns which they superintend, I am enabled to give the following concise summary of crime and disorder in those towns:—

* See the Rev. J. Clay's admirable Report on the Preston Gaol for 1849.

Comparative View of Criminality and Disorder in the manufacturing Towns of Manchester, Salford, Bolton, and Preston, and the Sea-port of Liverpool, founded on the Police Returns of the respective Places.

| | Manchester. | Salford. | Bolton. | Preston. | Total. | Per Cent. to Pop. | Liverpool. | Per Cent to Pop. |
|---|---|---|---|---|---|---|---|---|
| | 1848. | 1849. | 1848-9. | 1848. | | | 1848. | |
| Estimated Population - | 300,000 | 62,000 | 69,000 | 68,000 | 499,000 | | 390,000 | |
| Total of apprehensions | 6,277 | 1,624 | 1,950 | 1,626 | 11,477 | 2·3 | 22,036 | 5·64 |
| Committed for trial - | 825 | 149 | 127 | 81 | 1,182 | 0·24 | 937 | 0·24 |
| Summary convictions for robberies - - - | 126 | 11 | 65 | 41 | 243 | 0·05 | 3,440 | 0·88 |
| Total of summary convictions - - - | 2,885 | 900 | 997 | 546 | 5,328 | 1·07 | 13,849 | 3·55 |
| Total of *females* taken into custody - - | 1,842 | 433 | 387 | 299 | 2,961 | 0·6 | 6,274 | 1·6 |
| Young persons taken into custody on charges of felony - - - | under 20<br>838 | under 20<br>175 | under 20<br>64 | under 19<br>121 | 1,098 | 0·22 | under 19<br>2,342 | 0·6 |

"The very striking results appearing from the above statement are, that, comparing Liverpool with the *four* manufacturing towns *collectively*, and bearing in mind that its population is *one fifth less*,—

1. Its committals for trial are - - equal.
2. Its numbers taken into custody - $2\frac{1}{2}$ times greater.
3. Its females taken into custody - nearly 3 times greater.
4. Its juveniles charged with felony - nearly 3 times greater.
5. Its summary convictions for all offences $3\frac{1}{2}$ times greater.
6. Its summary convictions for *robberies - more than* 17 *times greater!*"

. . . . . . . . . . . . . . . .

* "If I have succeeded in removing from the manufacturing population of Lancashire the charge of excessive criminality, it has been at the expense of our great sea-port; and it is right that, having gone so far, I should proceed yet further, and shortly state the causes which have given to Liverpool its lamentable pre-

* The Rev. J. Clay's Report on the Preston Gaol for 1849.

eminence. It is scarcely necessary to say, that in every large sea-port, there exists a dissolute class, maintaining itself by preying on careless and drunken seamen, and by pilfering property lying exposed on the landing places. But this is not all, as affects Liverpool. It is her peculiar misfortune, that her harbour is too easily gained by a race of persons who, whatever may have been their habits at home, no sooner reach Liverpool, than such of them as are in a destitute state, either give way to the temptation to plunder round the docks, or become an oppressive and demoralising burden to the town. I am indebted to Mr. Rushton for much information on this subject, and for carefully prepared statistics, which should be taken into account, whenever the crime of Lancashire or Liverpool is adverted to. The Irish in Liverpool are estimated by Mr. Rushton at *one-fourth* of the entire population; *but they supply more than* ONE HALF *the number of criminals!* I have now before me a return, from which it appears, that in the eleven months ending 30th November last, 6194 persons were brought before the magistrates of Liverpool, charged with felony,—of whom 1489 were natives of Liverpool, 946 were from other parts of England, 338 from Scotland, Wales, and the Isle of Man, while 3266 *were natives of Ireland!* It also appears from the return, that, as regards the English, females are to the males in the proportion of 1 to 2; but as regards the Irish, they are in the proportion of 14 to 17. This constant influx of Irish misery and crime it is almost impossible to restrain. The open docks of Liverpool, where the quays are covered with costly articles of commerce, swarm with thieves, whose cunning and rapacity are in continual action. When apprehended, the process of committal to assizes or sessions would not promote the ends of justice, and it becomes an unavoidable necessity that 'crimes which, in other places, would be punished by long terms of imprisonment, are punished, here, by repeated summary convictions, under the powers of various local acts of parliament; and this must be, or the criminal would go without punishment altogether. For instance, a sailor is the necessary witness; his ship is going to sea; you cannot detain him, and therefore you enforce your summary powers. This happens in hundreds of cases in Liverpool.'* Thus, again, in cases of robbery from the person by prostitutes, or by *pickpockets*, seamen being the injured parties, it is necessary to dispose of the cases at once. According to the report of the Liverpool police, robberies from the person by 67 male and 20 female pickpockets, and 198 robberies from the person by prostitutes, were *summarily* punished in 1848.

"It is obvious from all this, that Liverpool, from its unfortunate proximity to Ireland, is undergoing an aggravation of moral and social evils of the severest character,—even to the extent of clogging and embarrassing the free action with which justice should deal with delinquents. From such evils North Lancashire enjoys an almost complete immunity. At the Preston sessions, known pickpockets seldom appear, and indictments against 'unfortunate women' for robberies from the person, are comparatively rare; but persons of either class, when convicted—former convictions being proved—have almost always been sentenced to transportation."†

From the above facts and extracts it is clear that,

* Mr. Rushton.

† Such offences as those now adverted to are never disposed of *summarily* in North Lancashire.

in estimating the criminality of the *manufacturing* districts, we ought to omit the amount of crime committed in Liverpool; first, because it is not a *manufacturing* town; and, secondly, because the majority of its criminals are not natives, or even permanent inhabitants of the town.

But, if we reckon the criminality of Liverpool as part of the criminality of the manufacturing districts of Lancashire, what is the result even then? Mr. Redgrave, in his valuable tables for 1848, shows* that, even *without* excluding Liverpool, Lancashire, *as a whole*, stands ELEVENTH on the list of counties arranged in the order of their criminality, and that there are TEN *agricultural* counties, where the proportion of criminals to population is greater than in the whole of Lancashire, including Liverpool! Mr. Clay exhibits this fact very clearly in the following table, extracted from his very able report for 1849:—

| Order in which the Ten Counties would stand, supposing Criminality proportioned to *Density* of Population. | | Order in which the Ten Counties would stand, supposing Crime to depend on the Excess of Manufacturing over Agricultural Population. | | Actual Order, in Ratio of Criminals to Population. (1848.) | |
|---|---|---|---|---|---|
| Counties. | Inhabitants to 100 Acres. | Counties. | Persons in Manufactures to 1 in Agriculture. | Counties. | Criminals to Population. |
| 1. Lancaster | 147·5 | Lancaster - | 9·3 | Warwick - | 1 to 358 |
| 2. Surrey - | 120· | Surrey - | 4· | Worcester - | " 364 |
| 3. Warwick | 70· | Chester - | 3·8 | Chester - | " 411 |
| 4. Chester - | 59· | Warwick - | 3·5 | Hereford - | " 428 |
| 5. Gloucester | 53·6 | Gloucester - | 2·1 | Rutland - | " 439 |
| 6. Worcester | 50·4 | Worcester - | 1·6 | Gloucester - | " 443 |
| 7. Hertford | 39· | Hertford - | 1· | Berks - | " 477 |
| 8. Berks - | 33·5 | Berks - | 0·8 | Hertford - | " 480 |
| 9. Rutland - | 22·3 | Hereford - | 0·7 | Surrey - | " 504 |
| 10. Hereford | 20·6 | Rutland - | 0·6 | Lancaster - | " 509 |

But if we consider the populous manufacturing dis-

* See Mr. Clay's Report for 1849.

tricts of North Lancashire *separately*, without considering the southern division of Lancashire, with its great sea-port, Liverpool, we shall arrive at still more remarkable results, showing how much more demoralised many of our rural districts are than the crowded cities of the north.

It appears, as shown by Mr. Clay, that there are 34 *counties whose proportion of crime to population is greater than that of North Lancashire;* that in regard to *juvenile* crime, *North Lancashire is very greatly surpassed by* 22 *counties*, most of which are agricultural; and that in *female* criminality *it is surpassed by* 17 *counties*, almost all of which are also agricultural!

Mr. Clay says, in Kent the ratio of criminals to the population is as 1 to 668; in Suffolk the ratio is greater than in Kent, being 1 to 647; while in North Lancashire it is only 1 to 999! In Suffolk, too, the extent of depravity among the female sex is in a greater ratio than in North Lancashire. In the former, it is 1 to 4,633, while in the latter it is only 1 to 5,441! "And as to juvenile offenders—taking the data from Captain Williams's 12th Report—*those of Suffolk are* THRICE *as numerous as those of North Lancashire!!*"

The following table shows the aggregate criminality for each of the English counties in the five years ending 1847; the increase or decrease which has taken place between those periods; and the *order* in the criminality of the counties—as evinced in 1841 and 1847; those counties being placed *first* in order, which furnish the greatest number of criminals in proportion to their population. It is extracted from Mr. Clay's report for 1848.

| Counties: in the Order of their Criminality (1847). | Population in 1841. | Estimated Population in 1847.* | Criminals in 1847. | Aggregate of Criminals in the Five Years ending | | Per-centage of Increase or Decrease in the Quinquennial Periods. | | Consecutive Order in Criminality as compared to Population. | |
|---|---|---|---|---|---|---|---|---|---|
| | | | | 1842. | 1847. | Incr. | Decr. | 1847. | 1841. |
| Middlesex - - | 1,576,636 | 1,728,700 | 5175 | 18,394 | 22,543 | 22·5 | - - | 1 | 7 |
| Worcester - - | 233,336 | 247,800 | 620 | 2,689 | 3,000 | 11·6 | - - | 2 | 5 |
| Gloucester - - | 431,383 | 460,700 | 1092 | 5,489 | 5,162 | - - | 5·9 | 3 | 1 |
| Warwick - - | 401,715 | 448,300 | 998 | 4,712 | 4,505 | - - | 4·4 | 4 | 4 |
| South Lancashire, including Liverpool - - | 1,264,383 | 1,471,740 | 3011 | 14,569 | 13,698 | - - | 6·0 | 5 | 3 |
| Surrey - - | 582,678 | 652,000 | 1315 | 4,842 | 5,023 | 3·7 | - - | 6 | 27 |
| Chester - - | 395,660 | 439,200 | 871 | 4,491 | 4,121 | - - | 8·2 | 7 | 6 |
| Bucks - - | 155,983 | 160,400 | 315 | 1,298 | 1,477 | 13·8 | - - | 8 | 18 |
| Berks - - | 161,147 | 171,600 | 335 | 1,600 | 1,460 | - - | 8·8 | 9 | 16 |
| Southampton - | 355,004 | 382,300 | 737 | 3,388 | 3,157 | - - | 6·8 | 10 | 15 |
| Wilts - - | 258,733 | 270,600 | 502 | 2,351 | 2,213 | - - | 5·9 | 11 | 14 |
| Hereford - - | 113,878 | 115,400 | 212 | 1,145 | 1,064 | - - | 7·1 | 12 | 10 |
| Rutland - - | 21,302 | 22,600 | 41 | 97 | 157 | 61·9 | - - | 13 | 40 |
| Oxford - - | 161,643 | 167,600 | 299 | 1,611 | 1,460 | - - | 9·4 | 14 | 13 |
| Stafford - - | 510,504 | 584,500 | 1028 | 5,165 | 4,656 | - - | 9·8 | 15 | 11 |
| Norfolk - - | 412,664 | 426,700 | 751 | 3,487 | 3,688 | 5·6 | - - | 16 | 25 |
| Hertford - - | 157,207 | 166,300 | 291 | 1,561 | 1,314 | - - | 15·8 | 17 | 12 |
| Monmouth - - | 134,355 | 163,800 | 282 | 1,385 | 1,234 | - - | 10·9 | 18 | 2 |
| Devon - - | 533,460 | 558,600 | 949 | 3,356 | 3,845 | 14·6 | - - | 19 | 31 |
| Somerset - - | 435,982 | 456,500 | 774 | 4,968 | 4,354 | - - | 12·3 | 20 | 8 |
| Essex - - | 344,979 | 362,900 | 608 | 3,266 | 3,065 | - - | 6·2 | 21 | 17 |
| Dorset - - | 175,043 | 185,300 | 307 | 1,348 | 1,205 | - - | 10·6 | 22 | 24 |
| Sussex - - | 299,753 | 317,800 | 522 | 2,665 | 2,301 | - - | 13·6 | 23 | 19 |
| Suffolk - - | 315,073 | 327,100 | 505 | 2,525 | 2,598 | 2·9 | - - | 24 | 28 |
| Bedford - - | 107,936 | 116,300 | 178 | 837 | 908 | 8·5 | - - | 25 | 20 |
| Kent - - | 548,337 | 594,900 | 889 | 5,000 | 4,423 | - - | 11·5 | 26 | 21 |
| Leicester - - | 215,867 | 228,200 | 335 | 2,201 | 2,011 | - - | 8·6 | 27 | 9 |
| Huntingdon - | 58,549 | 62,000 | 89 | 363 | 405 | 11·6 | - - | 28 | 33 |
| Cambridge - - | 164,459 | 177,800 | 255 | 1,157 | 1,324 | 14·4 | - - | 29 | 29 |
| Nottingham - | 249,910 | 266,300 | 343 | 1,623 | 1,597 | - - | 1·6 | 30 | 30 |
| Lincoln - - | 362,602 | 393,400 | 506 | 2,036 | 2,419 | 18·8 | - - | 31 | 35 |
| Northampton - | 199,228 | 212,300 | 243 | 1,496 | 1,379 | - - | 7·8 | 32 | 23 |
| Salop - - | 239,048 | 249,300 | 267 | 1,854 | 1,785 | - - | 3·7 | 33 | 22 |
| York - - | 1,591,480 | 1,745,600 | 1794 | 9,305 | 8,766 | - - | 5·8 | 34 | 32 |
| N. LANCASHIRE - | 402,672 | 444,550 | 445 | 2,907 | 2,252 | - - | 22·6 | 35 | 26 |
| Cornwall - - | 341,279 | 363,600 | 341 | 1,469 | 1,463 | - - | 0·4 | 36 | 37 |
| Durham - - | 324,284 | 378,100 | 279 | 1,022 | 1,407 | 37·7 | - - | 37 | 39 |
| Derby - - | 272,217 | 296,200 | 214 | 1,347 | 1,278 | - - | 5·1 | 38 | 34 |
| Northumberland | 250,278 | 268,600 | 189 | 965 | 1,131 | 17·2 | - - | 39 | 36 |
| Cumberland - | 178,038 | 183,200 | 120 | 698 | 632 | - - | 9·4 | 40 | 38 |
| Westmoreland - | 56,454 | 57,300 | 83 | 183 | 221 | 20·8 | - - | 41 | 41 |

* "The estimated population in 1847 is only a rough approximation to the probable truth. It has been derived from the known increase of the respective counties in the ten years between 1831 and 1841."

This table well deserves study. It shows, that the proportional amount of crime to population, calculated in two years, 1841 and 1847, was greater, in both years, in almost all the *agricultural* counties of England, than it was in the *manufacturing* and mining districts of North Lancashire, Yorkshire, Derbyshire, Northumberland, and Durham. It also shows, how fearfully the amount of crime is increasing in the agricultural districts of Westmoreland, Lincoln, Cambridge, Huntingdon, Leicestershire, Rutland, Bedfordshire, Buckinghamshire, Worcestershire, and Devonshire; whilst, in almost all the mining and manufacturing districts—*even reckoning South Lancashire, with its demoralised seaport, Liverpool*—the amount of crime has been, during the same period, actually decreasing!

With what terrible significance do these statistics plead the cause of the poor of our rural districts! Notwithstanding, that a town life *necessarily* presents so many more opportunities for, and temptations to, vice than a rural life; notwithstanding, that the associations of the latter are naturally so much purer and so much more moral than those of the former; notwithstanding, the wonderfully crowded state of the great manufacturing cities of Lancashire; notwithstanding, the constant influx of Irish, sailors, vagrants, beggars, and starving natives of the agricultural districts of England and Wales; and notwithstanding, the miserable state of most of the primary schools of those districts, and the great ignorance of the majority of the inhabitants; still, in face of all these, and other equally significant facts, the criminality of the *manufacturing* districts of Lancashire is LESS in proportion to the population, than that of most of the rural districts of England and Wales!

Does not this show, that the peasants of England

must be subjected to a singularly demoralising system, to produce so strange, so almost incredible, a result?

But let us consider the condition of the juvenile poor of our towns. The chief source and cause of the criminality of the poorer classes of our towns, is the neglected and frightfully wretched condition of a great part of their juvenile population. The children are not obliged by law to go to any school. The parents are often too vicious, or too ignorant, or too poor to care to send them, if not compelled and *enabled* to do so; and so a great part of the children are left in the streets to be educated and brought up in crime. This will always be the case, while the law does not at the same time oblige and enable poor, vicious, and ignorant parents to send their children to school. But in our country, the evil is worse than it otherwise would be, because we have not a sufficient number of schools in our towns, and because the greatest part of the schools we have, are so wretchedly insufficient in character.

The following account is quoted almost verbatim, but somewhat abridged, from Lord Ashley's admirable speech on juvenile destitution, delivered in the House of Commons on the 6th of June, 1848, clearly showing the awfully wretched condition of a great part of the children of London. But although this singular account refers to London alone, it does, in reality, give a very correct picture of the condition of a great part of the children of all the larger towns of England. In the towns of Lancashire, and in all the larger of the manufacturing and provincial towns, the life and character o an equal proportion of the whole number of the children is precisely similar to that of the juvenile population of the back streets of London.

Any one may convince himself of the truth of Lord

Ashley's account, and may learn how a great part of the juvenile population of every one of our larger towns is being bred in filth, immorality, and degradation, if he will only take the trouble to walk into the back streets, and observe what is going on around him. He will there see one of the principal nurseries of our criminals and paupers, and one of the numerous overwhelming proofs of the insane folly of supposing, that the unaided, voluntary efforts of charitable individuals will ever be able to reclaim and civilise the rapidly increasing masses of our juvenile poor.

Careful inquiries by Lord Ashley, and by the excellent men connected with that admirable society, the City Mission, have shown, that in the midst of London, there is a large and continually increasing number of lawless persons, forming a separate class, having pursuits, interests, manners, and customs of their own, and that the filthy, deserted, roaming, and lawless children, who may be called the source of 19-20ths of the crime, which desolates the metropolis, are not fewer in number than THIRTY THOUSAND!

These 30,000 are quite independent of the number of mere pauper children, who crowd the streets of London, and who never enter a school: but of these latter nothing will be said here.

Now, what are the pursuits, the dwelling-houses, and the habits of these poor wretches? Of 1,600, who were examined, 162 confessed, that they had been in prison, not merely once, or even twice, but some of them several times; 116 had ran away from their homes; 170 slept in the "lodging houses;" 253 had lived altogether by beggary; 216 had neither shoes nor stockings; 280 had no hat or cap, or covering for the head; 101 had no linen; 249 had never slept in a bed;

many had no recollection of ever having been in a bed; 68 were the children of convicts.

In 1847, it was found that of 4,000 examined, 400 confessed that they had been in prison, 660 lived by beggary, 178 were the children of convicts, and 800 had lost one or both their parents. Now, what was the employment of these people? They might be classed as street-sweepers; vendors of lucifer matches, oranges, cigars, tapes, and ballads; they held horses, ran errands, jobbed for "dealers in marine stores," that being the euphonious term for receivers of stolen goods,—an influential race in the metropolis, but for whose agency, a very large proportion of juvenile crime would be extinguished. It might be asked, how did the large number who never slept in bed pass the night? In all manner of places: under dry arches of bridges and viaducts, under porticoes, sheds, carts in out-houses, saw-pits, or staircases, or in the open air, and some in lodging-houses. Curious, indeed, was their mode of life. One boy, during the inclement period of 1847, passed the greater part of his nights in the large iron roller in the Regent's Park. He climbed over the railings, and crept to the roller, where he lay in comparative security.

Lord Ashley says, "many of them were living in the dry arches of houses not finished, inaccessible except by an aperture, only large enough to admit the body of a man. When a lantern was thrust in, six or eight, ten or twelve people might be found lying together. Of those, whom we found thus lodged, we invited a great number to come the following day, and there an examination was instituted. The number examined was 33. Their ages varied from 12 to 18, and some were younger. 24 had no parents, 6 had one, 3 had step-mothers, 20 had no shirts, 9 no shoes, 12 had been once in prison, 3 twice, 3 four times, 1 eight times, and 1 (only 14 years old) twelve times. The physical condition of these children was exceedingly bad; they were a prey to vermin, they were troubled with itch, they were begrimed with dirt, not a few were suffering from sickness, and two or three days afterwards several died from disease and the effects of starvation. I privately examined eight or ten. I was anxious to obtain from them the truth. I examined them separately, taking them into a room alone. I said, 'I am going to ask you a variety of questions, to which I trust you will give me true answers, and I will undertake to answer any question you may put.' They thought that a fair bargain. I put to several of them the question, 'How often have you slept in a bed during the last three years?' One said, perhaps twelve times, another three times, another could not remember that he ever had. I asked them, how they passed the night in winter. They said, 'We lie eight or ten together, to keep ourselves warm.' I entered on the subject of their employments and mode of living. They fairly confessed, they had no means of subsistence but begging and stealing. The only way of earning a penny in a legitimate way was by picking up old bones. But they fairly acknowledged for themselves and others scattered over the town, with whom they professed themselves acquainted, that they had not and could not have any other means of subsistence, than by begging and stealing. A large proportion of these young persons were at a most dangerous age for society. I met one very remarkable instance of a boy, past 17. I was struck at discovering, that the boy knew the French language, and I asked an account of his life. He said, he had been in France at the time of the Revolution, and had fought at the barricades. He and his mother had gone to Paris some four or five years ago. He there got into some employment, but, as the political atmosphere became warm, he yielded to its influence, and being enticed by French boys, his companions, he joined in the general warfare, fought at the barricades, was taken prisoner, tried, and sentenced to punishment. There were hundreds and thousands of others, as capable of being employed for the worst purposes, as the Garde Mobile of Paris. And therefore for the peace of society, I would direct the attention of the House to the subject. What was the moral condition of those persons? A large proportion of them, (it was no fault of theirs,) did not recognise the distinctive rights of *meum* and *tuum*. Property appeared to them to be only the aggregate of plunder. They held that everything which was possessed, was common stock; that he who got most was the cleverest fellow, and that every one had a right to abstract from that stock, what he could by his own ingenuity. Was it matter of surprise, that they entertained those notions, which were instilled into their minds, from the time they were able to creep on all fours,—that not only did they disregard all the rights of property, but gloried in doing so, unless they thought the avowal would bring them within the grasp of the law. To illustrate their low state of morality, and to show how utterly shameless they were, in speaking on these subjects, I would mention, what had passed at a ragged school, to which fourteen or fifteen boys, having presented themselves on a Sunday evening, were admitted as they came. They sat down, and the lesson proceeded. The clock struck eight. They all rose with the exception of one little boy. The master took him by the arm and said, 'You must remain; the lesson is not over.' The reply was, 'We must go to business.' The master inquired what business? 'We must all go to catch them, as they come out of the chapels.' It was necessary for them, according to the remark of this boy, to go at a certain time in pursuit of their calling. They had no remorse or shame, in making the avowal; because they believed, that there were no other means of saving themselves from starvation. I recollect a very graphic remark, made by one of those children in perfect simplicity, but which yet showed the horrors of their position. The master had been pointing out to him the terrors of punishment in after-life. The remark of the boy was, 'That may be so, but I don't think it can be any worse than this world has been to me.' Such was the condition of hundreds and thousands!"

Great numbers of these wretched beings live in the "*lodging-houses.*" These horrible dens will be described more fully hereafter; but I shall quote Lord Ashley's account of them here, in order to show, where and how a great part of the juvenile population of our towns are lodged and *educated.* Until the poor children are rescued from these hells, how can we hope to raise them from their present degraded condition? But how can we rescue them, unless the municipalities interfere, and at their own expense clothe and send all the poor children of their towns to good and religious schools, as they do in Germany and Switzerland? But listen to Lord Ashley's description given in his own words:—

"I will read a description of the lodging-houses. Many of them, which I have seen, were abominable; but the statement, I will lay before the House, was given on the authority of a city missionary, who had been appointed to inspect and report on the subject.

It is not an exaggerated description of those places, where hundreds and thousands of the human race are congregated. The city missionary, speaking of a lodging-house, and referring to the 'parlour,' — for there were many euphonious terms to be applied, — said, —

"'The parlour measures 18 feet by 10. Beds are arranged on each side of it, composed of straw, rags, and shavings. Here are 27 male and female adults and 31 children, with several dogs; in all, 58 human beings, in a contracted den, from which light and air are systematically excluded. It is impossible,' he says, 'to convey a just idea of their state,—the quantities of vermin are amazing! I have entered a room, and in a few minutes, I have felt them dropping on my hat from the ceiling like peas.' 'They may be gathered by handfuls,' observed one of the inmates. 'I could fill a pail in a few minutes. I have been so tormented with the itch, that on two occasions I filled my pockets with stones, and waited till a policeman came up, and then broke a lamp, that I might be sent to prison, and there be cleansed, as is required before new comers are admitted.' 'Ah!' said another, standing by, 'you can get a comfortable snooze and scrub there!'

"A vast number of boys of tender years resort to these houses. I wish to show, what a variety of circumstances stand in the way of their moral or physical improvement. The existence of these houses is one of those circumstances. I have given a sample of the houses these children are compelled to inhabit. It would be found true on inquiry, *not only of the metropolis, but of the smaller as well as of the great towns throughout the country, that seven-tenths of the crime perpetrated in the different localities are concocted by the society, which meet in those lodging-houses.* The Warwick magistrates say,—and it is applicable to London, —'such houses are the general receptacle of offenders. Here the common vagrants assemble in great numbers at nightfall, and, making the lodging-houses the common centre, traverse their several beats.' 'I have no hesitation,' says a public officer, 'in declaring my belief, that the principal robberies have been concocted in vagrant lodging-houses, and rendered effectual through the agency of the keepers.' That is not all. When a boy leaves the lodging-houses, he is exposed to influences quite as deleterious to his moral and physical well-being. I shall read a description of a court, which I have witnessed myself. It is in such places that a large mass of the community dwell. In one of those courts there are three privies to 300 people; in another, two to 200 people. Here is a statement made by a medical man:—'In a place, where these public privies exist, scenes of the most shocking character are of daily occurrence. It will scarcely be believed, that these public privies often stand *opposite* the doors of the houses: modesty and decency are therefore altogether impossible.' But, in a private house, is the boy exposed to better influences than in the lodging-house? Very often several families are found in one room. It is a fortunate family which has one room for itself. Everything is transacted in that room. Cleanliness is impossible; it is a scene of filth, misery, and vice. The House will permit me to give a description of a locality, which affords a fair sample of the class; for those children are a peculiar race, to be found in almost all instances, in the most filthy, destitute, unknown parts of the metropolis—places seldom trodden by persons of decent habits. These courts and alleys are in the immediate neighbourhood of uncovered sewers, of gutters full of putrified matter, nightmen's yards, and privies, the soil of which is openly exposed, and never or seldom removed. It is impossible to convey an idea of the poisonous condition, in which these places remain during winter and summer, in dry weather and wet, from the masses of putrifying matter which are allowed to accumulate. These statements are by no means exaggerations. I would not assert what I do, if I did not do so on my own personal knowledge, having gone over many parts of those districts, and having devoted a certain portion of my time to the prosecution of investigations on the subject, when, in 1846, I lost my seat in Parliament, being curious to find my way in those parts of the metropolis, which had hitherto been unexplored. In company with a medical man and a city missionary, I ventured to go over many of those places, and I am able to say, that the description, I have now given, is below the truth. I shall next advert to the physical condition of the children. They are thus described in a report by Dr. Aldis:—

"'They are emaciated, pale, and thin, and in a low condition. They complain of sinking, depression of the strength, loss of spirits, loss of appetite accompanied by pains in different parts of the body, with disturbed sleep.' 'The depressed and low condition of health, in which these people are always found, induces habits of intemperance, unfortunately so common among them.' 'The children,' says another, 'are diminutive, pale, squalid, sickly, irritable; I rarely saw a child in a really healthy state.'

"The report from one school says:—

"'The boys have been sent out daily by drunken parents to beg and steal, being often cruelly treated if unsuccessful; others are employed in vending and assist ing in the manufacture of base coin. . . . . Of 74 admitted this year between 8 and 14, 16 are known thieves, 27 are beggars and hawkers.' There is a most remarkable statement made on the authority of a city missionary in a district in the east of London. His house was the open resort of all, who chose to come to pay him a visit and ask his advice. From January to December he received from these children 2,343 visits, averaging 334 per month. Of these, under 10 years of age, there were 2 per cent.; under 12, 9 per cent.; above 12 and under 15, 44 per cent.; above 15 and under 18, 36 per cent.; above 18 and under 22, 8 per cent. Of these, 39 per cent. voluntarily acknowledged that they had been in prison; 11 per cent. had been in once; 4 per cent., *twice;* 5 per cent., *thrice;* 2 per cent., *four* times; 1 per cent., *six* times; 3 per cent., *seven* times; 1 per cent., *eight* times; 2 per cent., *ten* times; and there were 10 per cent. *uncertain as to the number of times!* This state of matters arises in a great measure, either from desertion, or from the bad example of parents. In many instances, it is good for the children that they are deserted; in many instances, it is good that they have no parents. But in many instances, they are misled by the bad example of their parents—in many instances, tempted by necessity. There are hundreds and thousands in this city who, from their earliest years, have never obtained, what they do obtain, except by begging, or by stealing, or by some avocation of a questionable kind. Children are encouraged by their parents in that course of life. Even in those instances, where parents do not bring their children up to steal, they take very good care, when property is brought in of a suspicious character, to ask no questions, and to bestow praise for adroitness in such transactions. But a very great deal of the evil, which surrounds the parents, arises from the sanitary condition, in which they are left. The same causes, which operate on the parents, operate on the children; and hundreds are found utterly reckless of decency, of comfort, of regard for the spiritual or temporal welfare of their children—reckless even of almost life itself."

What are the consequences of this terrible state of things? Hear what Lord Ashley says:—

"I wish to show the condition of the metropolis; and for that purpose, will state the number taken into custody by the metropolitan police in 1847, as contrasted with the number taken into custody in 1848. In 1847, 41,479 males were taken into custody; OF WHOM 8,405 WERE UNDER 20 YEARS OF AGE, 3,228 BETWEEN 10 AND 15, AND 306 UNDER 10. In 1848, 42,933 males were taken into custody; OF WHOM 8,776 WERE UNDER 20 YEARS OF AGE, 3,604 BETWEEN 10 AND 15, AND 312 UNDER 10. The total increase in 1848 of males taken into custody was 1,454, of whom one half was under 20 years of age. But of those, who had been taken into custody under 10 years of age—the class which chiefly attended school—there had been an increase of only six. THE WHOLE NUMBER OF MALES TAKEN INTO CUSTODY BETWEEN 10 AND 20, A PERIOD OF 10 YEARS, WAS 12,692; between 25 and 50, a period of 25 years, 18,591; only one-third more. But looking at the number of those tried and convicted, there appears a great disproportion. BETWEEN 10 AND 20 THE MALES TRIED AND CONVICTED WERE 1,237, *whereas the males tried and convicted between 25 and 50 were only 1,059.* The same rule prevails in Manchester, to which I refer as a very large town, the returns being characterised by the same accuracy as those for the metropolis. There were taken into custody in Manchester 1,037 *males between* 10 *and* 20, *and* 2,157 *between* 25 *and* 50. But there were tried and convicted 165 between 10 and 20, 193 between 25 and 50. *These returns show the preponderating amount of* JUVENILE *delinquency.* They show also the possibility of applying the preventive system. The crimes are perpetrated, at a period of life, when the parties are open to the best influences, and are most capable of receiving permanent impressions. It is also clear that the seeds of crime are sown in early life, and would not, if they were then rooted out, grow up into rank maturity. Being anxious to ascertain the opinions of persons best acquainted with the subject, I circulated among persons having the charge of ragged schools, missionaries, and others, the question, 'Do many adult males become criminals for the first time after 20 years of age?' From 43 committees I received the answer, 'Very few.' One said, 'A small proportion, and these chiefly through drunkenness, and want of employment. In London, many country people, and the Irish, become criminals after 20 years of age, and these chiefly from the abovementioned causes.' Another said, 'I should say not one in fifty.' Another, 'I believe that among the lowest classes of society, hardly any become criminal for the first time after 20 years of age.' That large class roaming over the streets of London, of habits, manners, feelings, and pursuits totally unlike anything, with which people are acquainted in ordinary life, forms a seed-plot for three-fourths of the crime, which prevails in this metropolis; *and what I say of the metropolis, I say of every great city in the empire.*

"The records of the tribunals and of the police

courts, show only, what are the numbers of those, whom the police are adroit and quick enough to apprehend. But there is a vast amount of unseen crime; there are breaches of the public peace, which are undetected; there is a great deal of that training, which formed those children to a character dangerous to society. I believe the majority of criminals, in and about London, arises out of that class. If you greatly improve, or even extinguish that class as such, I do not mean to say, that crime will be removed; but the amount will be considerably abated, because I have no doubt, the greater part of the crime perpetrated within this metropolis and the neighbourhood, is perpetrated by individuals, who are formed and trained in the class, to which I have alluded. A city missionary wrote to me, that he looked on several parts of his district, as breeding places for prisons. It is the concurring testimony of those persons, who are best acquainted with the class in question, that from that class, the major part of the crimes, which are perpetrated, take their rise. The House will recollect, how I have described the children, their necessities, moral and physical, the manner in which they are trained, the state in which they remain, believing that they have a right to prey on the whole world, having no knowledge of right and wrong, except that which arises in some way or other out of their fears. I have now to call your attention to the temptations to which these children were exposed. I beg you to recollect that we have in this city a mass of THIRTY THOUSAND children, such as I have described, in a state of great necessity, living entirely by their wits, and not knowing from one hour to another whether they will obtain anything for their sustenance during the day. I ask the House, then, just to look at the temptations to which these children are exposed—temptations which are often commented on in the police court—from the want of care on the part of owners of property. I find that, of the felonies, which have been perpetrated last year, within the jurisdiction of the metropolitan police, there were 814 cases of stealing tools, &c., from unfinished houses, where they had been left by workmen, without any care or supervision whatever; that the number of cases of stealing from carts and carriages, which have been left without any one to look after them, is 298; that the number of cases of theft from houses, in consequence of the doors being left open by the most wanton neglect on the part of servants and masters, is 2,208; and that the number of cases of theft of goods exposed for sale at shop-doors—and honourable gentlemen will recollect, how freely goods of all descriptions are so exposed, especially of all kinds of provisions, calculated to tempt the appetite of poor children—of these cases the number is 2,299. Now, every one of these felonies has increased in number, with the exception,—and this is a very curious fact,—with the exception of felonies of linen exposed to dry. These have considerably abated; and I do not hesitate to assert, that this has arisen, from the establishment of public baths and washhouses; which enable poor people to wash and dry their clothes by a short and speedy process, and keep them under proper care and supervision. Now, I wish to draw the attention of the House to the result of this system of things, of the total neglect and want of care, in which these children are left, because I am pressing upon you, the necessity of doing something to extricate them from their hopeless condition. I therefore wish to show the House, that the children are of that extraordinary description that they cannot be dealt with by means of ordinary agency, that they are utterly dissimilar in their habits from other children, and that they are in nothing more remarkable than in their insubordination. I cannot give a better proof of this than by relating the kind of scenes which take place whenever a school is opened in a new locality. I have heard teachers who have undertaken to open such schools as a sort of speculation—I do not mean a money speculation, but a kind of experiment—I have heard them describe the roaring and whistling with which their ears have been assailed, and the actual onslaughts they have had to resist, on first opening these schools. There is a school over the water well known to my honourable friend the member for Kinsale (Mr. Hawes), whom I have frequently met there, to which, when it was first opened, in 1846, there came twenty-four boys, all with tobacco-pipes, who kept possession of the school, and would neither learn nor dislodge; and, as it was necessary that they should be invited, and not coerced, the teachers had to wait with patience in the hope, that they would get tired of their "lark," and go away, and let those remain who desired to do better. They did go away at last. Others came who were more anxious to be taught; and now the school is in active operation, and producing, I thank God, good effects. Another similar school has been got up in the neighbourhood of Camden Town, the teachers of which had at first their hats knocked off, and stones thrown at them. This is the history of almost every such school I have known; tumults invariably take place at the opening, and you may always calculate upon a fortnight or three weeks passing before getting the children into habits of attention and order. It requires the highest exercise of patience to encounter obstacles so formidable and risks so peculiar."

The "Quarterly Review," not given to exaggerate on such subjects as these, describes the *juvenile population of the metropolis* as follows*:—"Every one, who walks the streets of the metropolis, must daily observe several members of the tribe—bold, and pert, and dirty as London sparrows, but pale, feeble, and sadly inferior to them in plumpness of outline. Their business, or pretended business, seems to vary with the locality. At the West-end they deal in lucifer-matches, audaciously beg, or tell a touching tale of woe. Pass on to the central parts of the town—to Holborn or the Strand, and the regions adjacent to them—and you will find the numbers very greatly increased: a few are pursuing the avocations above mentioned of their more Corinthian fellows; many are spanning the gutters with their legs, and dabbling with earnestness in the latest accumulation of nastiness; while others, in squalid and half-naked groups, squat at the entrances of the narrow fetid courts and alleys, that lie concealed behind the deceptive frontages of our larger thoroughfares. Whitechapel and Spitalfields teem with them like an ant's nest; but it is in Lambeth and Westminster, that we find the most flagrant traces of their swarming activity. There the foul and dismal passages are thronged with children of both sexes, and of every age from three to thirteen. Though wan and haggard, they are singularly vivacious, and engaged in every sort of occupation but that, which would be beneficial to themselves and creditable to the neighbourhood. Their appearance is wild; the matted hair, the disgusting filth, that renders necessary a closer inspection, before the flesh can be discerned between the rags, which hang about it, and the barbarian freedom from all superintendence and restraint, fill the mind

* See the volume for 1847.

of a novice in these things with perplexity and dismay. Visit these regions in the summer, and you are overwhelmed by the exhalations ; visit them in the winter, and you are shocked by the spectacle of hundreds shivering in apparel that would be scanty in the tropics; many are all but naked; those that are clothed are grotesque; the trousers, where they have them, seldom pass the knee; the tail coats very frequently trail below the heels. In this guise, they run about the streets and line the banks of the river at low water, seeking coals, sticks, corks, for nothing comes amiss as treasure trove. Screams of delight burst occasionally from the crowds, and leave the passer by, if he be in a contemplative mood, to wonder and rejoice that moral and physical degradation has not yet broken every spring of their youthful energies. . . . . .

"A large proportion of those who dwell in the capital" (and the writer might have added, in all the larger towns) "of the British empire, are crammed into regions of filth and darkness, the ancient but not solitary reign of the newts and toads.

"Here are the receptacles of the species we investigate; here they are spawned, and here they perish! Can their state be a matter of wonder! We have penetrated alleys terminating in a *cul-de-sac*, long and narrow, like a tobacco-pipe, where air and sunshine were never known. On one side rose walls several feet in height, blackened with damp and slime; on the other side stood the dwellings still more revolting, while the breadth of the wet and bestrewed passage would by no means allow us the full expansion of our arms! We have waited at the entrance of another of similar character and dimensions, but forbidden by the force and pungency of the odours to examine its recesses. The novelty of a visit from persons clad like gentlemen, gave the hope, that we were official; and several women, haggard, rough, and exasperated, surrounded us at once, imploring us to order the removal of the filth, which had poisoned their tenements, and to grant them a supply of water, from which they had been debarred for many days. Pass to another district; you may find it less confined, but there you will see flowing before each hovel, and within a few feet of it, a broad, black, uncovered drain, exhaling at every point the most unwholesome vapours. If there be not a drain, there is a stagnant pool: touch either with your stick, and the mephitic mass will yield up its poisonous gas like the coruscations of soda water.

"The children sit along these depositories of death, or roam through the retired courts, in which the abomination of years has been suffered to accumulate. Here reigns a melancholy silence, seldom broken, but by an irritated scold or a pugnacious drunkard. The pale, discoloured faces of the inhabitants, their shrivelled forms, their abandoned exterior, recall the living skeletons of the Pontine Marshes, and sufficiently attest the presence of a secret agency, hostile to every physical and moral improvement of the human race.

"The interior of the dwellings is in strict keeping; the smaller space of the apartments increasing, of course, the evils that prevail without—damp, darkness, dirt, and foul air. Many are wholly destitute of furniture; many contain nothing except a table and a chair; some few have a common bed for all ages and both sexes; but a large proportion of the denizens of these regions lie on a heap of rags more nasty than the floor itself. Happy is the family that can boast of a single room to itself, and in that room, of a dry corner. . . .

"The children that survive the noxious influences and awful neglect, are thrown, as soon as they can crawl, to scramble in the gutter, and leave their parents to amusement or business. . . . . . .

"The 'duris urgens in rebus egestas' stimulates these independent urchins; and at an age, when the children of the wealthy would still be in leading strings, they are off, singly or in parties, to beg, borrow, steal, and exercise all the cunning that want and a love of evil can stir up in a reckless race. . . . . . .

"They receive no education, religious or secular; they are subjected to no restraint of any sort; never do they hear the word of advice or the accent of kindness; the notions that exist in the minds of ordinary persons have no place in theirs; having nothing exclusively of their own, they seem to think such, in fact, the true position of society; and helping themselves, without scruple, to the goods of others, they can never recognise, when convicted before a magistrate, the justice of a sentence, which punishes them for having done little more than was indispensable to their existence."

This is a fair picture of the state of things in all our larger towns. In the Lancashire towns, a great part of the juvenile poor are in, at least, as wretched a state, while the democratic tendencies of society in Lancashire, and the crowds of poor, who are congregated on a small area, add immeasurably to the dangers of this state of things.

How far this state of things conduces to the increase of vice may be gathered from the fact, that—

Out of the total of 59,123 persons taken into custody in 1845,

15,263 could neither read nor write,

39,659 could read only, and write very imperfectly,

while in the year 1845, 14,887 persons of both sexes UNDER TWENTY YEARS OF AGE, were taken into custody *by the police in the metropolis alone!*

It is scarcely necessary for me again to remind my readers, that in none of the towns of Germany, or Switzerland, or Holland does any thing at all comparable to this state of things exist. Throughout Germany, Switzerland, Denmark, and the Austrian empire, every parent is *obliged* to send his children to school, while each municipality is *obliged* to pay the school fees for the poor children, and to provide them all with decent and comfortable clothing. The consequence is, that all the children between the ages of six and fifteen, in the German and Swiss towns, and nearly all the children in the French, Dutch, Danish, and Norwegian towns, spend *every day* in airy, roomy, clean, and well-furnished class-rooms, or in dry exercise grounds, and often in the company of children of the middle classes, and in the society of men who are fit to be the teachers of the children of the rich.

And yet, notwithstanding that such is the state of things in the English towns, and that such vast numbers of children are uncared for and uneducated in 1850, there are good and earnest men to be found, who tell us that the *laissez faire* system has been, and is, equal to the work of reforming the condition of our poor!

I have mentioned the London City Mission. Some of my readers may not know what this society is. It is an association supported by voluntary contributions, and formed for the purpose of supporting a body of intelligent and religious men,—selected from members of the English Church and of the Christian dissenting bodies, and of a lower grade of society, than that to which our clergymen belong,—as visitors and advisers of the poor in the more densely populated districts of London.

The funds of the society amount, at the present time, to between 15,000*l.* and 20,000*l.* a-year. Between 100 and 200 visitors have been appointed, each of whom receives a salary of 70*l.* per annum. The society is under the patronage of many excellent men, and is sanctioned by several of our bishops.

Each of the visitors or missionaries has a district allotted him. He acts under the direction of some clergyman, layman, or dissenting minister, and is required to give regular accounts of his daily work, of the houses and families he has visited, of the state in which he has found them, and of the advice and assistance which he has rendered them.

The results of the labours of this excellent society have been very admirable. They have disclosed the state of the poor of London—they have rescued hundreds from degradation and misery—they have shed rays of happiness in dens of wretchedness, and have made the poor feel that good men pity them. The civilising influence of all this cannot be exaggerated.

The English clergy throughout the whole country stand in need of such assistants as the visitors of the "City Mission." Personal intercourse, and personal advice have very much greater effect upon the poor than sermons, or than the public services of the Church, even when those services are attended by the poor; but the truth is, that where there is not a constant intercourse between the clergyman and his people, the poor do not go to church. Of the operatives in Lancashire, and of the workmen in our great towns, there is not—and I speak after considerable experience and numerous inquiries—there is not one out of every ten who ever enters a church, and still fewer who attend regularly.

Let any one go into nine out of every ten of the churches in the densest parts of the metropolis, or into nine out of every ten of the Lancashire churches, and count the labourers present, and then compare them with the numbers, who live in the district, which appertains to the church, and he will soon satisfy himself of the sad truth of these assertions.

Take, for instance, the case of the parish of St. Pancras in London. The London City Mission have made the most careful inquiries into the state of church and chapel attendance in this district. It was not under the charge of a careless clergyman at the time of the inquiry. On the contrary, one of the most earnest and philanthropic of our clergy, viz. the Rev. Thomas Dale, was labouring there. From what we all know of Mr. Dale, we may be sure that he had done all that lay in his power to foster religion among the inhabitants of his parish. And yet what was the state of things in January, 1848? In the number of the "City Mission Magazine" published in that month, I find it stated:—

1. That more than 100,000 inhabitants of the parish had NO sittings in either church or chapel.

2. That in 1841 the churches and chapels, which were opened on Sundays in the parish, were only HALF filled, small as was their size in comparison to the population of the parish.

3. That nearly one poor family in every six in the parish was without the Scriptures.

4. That the *majority* of all the poor children in the parish were growing up without receiving daily instruction.

I do not quote this instance of St. Pancras as that of a peculiarly neglected parish. I believe, that it is well off, when compared to many others both in London and in other towns. I only quote it, as a fair instance of the state of things throughout the country.

Now, what are the causes of this state of things? There are several. In the first place, the religion of the English Church is too much above the comprehension of the *uneducated* masses; or, perhaps, I should say, that the intelligence of the masses is too little developed to enable them to join in so intellectual and so unimaginative a form of worship, as that of the English Church, or as that of many of the sections of Dissenters. A Romanist service, or a Ranter's service, will attract crowds of poor, where the service of the English Church, or of the Independents, or of the Methodists, or of the Baptists will not attract fifty. But it will be said, that the Presbyterian churches of Scotland are filled, although the service is even less imaginative than that of the English Church. It is so because the Scotch poor are much better educated, and much more intelligent than our poor; because the Presbyterian clergymen are not nearly so far separated from the poor in their social origin, habits, and education, as our clergy; and because they visit their people in their cottages very much more than our English clergy can do.

A second cause of the small numbers of the poor who attend our churches, is the want of a much greater system of parochial visitation.

In the great towns, and especially in the metropolis and manufacturing districts of England, each poor family *ought* to be visited at least once a week, if their religious teachers are to have due influence upon them, and if the doctrines and precepts of religion are to be taught them, so as to be remembered. Of course, it is physically impossible for the clergy in the towns, however zealous they may be, to visit the families of their respective parishes nearly so often as this. In very many parishes and town districts, it would be utterly impossible for them, with the greatest efforts, to visit all the poor in their districts, *at the most*, more than once or twice a-year. The consequence is, that vast numbers are never visited at all by their religious ministers, whilst others are visited so seldom, that they cease to feel, that they are in any way connected with the clergyman of the district, and discontinue, or never begin, to attend the public services of his church.

But there is another cause, of still more potent influence, which prevents a vast majority of the clergy from ever visiting the lowest haunts of the poor in their districts—and that is their education and associations. They are educated gentlemen; brought up in comfortable homes, and in luxurious Universities; trained in the most splendid halls of learning in the world, in company with the sons of the highest, richest, and most influential people of the country; and accustomed to associate with the most literary, refined, and luxurious classes in the land. Now, however well their origin, education, and manners, fit them to be the patterns and advisers of the middle classes, to be the foci of a high order of civilisation in their respective districts, and to carry the politeness of the metropolis into the most remote corners and into the most secluded nooks of the island; it undoubtedly often unfits them for the difficult task of visiting the poor in the low haunts of our crowded towns. No one, but those who have actually tried the experiment, can imagine, how revolting it is to the senses of a refined man, to spend hours, or even minutes, in the foul retreats of the most degraded of our town poor. The atmosphere of the rooms, where two, three, and four families often live together in unwashed filth, and with scarce any ventilation; the manners, habits, food, and conversation of these people; the effluvia from their beds, where often as many as six individuals, parents and children, crowd in together, render these dens of misery intolerable to a man of refined habits.

When to all this are added the great number of inhabitants in many of these districts, and the little assistance, which the clergyman receives; it is very easy to understand why, even the most devoted of them find it often impossible, ever to see anything of a vast number of the inhabitants of their districts.

It is a common remark of the operatives of Lan cashire, and one which is only too true, "Your Church is a Church for the rich, but not for the poor. It was not intended for such people as we are."

The Roman Church is much wiser than the English in this respect. It selects a great part of its priests from the poorest classes of society, and educates them gratuitously in great simplicity of habits. The consequence is, that they feel no difficulty in mingling with the poor. Many of them are not men of refined habits themselves, and are not therefore disgusted at want of refinement in others. They understand perfectly what are the thoughts, feelings, and habits of the poor. They know how to suit their demeanour, conversation teaching, and actions, so as to make the poor quite at ease with them. They do not feel the disgust, which a more refined man cannot help feeling, in being obliged to enter the low haunts of the back streets and alleys.

It is singular to observe how the priests of Romanist countries abroad associate with the poor. I have often seen them riding with the peasants in their carts along the roads, eating with them in their houses, sitting with them in the village inns, mingling with them in their village festivals, and yet always preserving their authority. Besides this, the spectacles of the Romanist worship are much more attractive to the less educated masses, than the less imaginative forms of Protestant worship, and the services of the Roman Church are shorter and much more numerous than those of the English. These causes fill the Romanist churches, both abroad, and in our manufacturing districts, on the Sundays, and at the early matins of the weekdays, with crowds of poor, who go there to receive the blessing of their priests, to hear prayers put up, which they believe to be for blessings, although they do not understand them, and to see the glittering spectacles of the Romanist worship exhibited before them.

It behoves us to consider these things, if the English Church is not willing to give up the poor to the care of the Romanist priests. There are significant facts before us, if we would but see them. Within the last few years, splendid Romanist churches, full of free sittings, have been springing up in all the crowded districts of England, and especially in the manufacturing towns of the north. In Manchester alone, three beautiful Romanist churches, and one magnificent Romanist cathedral,—now by far the finest building in the town,—have been erected within the last twelve years. The priests seem to be able to obtain as much money as they require; and to spare no pains to attract the people. Their exertions among the poorest of the operatives, and in the lowest of their haunts, are praiseworthy in the extreme. They know that it is infinitely more important to have priests than churches. When they build a church, therefore, they generally attach to it, not one, but several, and often many priests, some of them chosen from the lowest classes of the community, and educated expressly for their labours. In the manufacturing districts of England, a large handsome building, of the same style of architecture as the church, and capable of serving as the dwelling-house of ten or twelve priests, is generally attached to each of the churches.

These churches and priest-houses are situated in the districts most densely populated with the poorest of the operative classes, and near their lowest haunts. The church and its servants, both arrayed and surrounded with all the ornaments and ceremonials of a very richly and beautifully adorned form of worship, are placed close to the doors of the worst and most degraded of the population. The churches are built with the greatest possible taste, both as regards their exteriors and their interiors, and are as splendidly ornamented, as beautifully painted, as well warmed and cleaned, and as comfortable, as they could be, if they had been intended for the use of the richest classes in the land; while nearly all the sittings in them are free to the humblest of the people.

When the poor enter, they find themselves treated in the Temple of their God, with the same respect as the richest; while all their senses are gratified in the highest degree. When to all this is added the fact, that the priests carry out an indefatigable and unostentatious system of visitation, it is not a matter of surprise, that they should be making many converts among our people.

I have been assured by clergymen of Lancashire, who are equally removed above bigotry and indifference, and who are themselves the most earnest labourers among the poor, that the progress of Romanism throughout the manufacturing districts is very extraordinary.

They attribute it to the following causes:—

1st. The astounding ignorance of the great mass of the operatives, which renders them unfit for the unimaginative and intellectual worship of the English Church.

2dly. The too great length of the services of the English Church, and the small number of services in the week, and on the Sunday.

3dly. The small number of clergy in the most thickly populated districts.

4thly. The want of an inferior order of clergy.

If, in addition to all this, we remember, that vast numbers of the poor of our towns cannot read or write a word, have never entered one of our churches, and have never heard the doctrines of Christianity; and that of the thousands of criminals who are convicted at our sessions and assizes, very few have ever received any instruction whatever, it certainly does behove us to stir ourselves.

The only way, by which we can hope to render the labours of our town clergy really efficient among the poor, is, to give them, as assistants, religious and intelligent men, chosen from among the poor themselves. Each clergyman ought to have two or three such assistants, whom he might employ, as the city missionaries are employed, in constantly visiting all the poor in his district, even in the most loathsome of their dwellings; in rendering him weekly accounts of their labours;

in advising, instructing, and admonishing the poor; in getting their children sent to school; in seeing that they were regular in attendance there; in urging the parents to attend a place of worship; and, in fine, in acting as their friends and religious instructors.

If the English Church does not soon adopt some such scheme, the poor of many of our towns will be entirely lost to her.

But to resume our description of the English poor.

Another very singular and very melancholy proof of the degradation and pauperism of a great part of our labouring population, is to be found, in the alarming magnitude of the numbers of vagrants, or wandering beggars, who now infest all parts of the country. This evil has become so enormous in the last six years, that the attention of the poor-law board, and of the government, has been attracted to it. An elaborate and very able Report upon the frightful extent of this growing evil has been drawn up, under the direction of the poor-law board, by Mr. Boase, and has been laid before the Houses of Parliament. From this Report, I have derived all the materials of the short sketch of this horrible phenomenon, which I now offer to my readers.

Large and ever-increasing hordes of vagrants, or wandering beggars, infest all the highways of England and Wales. These poor wretches are miserably clothed, filthily dirty, covered with vermin, and, generally, very much diseased; sometimes from debauchery, and sometimes—though this would appear to be the exceptional case—from the want of food. These vagrants consist, in some parts of the country, of nearly equal parts of Irish and English; while, in other parts, two-thirds of them are Irish, and the other third English. They are composed of persons of both sexes, and of all ages.

Very few are married. The women, of whom there are great numbers, are nearly all prostitutes. Each man is generally attended by one or two such companions in misery and crime.

They clothe badly, and keep themselves as filthy as possible, in order the better to excite the compassion of those to whom they apply for alms in the course of each day's march.

The manner of life of these creatures is singular. They beg, during the day, in the towns, or along the roads; and they so arrange their day's tramp, as to arrive, most nights, in the neighbourhood of some one of our workhouses. They then hide the money they have collected by begging, and present themselves, after sunset, at the gates of the workhouse, to beg a *night's lodging*. This, it appears, the guardians are obliged—or conceive they are obliged—to grant to all applicants.

To nearly every workhouse there are attached, what are called vagrant-wards, or buildings, which are specially set apart for the reception of tramps, such as those I have described. These wards are generally brick buildings, of one story in height. They have brick floors, and guard-room beds, with loose straw and rugs for the males, and iron bedsteads, with straw, for the females. They are badly ventilated, and unprovided with any means of producing warmth. It is, indeed, useless to attempt to keep them ventilated, as all holes for ventilation are sure to be stuffed up at night, by the occupants, with rags or straw, so that the stench of these sleeping-rooms is disgusting in the extreme. In some places, such is the filthy state of the poor wretches who are admitted at night, that it is necessary to have the framework of the beds whitewashed every day. In many places it is found impossible to give them beds, because the tramps swarm so horribly with vermin. In these cases, a rug is allowed to each, and the rug is washed in the morning.

Men are kept, in order to guard these foul receptacles every night; but it is needless to observe, that nothing can prevent scenes, which I may not attempt to describe.

The tramps are admitted from six to ten in the evenings. Those who arrive before nine are provided with a supper of milk and bread, and with a breakfast of the same kind, on condition, that they will remain in the workhouse, and perform from two to three hours' work, in breaking stones, picking oakum, or some other such employment, before they receive their breakfast.

Very often the poor wretches, and their women, prefer leaving early, without breakfast, to remaining, and obtaining breakfast on such terms as these.

Union workhouses are generally not more than ten miles apart, so that the vagrants can afford to spend time upon the road, or to make a detour, in order to beg in some town or village lying out of the direct route. If they start from the workhouse about nine in the morning, they have time to do a great deal of business before they cram into the next vagrant den for the night.

They often make as much as from five to ten shillings a day by begging, from charitable and inconsiderate people. They often carry about with them large sums of money. Before entering into a workhouse—where they would be searched—they deposit this money in shops, or hide it, or leave one of their party out of the house, with the charge of the money, while the others crowd into the ward free of expense.

The cost of receiving the crowds of these tramps,

who swarm on all the great roads, is become so heavy already, and is so rapidly increasing, that the boards of guardians find it absolutely impossible to attempt anything like classification or separation of the sexes. The expense is already so great, that the unions are beginning, in all directions, to cry to government to be delivered from this frightful plague by some means or another. It is quite certain that the present system is aggravating the evil every day.

The degradation of these poor wretches is hardly conceivable. Mr. Boase says, that it is quite incomprehensible how they can themselves endure the air and condition of the wards, unless it be explained, by the fact, that their senses have become dulled, and incapable of fulfilling their functions. Night-stools, or privies, are generally provided in connection with the wards; the wretched beings, however, will not use them, but defile the sleeping wards. It is found necessary to have the floors of the wards washed down every morning with buckets of water.

The conduct of the poor wretches is reported to be bad in the extreme. They are described as being noisy and turbulent; as making the wards resound with the vilest songs and language; as being ungrateful and refractory towards the ward-officers; and as having habits too filthy and indecent to be named.

This evil is rapidly increasing, and is a strange and melancholy commentary upon the state of our poorer classes, especially as compared with the improving state of the same classes in Germany and Switzerland, where no such phenomenon exists at all.

The following selections from the returns, will show the rapid increase of the numbers of tramps relieved in different unions during the last few years. These are only instances of a state of things which is almost universal.

| | Year. | No. of Vagrants relieved. |
|---|---|---|
| Watford Union | 1844 | 627 |
| | 1845 | 918 |
| | 1846 | 953 |
| | 1847 | 2,486 |
| | 1848 | 3,487 |
| Derby Union | 1845 | 2,442 |
| | 1846 | 2,960 |
| | 1847 | 6,293 |
| Newport House of Refuge | 1846 | 3,953 |
| | 1847 | 25,120 |
| | Year ending March, | |
| Chepstow Union | 1846 | 1,441 |
| | 1847 | 1,640 |
| | 1848 | 4,525 |
| | Year ending 25th March, | |
| Brentford Union | 1841 | 1,368 |
| | 1842 | 3,000 |
| | 1843 | 5,444 |
| | 1844 | 6,865 |
| | 1845 | 5,267 |
| | 1846 | 4,530 |
| | 1847 | 5,857 |
| | 1848 | 14,368 |
| Uxbridge Union | 1845 | 2,835 |
| | 1846 | 2,965 |
| | 1847 | 6,322 |
| | Year ending Lady-day, | |
| Windsor Union | 1846 | 1,708 |
| | 1847 | 2,033 |
| | 1848 | 5,368 |

| | Year. | No. of Vagrants relieved. |
|---|---|---|
| | Year ending Michaelmas, | |
| Eton Union | 1844 | 2,666 |
| | 1845 | 2,924 |
| | 1846 | 2,903 |
| | 1847 | 4,375 |
| | Year ending Lady-day, | |
| Newcastle-under-Lyne Union | 1846 | 1,953 |
| | 1847 | 2,736 |
| | 1848 | 4,967 |
| | Year ending 25th March, | |
| Stafford Union | 1845 | 3,126 |
| | 1846 | 3,047 |
| | 1847 | 5,264 |
| | 1848 | 11,108 |
| | Year ending Midsummer, | |
| Aylesbury Union | 1845 | 1,344 |
| | 1846 | 1,430 |
| | 1847 | 2,077 |
| | 1848 | 2,847 |
| | Years. | |
| City of London Union | 1840 | 2,403 |
| | 1844 | 24,574 |
| | 1845 | 26,003 |
| | 1846 | 33,655 |
| | 1847 | 41,743 |

These returns will suffice to show the alarming extent of this evil, and the way in which it is growing in almost all parts of the island. This will be made all the more apparent by the following table:—

| | |
|---|---|
| Average number of vagrants relieved in one night in 603 unions in England and Wales, in the week ending 20th of Dec. 1845 | 1,791 |
| Average number relieved in one night in 603 unions, in the week ending 19th of Dec. 1846 | 2,224 |

| | |
|---|---|
| Average number relieved in one night in 596 unions, in the week ending 18th Dec. 1847 . . . | 4,508 |
| Number relieved in 626 unions on 25th of March, 1848 | 16,086 |

If, however, I were only to state that 16,086 of such poor wretches as I have described were wandering about our roads begging alms in March, 1848, I should give no idea of the magnitude of this plague. Hitherto, I have only spoken of those, who seek shelter for the night in the workhouse vagrant-wards. But, besides these, there are vast numbers, who sleep every night in the vagrant lodging-houses in the towns.* These lodging-houses, which are to be found in most of our towns, consist of long low rooms, filled with beds or mattresses, upon which the vagrants of all ages and of both sexes, sleep, two or three in one bed or upon one mattress. These rooms are unventilated, seldom cleaned, filthy and close beyond comprehension, to those who have not been into them. In these dens, the vagrants, pickpockets, beggars, and, in fine, all the homeless wanderers of our streets, sleep crowded together. Old men and young men, old women and young women, and, worst of all, children of all ages, from the infant at the breast to the boy, who is just ripening into the felon, are crowded together. The scenes, which take place in these places, are horrible. In one bed sleeps a man with two women; in another, a woman with two men; in another, two or three women or men; in another, a poor mother and her children. Drunkards, pickpockets, prostitutes, and beggars, covered with vermin, are packed in together. Foul

* For a description of these horrid dens, see Mr. Chadwick's sanitary Reports, the reports of the City Mission, the Police Reports, and Lord Ashley's speeches.

songs, oaths, drunken yells, and groans, mingle every night in one sad chorus, until sleep closes the eyes of all.

In such scenes as these, and surrounded by such companions as these, the women are often delivered of children, thus adding to the foul indelicacy and barbarity of the scene.

The sleep of the poor wretches is often broken by the entrance of the police to seek some offender, whom they are ordered to find out and give up to justice; for the police, who know all these haunts, regard them as the general rendezvous of the offscouring of the towns.

One of the city missionaries, describing the state of the Mint district in the city of London, says, "it is utterly impossible to describe the scenes, which are to be witnessed here, or to set forth in its naked deformity the awful characters sin here assumes . . . . . . *In Mint Street, alone, there are nineteen lodging-houses.* The majority of these latter are awful sinks of iniquity, and are used as houses of accommodation. In some of them, both sexes sleep together indiscriminately, and such acts are practised and witnessed, that married persons, who are in other respects awfully depraved, have been so shocked, as to be compelled to get up in the night and leave the house. Many of the half-naked impostors, who perambulate the streets of London in the day-time, and obtain a livelihood by their deceptions, after having thrown off their bandages, crutches, &c., may be found here in their true character; some regaling themselves in the most extravagant manner; others gambling or playing at cards, while the worst of language proceeds from their lips. Quarrels and fights are very common, and the cry of murder is frequently heard. The public houses in this street are crowded to excess, especially on the Sabbath evening."*

In the Police Reports published in the "Sun" newspaper of the 11th of October, 1849, the following account is given of "*a penny lodging-house*" in Blue Anchor Yard, Rosemary Lane. One of the policemen examined, thus describes a room in this lodging-house:—"It was a very small one, extremely filthy, and there was no furniture of any description in it. *There were sixteen men, women, and children, lying on the floor, without covering. Some of them were half-naked.* For this miserable shelter, each lodger paid a penny. The stench was intolerable, and the place had not been cleaned out for some time."

If the nightly inmates of these dens are added to the tramps who seek lodging in the vagrant-wards of the workhouses, we shall find that there are at least between 40,000 and 50,000 tramps who are daily infesting our roads and streets!

I might crowd my pages with such accounts.

And yet with this plague-spot spreading in this horrible manner, and distinguishing us from all the other nations of Europe, we are still wrangling and disputing HOW and WHO are to educate the poor. And with such facts as these staring them in the face, there are men who tell us, that it is better that the poor should not be educated, than that the government should be allowed to aid in carrying out this great national undertaking.

Another sad symptom of the condition of the poor of our own towns is the use they make of the "burial clubs." In some of our towns the degradation of many of the poor is such, that parents often cause the death

* City Mission Magazine, Oct., 1847.

of their children, in order to obtain the premiums from the societies.

The accounts of these "burial clubs," and of the extent to which infanticide is practised in some parts of this country, may be found in Mr. Chadwick's able Reports upon the sanitary condition of the poor.

It appears, that in our larger provincial towns the poor are in the habit of entering their children in what are called "burial clubs." A small sum is paid every year by the parent, and this entitles him to receive from 3*l.* to 5*l.* from the club, on the death of the child. Many parents enter their children in several clubs. One man in Manchester has been known to enter his child in *nineteen* different clubs. On the death of such a child, the parent becomes entitled to receive a large sum of money; and as the burial of the child does not necessarily cost more than 1*l.*, or, at the most, 1*l.* 10*s.*, the parent realises a considerable sum after all the expenses are paid!

It has been clearly ascertained, that it is a common practice among the more degraded classes of poor in many of our towns, to enter their infants in these clubs, and then to cause their death either by starvation, ill-usage, or poison! What more horrible symptom of moral degradation can be conceived? One's mind revolts against it, and would fain reject it as a monstrous fiction. But, alas! it seems to be but too true.

Mr. Chadwick says,* "officers of these burial societies, relieving officers, and others, whose administrative duties put them in communication with the lowest classes in these districts" (the manufacturing districts), "express their moral conviction of the operation of such bounties to produce instances of the visible neglect

* Sanitary Inquiry Report, 1843, p. 64.

of children of which they are witnesses. They often say, 'You are not treating that child properly; it will not live: *is it in the club?*' And the answer corresponds with the impression produced by the sight.

"Mr. Gardiner, the clerk to the Manchester union, while registering the causes of death, deemed the cause assigned by a labouring man for the death of a child unsatisfactory, and staying to inquire, found that popular rumour assigned the death to wilful starvation. The child (according to a statement of the case) had been entered in at least *ten* burial clubs; *and its parents had had six other children, who only lived from nine to eighteen months respectively.* They had received from several burial clubs 20*l.* for *one* of these children, and they expected at least as much on account of this child. An inquest was held at Mr. Gardiner's instance, when several persons, who had known the deceased, stated, that she was a fine fat child shortly after her birth, but that she soon became quite thin, was badly clothed, and seemed as if she did not get a sufficiency of food. . . . . The jury, having expressed it as their opinion, that the evidence of the parents was made up for the occasion, and entitled to no credit, returned the following verdict: —'Died through want of nourishment, but whether occasioned by a deficiency of food, or by disease of the liver and spine, brought on by improper food and drink, or otherwise, does not appear.'

"Two similar cases came before Mr. Coppock, the clerk and superintendent-registrar of the Stockport union, in both of which he prosecuted the parties for murder. In one case, where three children had been poisoned with arsenic, the father was tried with the mother, and convicted, at Chester, and sentenced to be transported for life, but the mother was acquitted.

In the other case, where the judge summed up for a conviction, the accused, the father, was, to the astonishment of every one, acquitted. In this case the body was exhumed after interment, and *arsenic was detected in the stomach.* In consequence of the suspicion raised upon the death, on which the accusation was made in the first case, the bodies of two other children were taken up and examined, when *arsenic was found in their stomachs.* In all these cases payments on the deaths of the children were insured from the burial clubs; the cost of the coffin and burial dues would not be more than about 1*l.*, and the allowance from the club is 3*l.*

"It is remarked on these dreadful cases by the superintendent-registrar, *that the children who were boys, and therefore likely to be useful to the parents, were not poisoned;* the female children were the victims. It was the clear opinion of the medical officers that infanticides have been committed in Stockport to obtain the burial money."

The town clerk of Stockport says,* "*I have no doubt that infanticide, to a considerable extent, has been committed in the borough of Stockport.*

"I know it to be the opinion of some of the respectable medical practitioners in Stockport, that infanticides have been commonly influenced by various motives—to obtain the burial moneys from the societies in question, and to be relieved from the burden of the child's support. The parties generally resort to a mineral poison, which, causing sickness, and sometimes purging, assumes the appearance of the diseases, to which children are subject; and as they then take the child to a surgeon, who prescribes after a very cursory examination, they

* Sanitary Inquiry Report, 1843, p. 235.

thus escape any suspicion on the part of their neighbours."

Mr. Chadwick again says,* "At the Liverpool assizes in 1843, a woman named Eccles was convicted of the murder of one child, and was under the charge of poisoning two others with arsenic. Immediately the murders were committed, it appeared she went to demand a stated allowance of burial money from the employers of the children. The collector of a burial society, one of the most respectable in Manchester, stated to me strong grounds for believing, that it had become a practice to neglect children for the sake of the money allowed."

The able author of the "Letters on Labour and the Poor in the Rural Districts," lately published in the "Morning Chronicle," writing of the "burial clubs" in the eastern counties, says "The suspicion that a great deal of 'foul play' exists with respect to these clubs is supported, not only by a comparison of the different rates of mortality, but it is considerably strengthened, by the facts proved upon the trial of Mary May. The Rev. Mr. Wilkins, the vicar of Wickes, who was mainly instrumental in bringing the case before a court of justice, stated to me, that from the time of Mary May coming to live in his parish, he was determined to keep a very strict watch upon her movements, as he had heard that *fourteen of her children had previously died suddenly.* A few weeks after her arrival in his parish, she called upon him to request him to bury one of her children. Upon his asking her which of the children it was, she told him that it was 'Eliza,' a fine healthy-looking child of ten years old. Upon his expressing some surprise, that she should have died so suddenly, she said,

* Sanitary Inquiry Report, 1843, p. 65.

'Oh, sir, she went off like a snuff; all my other children did so, too.' A short time elapsed, and she again waited upon the vicar, to request him to bury her brother as soon as he could. His suspicions were aroused, and he endeavoured to postpone the funeral for a few days, in order to enable him to make some inquiries. Not succeeding in obtaining any information, which would warrant further delay in burying the corpse, he most reluctantly proceeded in the discharge of his duty. About a week after the funeral Mary May again waited upon him, to request him to sign a certificate to the effect that her brother was in perfect health a fortnight before he died,—that being the time at which, as it subsequently appeared, she had entered him as nominee in the Harwich Burial Club. Upon inquiring as to the reason of her desiring this certificate, she told him, that unless she got it, she could not get the money for him from the club. This at once supplied the vicar with what appeared to be a motive for 'foul play' on the part of the woman. He accordingly obtained permission to have the body of her brother exhumed; doses of arsenic were detected, and the woman was arrested. With the evidence given upon the trial, the reader is, no doubt, perfectly conversant, and it will be unnecessary for me to detail it. She was convicted. Previously to her execution, she refused to make any confession, but said, '*If I were to tell all I know, it would give the hangman work for the next twelve months.*' Undue weight ought not to be attached to the declaration of such a woman as Mary May, but coupled with the disclosures, that took place upon the trial, with respect to some of her neighbours and accomplices, and with the extraordinary rate of mortality among the clubs, it certainly does appear, that the general opinion with respect to the mischievous effects of these societies is not altogether without foundation.

" Although there are not in Essex, at present, any burial clubs, in which children are admitted under fourteen years of age, as members or nominees, still, as illustrating the evils arising from these clubs, I may state that many persons who are fully conversant with the working of such institutions, have stated, that they have frequently been shocked by hearing women of the lower classes, when speaking of a neighbour's child, make use of such expressions as, ' *Oh, depend upon it, the child 'll not live; it's in the burial club.*' When speaking to the parents of a child who may be unwell, it is not unfrequently that they say, 'You should do so and so,' or 'you should not do so and so;' '*you should not treat it in that way; is it in the burial club?*' Instances of the most culpable neglect, if not of graver offences, are continually occurring in districts, where clubs exist, in which children are admitted. A collector of one of the most extensive burial societies gave it as his opinion, founded upon his experience, that it had become a constant practice to neglect the children for the sake of the allowance from the clubs, and he supported his opinion by several cases, which had come under his own observation."

From a very remarkable letter published in "The Times" of the 18th of January, A.D. 1849, by that indefatigable and earnest man, the Rev. J. Clay, chaplain of the Preston House of Correction, I collect the following particulars, still further illustrating this horrible symptom of our social state.

Mr. Clay says,—" Let me recall to your recollection *some* of the murders for burial money perpetrated since the publication of Mr. Chadwick's admirable Report on interment in towns. 1. A Liverpool paper of April, 1846, gives the details of an inquiry before the coroner in a case of 'infanticide, at Runcorn, to obtain funeral money.' It appeared, in evidence, that James Pimlet, aged ten months, died on the 6th of March, and that on the 21st of the same month died Richard Pimlet, aged four years and a half. On the 27th of the same month a *third* child was taken ill. The medical man's suspicions were roused. The authorities caused the bodies of the two dead infants to be exhumed. It was found, that the *mother* had purchased arsenic before the children's illness. Dr. Brett showed the presence of arsenic in the bodies 'in quantities more than sufficient to cause death.' The collector of the Liverpool Victoria Legal Burial Society proved, that the three children were all enrolled members; that he had paid 1*l.* 5*s.* on the death of one child, and 5*l.* on the death of the other. The steward of another society proved the payment of 1*l.* 5*s.* and 1*l.* 15*s.* on the two deaths. Verdict, 'wilful murder' against the mother.

2. "At York assizes, in July, 1846, John Rodda was convicted of the wilful murder of his own child, aged one year. The evidence proved, that the wretch poured a spoonful of sulphuric acid down his helpless infant's throat. It was proved that he had said, he did not care how soon the child died, for whenever it died, he should have 2*l.* 10*s.*, as it was in a 'dead list.' He said he had another that would have the same when it died, and two others that would have 5*l.* apiece when they died.

3. "In June, 1847, Mary Ann Milner was charged with the wilful murder—by arsenic—of her mother-in-law, her sister-in-law, and her niece; her father-in-law had also well nigh become her victim, and was reduced to imbecility from the effects of the poison. The only

imaginable motive for the conduct of the prisoner, as suggested by the counsel for the prosecution, and as supported by the evidence, was the obtaining moneys from a burial society.

4. "In July, 1848, Mary May took her trial for the murder of Spratty Watts, by the favourite means —arsenic. This horrible case will be still in the recollection of your readers. The woman had put her victim into a 'death list,' which lured her to her crime, by promising 9*l.* or 10*l.* on its perpetration. 'The private confession of Mrs. May afforded'—I quote from 'The Times' of September 21,—'a due clue to a system, *which it is feared is capable of most extensive proof, and will result in the conviction of a large number of women*, who have adopted the practice of poisoning their husbands and children for the purpose of obtaining the fees which are granted by what are, in this part of the country, termed *death lists.*'

5. "I must add to this imperfect, but too full catalogue, the name of Ann Mather, against whom, in August, 1847, a coroner's jury, at Warrington, returned a verdict of 'wilful murder.' Her husband's name being in three separate '*death lists*,' the usual means—arsenic —was resorted to, and the desperate gamestress won 20*l.* I shall merely name the 'Essex poisonings;' their horrible notoriety has not yet subsided. Let it be remembered, that we have here only a portion of the positive murders resulting from the temptations offered by burial clubs. No one can guess how many more victims— infants especially—have been poisoned, or otherwise destroyed, for the sake of the coveted burial money, though neither inquiry nor suspicion may have been excited; nor, how many children, entered by their parents in burial clubs, are, when attacked by sickness,

suffered to die without any effort being made to save their lives.

"My report on the sanitary condition of Preston, given in the 'First Report of the Health of Towns Commission,' furnishes startling evidence of the wide prevalence of this feeling. A collector of cottage rents states, that '*almost all the children of the families where he collects are members of burial societies. . . . The children of the poor when sick are greatly neglected; the poor seldom seek medical assistance for sick children, except when they are at the point of death.*' Another collector states, '*the poor people have often told me that they were unable to pay at that time; but when a certain member of the family—generally a child—died, they would be able to pay.*' . . . . A lady states, that a young woman, whose services she required as wet nurse, having a child ill, she offered to send her own medical friend to attend it; the reply of the nurse was, '*Oh! never mind, ma'am, it's in two burial clubs.*' It also appears, on the unimpeachable authority of a burial-club official, that '*hired nurses speculate on the lives of infants committed to their care, by entering them in burial clubs;*' that 'two young women proposed to enter a child into his club, and to pay the weekly premium alternately. Upon inquiring as to the relation subsisting between the two young women and the child, he learned that the infant was placed at nurse with the mother of one of these young women.' The wife of a clergyman told me that, visiting a poor district just when a child's death had occurred, instead of hearing from the neighbours the language of sympathy for the bereaved parent, she was shocked by such observations as—'Ah! it's a fine thing for the mother, the child's in two clubs!' . . . . As regards one town, I possess some evidence of the amount of burial-club membership, and of infant mortality, which I beg to lay before you. . . . The reports of this town refer to 1846, when the population of the town amounted to about 61,000. I do not name the town, because, as no actual burial-club murders are known to have been committed in it, and as such clubs are not more patronised there, than in other places, it is, perhaps, not fair to hold it up to particular animadversion; indeed, as to its general character, this very town need not fear comparison with any other. Now, this place, with its 61,000 people of all classes and ages, maintains at least eleven burial clubs, the members of which amount in the aggregate to nearly 52,000; nor are these all. Such clubs, remember, act as burial clubs. Of these there are twelve or fourteen in the town, mustering altogether, probably, 2000 members. Here, then, we have good data for comparing population with '*death lists*;' but it will be necessary, in making the comparison, to deduct from the population all that part of it, which has nothing to do with these clubs; viz., all infants under two months old, and all persons of unsound health (both of these classes being excluded by the club rules); all those also of the working classes, whose sound intelligence and feeling lead them to abhor burial-club temptations; and all the better classes, to whom 5*l.* or 20*l.* offer no consolation for the death of a child. On the hypothesis that these deductions will amount to one-sixth of the entire population, it results, that the *death lists* are more numerous by far than the entire mass—old, young, and infants—which support them; and according to the statement of a leading death-list officer, THREE-FOURTHS of the names on these catalogues of the doomed are the names of children. Now, if this be the truth—and I believe it is—hundreds, if not thousands, *of children must be entered each into* FOUR, FIVE, *or even* TWELVE *clubs*, their chances of life diminishing, of course, in proportiou to the frequency with which they are entered. Lest you should imagine, that such excessive addiction to burial clubs is only to be found in one place, I furnish you with a report for 1846, *of a single club, which then boasted* 34,100 *members—the entire population of the town to which it belongs having been in* 1841 *little more than* 36,000 ! ! !

"I would now bespeak your attention to the infantile mortality in places where burial clubs flourish. In Dr. Lyon Playfair's 'Report on the Sanitary Condition of large Towns in Lancashire,' p. 53., it is stated, that *among the poor of Manchester, out of* 100 *deaths*, 60 *to* 65 *are of infants under five years old. One man put his children into nineteen clubs !* . . . . . Dr. Lyon Playfair again shows (p. 54.) that children die in Manchester, when wages are high, at a rate more than that, at which they die among the poverty-stricken labourers of Dorsetshire. . . . .

"I have now before me communications from five medical gentlemen, resident in the town of 61,000 inhabitants above alluded to (four of them surgeons to the union, and the fifth the medical officer of au institution furnishing gratuitous medical aid to the poor), showing their attendance on poor children under five years old, contrasted with their attendance on the poor above that age. The older patients, for whom medical aid was sought, constitute 87 per cent., the younger ones 13 per cent. Poor little creatures ! 56 per cent. die, but only 13 per cent. of them have the doctor's help, though it may be had for asking. I extract the following from the communications alluded to :—

"1. 'The above numbers (247 patients above five years of age, and 26 under five years of age,) very strikingly illustrate what I have frequently remarked otherwise,—the great indifference displayed by parents and others in the lower ranks of life with regard to infant life.'

"2. 'With respect to the attendance which the poorer classes give to their children in sickness, I am sorry to say it is generally anything but what it ought to be. . . . . If they seek medical aid at all, it is too often when there is not the slightest chance of recovery.'

"3. 'My impression is, that very few of the children of the operative class, in sickness, fall under the notice of the medical men of the town. But latterly there has been a disposition to call us in, in the last stage of disease, *for the purpose of obtaining a certificate of death*, for the registrar.'

"4. 'My general impression, derived from three years' experience at this institution, compels me to admit, what is very painful to acknowledge, that there is *among the poorer classes a manifest* and cold indifference to the health of infants, and especially so when suffering from disease.'

"The above extracts are from letters written in 1846. Since then, the medical certificate necessary to the registration of death has been more stringently required, and it was hoped would produce better attention to sick children. How far that hope has been realised, is showr in the following extract from a letter, written by th present medical officer of the charitable institution adverted to, a gentleman of distinguished zeal and ability:—'The return rather understates the mortality of infantile life; for in several instances, where very gross neglect has been apparent, and where our aid has only been requested in extremes, I have declined to give certificates, and such cases do not appear in the list. The whole number of patients admitted during the year 1847, was 3052: of these 341 were under five years of age, 2711 were above five years of age. It would thus appear, that although one half of all the deaths in the town consists of children under five years of age, the proportion of those who become patients of the only charitable medical institution in the place is only one-eighth of that above five years! Of the cases under five years, 1 in 6 proved fatal; of those above five years, 1 in 19¼. . . . . The difference between a mortality of 1 in 6 and 1 in 19¼ is too great to be accounted for on any other supposition, than that of the existence of great neglect on the part of the parents."

These accounts are really almost too horrible to be believed at all; and were they not given us on the authority of men of such great experience and benevolence, we should totally discredit them.

But, alas, they are only too true! There can be no doubt, that a great part of the poorer classes of this country are sunk into such a frightful depth of hopelessness, misery, and utter moral degradation, that even mothers forget their affection for their helpless little offspring, and kill them, as a butcher does his lambs, in order to make money by the murder, and therewith to lessen their pauperism and misery!

And yet we are sending hundreds of thousands of our savings every year to convert and comfort the heathen, who are seldom so morally degraded; while we are wrangling about the *way* in which we shall educate the poor; and are still telling Government that *volun-*

*tary* efforts will enable us to accomplish this great work.

I might greatly multiply the proofs of the universal existence of this evil; but the above quotations are, I think, sufficient to give an idea of this terrible sign of the social state of many of our poor.

Another melancholy symptom of the same fact is to be found in the great numbers and miserable condition of the inhabitants of the cellars of our towns.

In all our larger towns, and especially in those in which manufactures are carried on, there are a great number of cellars beneath the houses of the small shop-keepers and operatives, which are inhabited by crowds of poor inhabitants. Each of these cellar-houses contains at the most two, and often, and in some towns generally, only one room. These rooms measure, in Liverpool, from 10 to 12 feet square. In some other towns they are rather larger. They are generally flagged. The flags lie directly upon the earth, and are generally wretchedly damp. In wet weather they are very often not dry for weeks together. Within a few feet of the windows of these cellars, rises the wall which keeps the street from falling in upon them, darkening the gloomy rooms, and preventing the sun's rays penetrating into them.

Dr. Duncan, in describing the cellar-houses of the manufacturing districts, says *,—"The cellars are 10 or 12 feet square; generally flagged, but frequently having only the bare earth for a floor, and sometimes less than 6 feet in height. There is frequently no window, so that light and air can gain access to the cellar only by the door, the top of which is often not higher than the level of the street. In such cellars ventilation is

* Reports of the Health of Towns Commission, vol. i. 127.

out of the question. They are of course dark; and from the defective drainage, they are also very generally damp. There is sometimes a back cellar, used as a sleeping apartment, having no direct communication with the external atmosphere, and deriving its scanty supply of light and air solely from the front apartment."

But the character of the cellars themselves is by no means the worst feature of this miserable class of dwellings. I have already mentioned that they have never more than two, and generally only one room each, and that these rooms are very small; but small as they are, they are generally crowded to excess. It is no uncommon thing for two and three, and sometimes for four, families to live and sleep together in one of these rooms, without any division or separation whatever, for the different families or sexes. There are very few cellars, where at least two families do not herd together in this manner. Their beds are made sometimes of a mattress, and sometimes of straw in the corners of the cellar, and upon the damp, cold, flag floor; and on these miserable sleeping-places, the father, mother, sons, and daughters, crowd together in a state of filthy indecency, and much worse off than the horses in an ordinary stable. In these cellar-houses no distinction of sex and age is made. Sometimes a man is found sleeping with one woman, sometimes with two women, and sometimes with young girls; sometimes brothers and sisters of the age of 18, 19, and 20, are found in bed together; while at other times a husband and his wife share their bed with all their children.

The poor creatures who inhabit these miserable receptacles are of the most degraded species: they have never learned to read; have never heard of the existence of a Deity; have never been inside a church, being scared from the doors by their own filth and wretchedness; and have scarcely any sense of a distinction between right and wrong.

I have heard gentlemen, who have visited these kinds of dens in London, say, that they have found men and women sleeping together, three and four in a single bed, that they have not disturbed or ashamed them in the least, by discovering them in these situations, but that on the contrary their remonstrances have been answered only by a laugh or by a sneer.

In these places criminals are raised, and from these dens a moral pestilence creeps forth, and contaminates the moral life of even the more virtuous town-labourers. While such places exist, and continue to harbour so much immorality, it is as hopeless to expect to materially raise the character of our town poor, as it is to improve the sanitary condition of London while the Thames continues to receive the contents of all the London sewers, and to emit the gases of its poisoned waters in the very centre of the great metropolis.

It is impossible to give anything like an exact account of the number of cellar-houses in the different towns of England and Wales; we are not possessed of such information; but some idea of them may be formed by the statistics, which have been collected of the numbers of these cellar-houses in some of the larger towns of England.

Dr. Duncan says,* that in the twelve wards forming the parish of Liverpool, there are 6,294 inhabited cellars, containing 20,168 inhabitants, "exclusive of the inhabited cellars in courts (of which there are 621, containing probably 2,000 inhabitants). From pretty extensive data which I have in my possession, I

* Report of the Health of Towns Commission, vol. i. 127.

should be inclined to think these numbers, both of the court and cellar population, to be under the mark; but as they profess to be from actual enumeration, I am of course obliged to take them as I find them. Of the entire number of cellars, 1,617 have a back apartment; while of 5,297, whose measurements are given, 1,771, or one third, are from 5 to 6 feet deep; 2,324 are from 4 to 5 feet, and 1,202 from 3 to 4 feet below the level of the street; 5,273, or more than five-sixths, have no windows to the front; and 2,429, or about 44 per cent., are reported as either being damp or wet.

"It may be stated, that the whole of the cellar-population of the parish (upwards of 20,000), are absolutely without any place of deposit for their refuse matter."

In some instances, Dr. Duncan says, the fluid contents of the ash-pits of the houses above ooze through into these cellar-houses, filling them with pestilential vapours, and rendering it necessary to dig wells to receive it, in order to prevent the inhabitants being inundated. One of these wells, 4 feet deep, filled with this stinking fluid, was found in one cellar under the bed where the family slept.

To give an idea of the number of families, who reside in cellars, in some of our towns, I may mention, that in 1844, 20 per cent. of the working classes of Liverpool, 11¾ per cent. of those of Manchester, and 8 per cent. of those of Salford inhabited cellars such as I have described.

Mr. Holme, in describing some of the cellars in Liverpool, says,*—"The melancholy facts elicited by previous inquiries, clearly show, that Liverpool contains a multitude of inhabited cellars, close and damp, with no

* Report of the Health of Towns Commission, vol. i. 277.

drain, nor any convenience; and these pest-houses are constantly filled with fever. Some time ago I visited a poor woman in distress, the wife of a labouring man; she had been confined only a few days, and herself and infant were lying on straw in a vault, through the outer cellar, with a clay floor, impervious to water. There was no light or ventilation in it, and the air was dreadful. I had to walk on bricks across the floor to reach her bed-side, as the floor itself was flooded with stagnant water. This is by no means an extraordinary case, for I have witnessed scenes equally wretched; and it is only necessary to go into Crosby Street, Freemason's Row, and many cross streets out of Vauxhall Road, to find hordes of poor creatures living in cellars, which are almost as bad and offensive as charnel-houses. In Freemason's Row, I found, about two years ago, a court of houses, the floors of which were below the public street, and the area of the whole court was a floating mass of putrified animal and vegetable matter, so dreadfully offensive that I was obliged to make a precipitate retreat. Yet the whole of the houses were inhabited."

Since these accounts were first published the members of cellar-houses in Liverpool have, I believe, been diminished by the exertions of the municipality, but in most of our great towns they remain just as foul and just as numerous as ever.

But what is the condition of the houses of the poor in our towns and in our villages?

The further we examine, the more painful, disgusting, and incredible does the tale become.

We see on every hand, stately palaces, to which no country in the world offers any parallel. The houses of our rich are more gorgeous and more luxurious than those of any other land. Every clime is ransacked to adorn or furnish them. The soft carpets, the heavy rich curtains, the luxuriously easy couches, the beds of down, the services of plate, the numerous servants, the splendid equipages, and all the expensive objects of literature, science, and the arts, which crowd the palaces of England, form but items in an *ensemble* of refinement and magnificence, which was never imagined or approached, in all the splendour of the ancient empires.

But look beneath all this display and luxury, and what do we see there? A pauperised and suffering people.

To maintain show, we have degraded the masses, until we have created an evil so vast, that we now despair of ever finding a remedy. The Irish poor have drunk the dregs of the cup of misery, and are hardly kept from revolution by the strong arm of the soldiers and police; while the English poor are only saved from despair and its dread consequences, by the annual expenditure of MANY MILLIONS in relief, which our own neglect and misgovernment have rendered necessary.

The dwellings of the poor in the back streets and alleys of our towns are as wretched as they are degrading. The inquiries made in 1849, during the spread of the cholera, and those made in late years by the City Mission, by the correspondents of the "Morning Chronicle," and by private individuals, have disclosed a state of things which would disgrace a country of barbarians. Even leaving out of consideration the cellar-dwellings and the "lodging-houses," which I have mentioned above, the state of many of the houses in the back streets and alleys is wretched in the extreme. The amount of dwelling room occupied by many of the families is miserably small. Even in the manufacturing towns of the north, where the houses of the operatives are generally much superior to the wretched dwellings of the poor in the larger towns of the south of England, even there the accommodation afforded in a great part of the houses is miserable. Great numbers have only one bed-room for the whole family, whose father, mother, brothers, and sisters, all sleep together, often in the same bed.

Many even of the houses most recently built for operatives in Lancashire have only one bed-room. Scarcely one family in ten has more than two; so that, in the majority of cases, it is impossible to preserve anything like a decent separation of the sexes in the sleeping rooms. I have been assured on all hands in Lancashire, —by magistrates, manufacturers, and operatives,—that the immoral consequences of this state of things are terrible. Both in London, and in our larger provincial towns, it is no uncommon thing for two, three, and even four families to sleep in *one* room without any screen between the beds.

The evils resulting from this want of accommodation are still further enhanced by the wretched state of the back streets and alleys of our towns. In the larger of the provincial towns of England and Wales, the condition of these streets and alleys is as bad as it can be. They are built after no plan. They are narrow and often closed at one end. They are very badly drained. The openings of what drains there are, are generally close to the windows or doors of the houses. There is often only one privy for three, four, and sometimes as many as ten houses.

The streets and yards themselves are used for the filthiest purposes. Night-soil is spread about in the yards and on the pavements. The stench of these haunts is often insufferable.

The misery of life in these places is greatly increased by the fact, that there is often a very poor supply of water, and that the inhabitants are without the means, even if they had the will, to cleanse the streets of the filth, which accumulates upon their pavements. There is scarcely a town of any magnitude in England or Wales, which has not many quarters of this description.

What renders the demoralising effects of this state of things all the more appalling, is the fact, that most of the young children born in these places are left from morning to night for many years of their lives to grow up in the filth, amid the horrible scenes, and under the continued degrading influences of these streets,—unaccustomed to clean habits, clean dress, or to happy or healthy associations, but in the darkest ignorance; and that these poor little wretches have to creep back at night into crowded, loathsome, and immoral sleeping rooms, without having enjoyed any purer or more moral atmosphere or associations during the whole of the past day. If we reflect on the *necessary* effects of such a life as this, we shall not wonder at the vast numbers of our criminals and paupers, or at the degraded condition of so many of our town labourers.

Thus, while throughout Western Europe the schools are tending to improve the cleanliness, order, comfort, and propriety of the life of the town poor, by improving and forming the tastes and habits of the young, and by snatching them from the degrading scenes and associations to which the young of our towns are exposed; in our country, the way in which the children are growing up in the streets, renders the horrible state of our back streets even more injurious and demoralising than they otherwise would be, to the habits and the character of our town labourers.

The following accounts of the condition of the poor in the back streets of London will serve to illustrate the condition of our town poor in the back streets of most of the larger towns of England. If my space would permit, I could indefinitely multiply such instances. I could add similar accounts of almost every large town in England.

But as my space will not suffice, I beg to refer my readers to those published in Mr. Chadwick's Reports; in the City Mission Reports; in the Statistical Journal; and in the columns of "The Times," and "Morning Chronicle."

The Statistical Society, in 1848, appointed a committee of members to investigate the state of the inhabitants and their dwellings in Church Lane, St. Giles, London.

The committee represent* the state of this place as horrible. They give a minute account of the houses, and comment on their own report as follows:—

"Your committee have thus given a picture in detail of human wretchedness, filth, and brutal degradation, the chief features of which are a disgrace to a civilised country, and which your committee have reason to fear, from letters, which have appeared in the public journals, *is but the type of the miserable condition of masses of the community, whether located in the small, ill-ventilated rooms of manufacturing towns, or in many of the cottages of the agricultural peasantry.* In these wretched dwellings, all ages and all sexes,—fathers and daughters, mothers and sons, grown-up brothers and sisters, stranger adult males and females, and swarms of children,—the

* Journal of the Statistical Society of London, vol. xi. p. 17.

sick, the dying, and the dead,—are herded together *with a proximity and mutual pressure* which brutes would resist; where it is physically impossible to preserve the ordinary decencies of life; where all sense of propriety and self-respect must be lost, to be replaced only by a recklessness of demeanour, which necessarily results from vitiated minds. . . . . ."

In 1848, Mr. Hallam and Mr. Slaney furnished funds, wherewith to defray the expense of investigating the condition of the poorer classes in the parish of *St. George's in the East of London.* This parish was fixed upon, not as being the worst of the metropolitan districts, but as affording an example of the AVERAGE condition of the poorer classes of the metropolis.

1954 families, containing a population of 7711 individuals, were visited. The report upon their condition may be found in the eleventh volume of the Journal of the Statistical Society of London.

Out of these 1954 families—

551 families, containing a population of 2025 persons, have only *one* room each, where father, mother, sons, and daughters, live and sleep together.

562 families, containing a population of 2454 persons, have only *two* rooms each, in one of which people of different sexes must undress and sleep together.

705 families, containing a population of 1950 persons, have only *one bed* each, in which the whole family sleep together.

728 families, including a population of 3455 persons, have only *two* beds each, in one of which the parents sleep, and in the other of which all the sons and daughters sleep together.

In more than one-fourth of the houses, there were no serious books, Prayer-book, or Bible, and the impression of the agents employed in visiting the houses was, that of all the books which they found in the houses, the Bible was the least read.

In the number of the "City Mission Reports" for July, 1848, a description is given of Orchard's Place and Gray's Buildings, in the west end of London.

The report is as follows:—

"Orchard Place is (including two nooks) less than 45 yards long, and 8 broad, and contains 27 houses. Resident in this court, in 1845, *were no less than* 217 *families, consisting of* 882 *persons*, of whom 582 were above 14 years of age! The population of a large village, or a small town, is here comprised in one court. Kew, for instance, at the last census, had a population which exceeded it but by 41, and Abingdon exceeded it but by 38. Strathfieldsaye is less populous by 43; while the population of Brixton, in the Isle of Wight, is only 710; of Yarmouth, in the same island, but 567; and of Broxbourne, in Hertfordshire, but 643. . . . The description, which we presented to our readers of the district of St. Giles's, in the Magazine for November, 1847, showed that *each of the houses there contained* 100 *persons*. . . . ."

In 1847, however, the population of Orchard Place had considerably increased, notwithstanding the way in which the houses were crowded in 1845. It appears that, in 1847, THE 27 HOUSES CONTAINED 476 FAMILIES, AND FROM 882 TO 1222 INDIVIDUALS, and this, too, in the month of March, when the court is much more thinly populated than at any other season of the year!!

In the back streets of Kensington, and of Oxford Street, I know, from personal inspection, that the state of the poor is just such as I have described above. In

Westminster it is even worse. In the extreme parts of the city, and in the neighbourhood of the docks, it is even more horrible. And yet nothing worth speaking of is being done to check the continued growth of this terrible social cancer. It increases with the increase, and even faster than the increase in the multitudes of London, unchecked, as if there were no social remedy, and as if it were a necessary consequence of the system of great towns. And yet nothing like this state of things exists to any extent in the capitals of Germany. Certainly we have no right to say it cannot be cured, until we have tried all possible means of curing it; and as long as at least one half of the juvenile population is left to grow up without any education, we cannot say that we have done all that is possible.

In describing the wretched state of many of the houses in the parish of St. Giles's, in London, another of the city missionaries says* that in this district "there are 5 PRIVATE HOUSES, AND 8 LODGING HOUSES, IN ALL 13 HOUSES, WHICH ARE EACH INHABITED BY 100 INDIVIDUALS, *so that* 1300 *persons, or more than half a district, is comprised in only* 13 *houses.*

"Nor let it be supposed that these houses are so enormously large; for such is not the case. But the rooms are close packed with human beings, in a manner which would hardly be believed by those who had not actually seen them. Church Lane consists of 32 houses, which contain 190 rooms, IN EACH OF WHICH ROOMS LIVE AN AVERAGE OF 9 INDIVIDUALS, MAKING A TOTAL OF 1710 PERSONS. Separate families live in separate corners of the rooms. The party who hires the entire room ré-lets it in portions. And such rooms are the private and *respectable* rooms of the district, in

* City Mission Magazine, Nov., 1847.

distinction to the lodging-houses. The persons living in them profess to be respectable and virtuous members of society. But we will give a few examples of the manner in which rooms of this description were tenanted only last month. In *one* room of a house in Church Lane were found—

| | |
|---|---|
| Widow with three children . . . . | 4 |
| Widow with one child . . . . | 2 |
| Three single women . . . . | 3 |
| A man and his wife . . . . | 2 |
| A single man . . . . | 1 |
| A man and his wife . . . . | 2 |
| | 14 |

"These fourteen persons live by day, and sleep by night, in the same small room. The missionary put to one of the married men the question, 'Are you not ashamed?' His answer was, 'At first I was; but when I saw the other people thought nothing of it, I got to do so too.' The last enumerated couple are the landlord and his wife, who pay 3*s*. per week for the room. The two widows and the three single women, by dividing the four children between them, slept in two beds, and there were two other beds besides the landlord's. The landlord thus managed to use the room himself, and to let parts of it to others, from whom he received 8*s*. a week. He therefore lived himself rent free, and made 5*s*. a week profit of his furnished room, the furniture of which was only worth a few shillings. And yet this room was not reckoned as quite full!

"In a first-floor front room in Fletcher's Court were found—

| | |
|---|---|
| A man, his wife, and three children . . | 5 |
| A man, his wife, and child . . . | 3 |
| A widow and her two children . . | 3 |

| | |
|---|---|
| A man and his wife . . . . | 2 |
| A single woman, aged twenty years . . | 1 |
| | 14 |

"Of the above persons, only the first party enumerated had a bed; the others sleep on straw, and their only covering by night are the clothes they take off when the day is ended.

"In a ground-floor front of the same court were found—

| | |
|---|---|
| A woman and her five children . . | 6 |
| A woman and her two children . . | 3 |
| A man and his wife . . . . | 2 |
| A man and his wife . . . . | 2 |
| A single woman, sister to the above wife . | 1 |
| | 14 |

"The ages of the above children were from four to sixteen.

"Straw was the only bed in the room, and day clothes their only covering by night. Neither of the rooms in this court exceeded 7 feet by 10, and of the twenty-eight people living in them *not one could read.*

"Many women, now living with men in an unmarried state on the district, have stated to the missionary, *that it was by such crowded rooms they were led into temptation*, and that when they entered these houses they had no idea to what they were to be exposed. Some of these were servants out of place, who thought that because the houses looked respectable outside, they were the same within. They came up to London in search of situations, found they could not obtain them so immediately as they expected, were ignorant of this great city, and fell into company with the men with whom they now reside.

"Since the new street has been made the district has become more crowded than it was ever known to be before; and since the hopping season has closed, the missionary reckons that there are 500 more persons on the district than there were previously.

"THERE ARE FORTY LODGING-HOUSES OF THE LOWEST CHARACTER ON THE DISTRICT."

Mr. Riddall Wood was examined as to the effects of over-crowded tenements on the moral habits of the inmates in the various towns he had examined.*

"In what towns did you find instances of the greatest crowding of the habitations?—In Manchester, Liverpool, Ashton-under-Lyne, and Pendleton. In a cellar in Pendleton, I recollect there were three beds in the two apartments of which the habitation consisted, but having no door between them, in one of which a man and his wife slept; in another, a man, his wife, and child; and in a third, two unmarried females. In Hull, I have met with cases somewhat similar. A mother, about fifty years of age, and her son, I should think twenty-five, at all events above twenty-one, sleeping in the same bed, and a lodger in the same room. I have known two or three instances in Hull in which a mother was sleeping with her grown-up son; and in most cases there were other persons sleeping in the same room in another bed. In a cellar in Liverpool, I found a mother and her grown-up daughters sleeping on a bed of chaff on the ground in one corner of the cellar, and in the other corner three sailors had their bed. I HAVE MET WITH UPWARDS OF FORTY PERSONS SLEEPING IN THE SAME ROOM, MARRIED AND SINGLE, INCLUDING, OF COURSE, CHILDREN, AND SEVERAL YOUNG ADULT

* See Report on the Sanitary Condition of the Labouring Population.

PERSONS OF EITHER SEX. In Manchester, I could enumerate a variety of instances in which I found such promiscuous mixture of the sexes in sleeping rooms. I may mention one—a man, his wife, and child sleeping in one bed; in another bed, two grown-up females; and in the same room, two young men unmarried.

"I have met with instances of a man, his wife, and his wife's sister sleeping in the same bed together. I have known at least half-a-dozen cases in Manchester in which that has been regularly practised, the unmarried sister being an adult.

"In the course of your own inquiry, how many instances, if you were to look over your notes, of persons of different sexes sleeping promiscuously, do you think you met with?—I think I am speaking within bounds when I say I have amongst my memoranda above 100 cases, including, of course, cases of persons of different sexes sleeping in the same room.

"Was it so common as to be in no wise deemed extraordinary or culpable among that class of persons?—It seemed not to be thought of.

"As a proof of this, I may mention one circumstance which just occurs to me. Early in my visitation of Pendleton, I called at the dwelling of a person whose sons worked with himself in a colliery. It was in the afternoon, when a young man, one of the sons, came down stairs in his shirt, and stood before the fire, where a very decently dressed young female was sitting. The son asked his mother for a clean shirt, and on it being given to him, very deliberately threw off the shirt he had on, and, after warming the clean one, put it on.

"In another dwelling in Pendleton, a young girl, eighteen years of age, sat by the fire in her chemise during the whole time of my visit. Both these were houses of working people (colliers), and not by any means of ill fame.

"During your inquiries, were you able to observe any further demoralisation attendant upon these circumstances?—I have frequently met with instances in which the parties themselves have traced their own depravity to these circumstances. As, for example, while I was following out my inquiries in Hull, I found in one room a prostitute, with whom I remonstrated on her course of life, and asked her whether she would not be in a better condition if she were an honest servant, instead of living in vice and wretchedness. She admitted she should; and, on asking the cause of her being brought to her present condition, she stated that she had lodged with a married sister, *and slept in the same bed with her and her husband; that hence improper intercourse took place, and from that she gradually became more and more depraved, and at length was thrown upon the town*, because, having lost her character, the town was her only resource. Another female of this description admitted that her first false step was in consequence of her sleeping in the same room with a married couple. In the instance I have mentioned, of the two single women sleeping in the same room with the married people, I have good authority for believing that they were common to the men. In the case which I have mentioned of the two daughters and the woman where I found the sailors, I learned from the mother's admission, that they were common to the lodgers. In all of these cases the sense of decency was obliterated."

Mr. Baker, in his report on the condition of the labour ing classes in Leeds, corroborates this statement*:—

* See Report on the Sanitary Condition of the Labouring Population.

"*In the houses of the working classes, brothers and sisters, and lodgers of both sexes, are found occupying the same sleeping room with the parents, and consequences occur which humanity shudders to contemplate.* It is but three or four years ago since a father and daughter stood at the bar of the Leeds sessions as criminals, the one in concealing, and the other in being an accessory to concealing the birth of an illegitimate child, born on the body of the daughter by the father; and now, in November, 1841, one of the registrars of Leeds has recorded the birth of an illegitimate child, born on the body of a young girl only sixteen years of age, who lived with her mother, who cohabited with her lodger, the father of this child of which the girl had been pregnant five months when the mother died."

The over-crowding of the tenements of the labouring classes is productive of demoralisation in a mode pointed out by Mr. Barnett, the clerk to the Nottingham union, who states * :—

"That the houses are generally too small to afford a comfortable reception to the family, and the consequence is that the junior members are generally in the streets. Girls and youths destitute of adequate house-room, and freed from parental control, are accustomed to gross immoralities."

Mr. Chadwick says :†—

"It would require much time, and various opportunities of observation, to attempt to make an exact analysis of the combined causes, and an estimate of the effect of each separate cause, which operates to produce the masses of moral and physical wretchedness met

* See Report on the Sanitary Condition of the Labouring Population.

† See Ibid.

with in the investigation of the condition of the lowest population. But it became evident in the progress of the inquiry, that several separate circumstances had each its separate moral as well as physical influence. Thus, tenements of inferior construction had manifestly an injurious operation on the moral as well as on the sanitary condition, independently of any over-crowding. For example, it appears to be matter of common observation in the instance of migrant families of work-people, who are obliged to occupy inferior tenements, that their habits soon became of a piece with the dwelling. A gentleman, who has observed closely the condition of the workpeople in the south of Cheshire and the north of Lancashire—men of similar race and education, working at the same description of work, namely, a cotton-spinner's mill hands, and earning nearly the same amount of wages—states that the workmen of the north of Lancashire are obviously inferior to those in the south of Cheshire in health and habits of personal cleanliness, and general condition. The difference is traced mainly to the circumstance, that the labourers in the north of Lancashire inhabit stone houses of a description that absorbs moisture, the dampness of which affects the health and causes personal uncleanliness, induced by the difficulty of keeping a clean house. The operation of the same deteriorating influences was also observable in Scotland."

Even in Windsor, the city of our monarchs, the condition of the dwellings of the poor is wretched and horrible in the extreme. The following is a description of a part of the town called Garden Court, where the cholera made such ravages in 1849. I extract it from "The Times" of the 13th of October, 1849:—

"In the court there are twenty-one small houses, each

consisting of three rooms, the whole of which are occupied; *each room containing upon an average not less, including children, than five persons.* These rooms are generally let out to separate families. The back doors of each house open close to the privies, which are in a horribly filthy state, the stench arising from them being most offensive to the whole neighbourhood. Within 5 feet of the court there is an open stinking ditch running into the Thames, into which it carries the soil from some other houses in the neighbourhood.

"This ditch at times is most offensive, especially during the hot summer months. Into the rooms of four of the houses, the soil from the privies in Thames Street absolutely oozes, rendering these habitations unfit even for a dog, and much less for human beings. In the centre of the small yard there is a pump, from which water is supplied to all the inmates of this pestiferous court. This water is strongly impregnated with the stinking water of the ditches and drains by which the pump is surrounded."

I have lying under my hand accounts, precisely similar to those I have given of London, of the back streets of Liverpool, Manchester, Wigan, Preston, Rochdale, Durham, York, Lancaster, Carlisle, Stafford, Nottingham, Cambridge, Ely, Norwich, and of many other towns in all parts of England and Wales, but want of space prevents my publishing more than the few extracts which I have given.

Before however I dismiss this part of my subject, I would repeat that the *only* way by which we can hope to reform the habits and character of the poor, who live in the back streets and alleys of our towns, is, to snatch their children from the horrible influences of such a life as most of them now lead; and to endeavour, by means of good teachers and good schools, to keep them out of the streets during their younger years, to give them good principles, good habits, and useful knowledge; to make them *desire* to escape from their present social degradation; to enable them to act wisely and prudently; and to stimulate them to improve their own social condition. Before we can hope to civilise the poor of our back streets and alleys, we must teach them to become dissatisfied with their present miserable condition.

But so long as the greatest number of the children of the town poor are left, as at present, during the most susceptible period of their lives, to spend their days in such foul and degrading scenes as now surround the majority of them from morning to night, so long will our criminal calendars continue to increase, so long will the character of our poorer classes continue to degenerate, and so long will our towns remain hotbeds of vice, of misery.

If our poor were educated, as the German town poor are, they would not be able to endure such a life as they now lead. It would become as intolerable to them, as it would be to the richer and better educated classes of society.

Educate the habits of the poor, and the poor will soon find out a way to improve their homes. The homes will then aid the schools, by surrounding the children from their earliest years with improving instead of demoralising associations.

But miserable as the habitations of a great part of the poor of our towns are, the cottages and the cottage life of the peasants in our villages are still worse; and what is more, they have been for some time past, and still are, rapidly deteriorating. The majority of the cottages are wretchedly built, often in very unhealthy sites; they are miserably small, and are crowded to excess; they are very low, seldom drained, and badly roofed; and they scarcely ever have any cellar or space under the floor of the lower rooms. The floors are formed either of flags, which rest upon the cold undrained ground, or, as is often the case, of nothing but a mixture of clay and lime. The ground receives, day after day and year after year, between the crevices of the flags, or in the composition of clay and lime, water and droppings of all kinds, and gives back from them and from its own moisture combined, pestilential vapours, injurious to the health and happiness of the inmates of the cottage.

The cottages are fit abodes for a peasantry pauperised and demoralised by the utter hopelessness of their situation.

They may be classified as follows:—

1. Small cottages built of brick, of only one story in height, with a thatched roof, and without any cellar, so that the bricks or flags of the room rest immediately on the earth; with two small rooms between seven and eight feet in height, one used as the day-room and cooking-room, the other as the bed-room, where husband and wife, young men and young women, boys and girls, and very often a married son and his wife, all sleep together; without any garden, and with only a very small yard at the back, in which the privy stands almost close to the back door, pouring its gases into the house at all hours. This species of cottage is to be found in all parts of England and Wales. In some counties they are very numerous, as in Cambridgeshire, and especially in that part called the Isle of Ely, in Hertfordshire, in Leicestershire, in Dorsetshire, Devonshire, Somersetshire, Cornwall, Surrey, Sussex, Kent, Essex,

Bedfordshire, Buckinghamshire, Berkshire, the northern counties, and in Wales.

2. Cottages which have two stories with one small kitchen room on the ground floor, and with another small room above on the first floor, in which the whole family, father, mother, and children of both sexes sleep together. These houses have generally no garden, and only a small yard behind, in which the privy stands close to the back door. This class is very numerous throughout the country.

3. The third class of cottages are those, which have two stories,—the ground floor, where there is a day-room and a little scullery, and the upper floor, on which there are *two* bed-rooms, in one of which the parents sleep, and in the other of which the children, boys and girls, and young men, and young women, all sleep together. In many parts of England and Wales this class of cottages is very rare.

The accounts we receive from all parts of the country show that these miserable cottages are crowded to an extreme, and that the crowding is progressively increasing. People of both sexes, and of all ages, both married and unmarried—parents, brothers, sisters, and strangers—sleep in the same rooms and often in the same beds. One gentleman tells us of six people of different sexes and ages, two of whom were man and wife, sleeping in the same bed, three with their heads at the top and three with their heads at the foot of the bed. Another tells us of adult uncles and nieces sleeping in the same room close to each other; another of the uncles and nieces sleeping in the same bed together; another of adult brothers and sisters sleeping in the same room with a brother and his wife just married; many tell us of adult brothers and sisters sleeping in the same beds; another tells us of rooms so filled with beds that there is no space between them, but that brothers, sisters, and parents crawl over each other half naked in order to get to their respective resting-places; another of its being common for men and women, not being relations, to undress together in the same room, without any feeling of its being indelicate; another of cases where women have been delivered in bedrooms crowded with men, young women, and children; and others mention facts of these crowded bedrooms much too horrible to be alluded to. Nor are these solitary instances, but similar reports are given by gentlemen writing in ALL parts of the country.

The miserable character of the houses of our peasantry is, of itself, and independently of the causes, which have made the houses so wretched, degrading and demoralising the poor of our rural districts in a fearful manner. It stimulates the unhealthy and unnatural increase of population. The young peasants from their earliest years are accustomed to sleep in the same bedrooms with people of both sexes, and with both married and unmarried persons. They therefore lose all sense of the indelicacy of such a life. They know, too, that they can gain nothing by deferring their marriages and by saving; that it is impossible for them to obtain better houses by so doing; and that in many cases they must wait many years before they could obtain a separate house of any sort. They feel, that if they defer their marriage for ten or fifteen years, they will be at the end of that period in just the same position as before, and no better off for their waiting. Having then lost all hope of any improvement of their social situation, and all sense of the indelicacy of taking a wife home to the bed-room already occupied by parents, brothers, and sisters, they marry early in life,—often, if not generally, before the age of twenty,—and very often occupy, for the first part of their married life, another bed in the already crowded sleeping-room of their parents! In this way the morality of the peasants is destroyed; the numbers of this degraded population are unnaturally increased, and their means of subsistence are diminished by the increasing competition of their increasing numbers.

A low standard of living always tends to stimulate improvident marriages, to unduly increase the numbers of the population, and to engender pauperism, vice, degradation, and misery.

As I have said before, the landlords are unwilling to increase the number of cottages in the rural districts, because they fear to increase the numbers of the resident labouring population, and the amount of their poor-rates; and they are generally unwilling, even when they are able, to spend money in improving the size or character of the cottages, because they know, that they can easily let any of the existing cottages, no matter how wretched, owing to the great demand for house-room.

The crowding of the cottages has, therefore, of late been growing worse and worse. The promiscuous mingling of the sexes in the bed-rooms has been increasing very much, and is productive of worse consequences every year. Adultery is the very mildest form of the vast amount of crime which it is engendering. We are told by magistrates, clergymen, surgeons, and union officers, that in many parts of the country, cases of incest, and reports of other cases of the same enormity, are becoming more and more common among the poor. And there is no doubt whatsoever,—and in this all accounts and authorities agree,—that the way in which the married and unmarried people, and the different sexes, are mingled together, in the same bed-rooms, and even in the same beds, throughout the rural districts, is tending to destroy the modesty and virtue of the women, to annihilate the foundations, on which are based all the national and domestic virtues, and to make want of chastity before marriage, and want of delicacy and purity after marriage, common characteristics of the mothers and wives of our labouring population.

An eminent writer represents the consequences of the state of peasants' cottages in England and Wales, in the following powerful terms:—"A man and woman intermarry, and take a cottage. In eight cases out of ten it is a cottage with but two rooms. For a time, so far as room at least is concerned, this answers their purpose; but they take it, not because it is at the time sufficiently spacious for them, but because they could not procure a more roomy dwelling, even if they desired it. In this they pass with tolerable comfort, considering their notions of what comfort is, the first period of married life; but, by-and-by they have children, and the family increases, until, in the course of a few years, they number, perhaps, from eight to ten individuals. But all this time there has been no increase to their household accommodation. As at first, so to the very last, there is but the ONE SLEEPING-ROOM. As the family increases, additional beds are crammed into this apartment, until at last it is so filled with them, that there is scarcely room left to move between them. *I have known instances in which they had to crawl over each other, to get to their beds.* So long as the children are very young, the only evil connected with this is the physical one arising from crowding so many people together into what is generally a dingy, frequently a damp, and invariably an ill-ventilated apartment. But years steal on, and the family continues thus bedded together. Some of its members may yet be in their infancy, but others of both sexes have crossed the line of puberty. But there they are, still together in the same room—the father and mother, the sons and the daughters—young men, young women, and children. Cousins, too, of both sexes, are often thrown together into the same room, *and not unfrequently into the same bed.* I have also known of cases in which uncles slept in the same room with their grown-up nieces, and newly-married couples occupied the same chamber with those long married, and with others marriageable but unmarried. A case also came to my notice, already alluded to in connection with another branch of the subject, in which two sisters, who were married on the same day, occupied adjoining rooms in the same hut, with nothing but a thin board partition, which did not reach the ceiling, between the two rooms, and a door in the partition which only partly filled up the doorway. For years back, in these same two rooms, have slept twelve people of both sexes and ages. Sometimes, when there is but one room, a praiseworthy effort is made for the conservation of decency. But the hanging up of a piece of tattered clothes between the beds, which is generally all that is done in this respect, and even that but seldom, is but a poor set-off to the fact, that a family, which, in common decency, should, as regards sleeping accommodations, be separated at least into three divisions, occupy, night after night, but one and the same chamber. This is a frightful position for them to be in when an infectious or epidemic disease enters their abode. But this, important though it be, is the least important consideration connected with their circumstances. That which is most so, is the effect produced by them upon their habits and morals. In the illicit intercourse to which such a position frequently gives rise, *it is not always that the tie of blood is respected.* Certain it is that when the relationship is even but one degree removed from that of brother and sister, that tie is frequently overlooked. And when the circumstances do not lead to such horrible consequences, the mind, particularly of the female, is wholly divested of that sense of delicacy and shame, which, so long as they are preserved, are the chief safeguards of her chastity. She therefore falls an early and an easy prey to the temptations which beset her beyond the immediate circle of her family. People in the other spheres of life are but little aware of the extent to which this precocious demoralisation of the female amongst the lower orders in the country has proceeded. But how could it be otherwise? The philanthropist may exert himself in their behalf, the moralist may inculcate even the worldly advantages of a better course of life, and the minister of religion may warn them of the eternal penalties, which they are incurring; but there is an instructor constantly at work, more potent than them all,—an instructor in mischief, of which they must get rid ere they can make any real progress in their laudable efforts—and that is, *the single bed-chamber in the two-roomed cottage.*"

But what are the poor to do? So long as the law prevents their purchasing land; so long as they cannot obtain ground, on which to build their own cottages, as the foreign peasants do; so long, too, as the government will not interfere to educate the children of the peasants in higher tastes and better habits; and so long as they are only the tenants at the will of the agent of a landlord, one does not see how the peasant has a chance of improving the condition of his cottage, or the social position of his family.

I cannot too often repeat, that the great primary causes of the pauperism and degradation of our peasants are the utter *hopelessness* and *helplessness* of their position. We have done all we can to prevent their helping themselves; and to deprive them of every strong inducement to practise self-denial, prudence, and economy.

A man will not practise self-denial, economy, and prudence without an object. What object has an English peasant to practise them?

A peasant cannot possibly buy land as the foreign peasant does. He cannot get a farm even as a tenant-at-will of it. He cannot buy a house, or a plot of ground on which to build a house. He cannot even get the lease of a cottage. He cannot buy or get the lease of a garden. He often cannot even get the mere occupation of a cottage for himself. He is often obliged to take his wife to his father's or his brother's cottage, and to sleep with her in their bed-room.

What earthly inducement, then, has such a peasant to practise self-denial and economy? Absolutely none. He does not, therefore, practise any. He says to himself, if I put off my marriage and save, what should I gain by such a course? I'll marry early. If I cannot get a cottage, I'll take my wife to my father's cottage; and if bad times come, I'll apply to the union.

Such is the hideous social system to which we have subjected our poor.

How different is the condition of the foreign peasant! The majority of even the French peasants, who have attained the age of thirty-five, possess houses and farms of their own, the latter averaging from five to eight acres in size. The foreign peasant feels that his fate is in his own hands. He knows, that if he postpones his marriage, he will be able to purchase a house and farm of his own, and thus to establish his own complete independence. He is not dependent on agents of landlords or on landlords for the condition of his house, or for its tenure, or for the tenure of his farm, or for the social position of his family. All this, as well as his own future success in life, depends solely and entirely on his own exertions. This stimulates his energies and exertions. This makes his life hopeful and happy. This ennobles and developes his own character. This makes him a good citizen. This makes him a successful farmer. This increases his intelligence; and, while it makes his life hopeful and happy even amid privations, it makes him a good and conservative citizen even in times of suffering and distress.

I have myself examined, during the present year, the condition of the peasants' cottages in Cambridgeshire, and particularly in that part of Cambridgeshire called the Isle of Ely, in Hertfordshire, and in Leicestershire.

These are agricultural counties, where the land is very rich and very well cultivated. The farms are generally of considerable size. The peasants have no chance of ever rising to the farmer class. The cottages have scarcely ever a garden attached to them. The land is all divided between great farms and parks.

Now, what is the condition of the majority of cottages of the peasants of these counties?

They are almost as wretched as they can be. The majority of them are small low huts of one story in height. The walls are about eight feet high. The roofs are very often thatched. The thatch is very seldom repaired. Through the top of the thatch projects the chimney. There is no cellar beneath the rooms. The floors are made of bricks or flags, which are laid upon the earth, and, as may be conceived, are damp and cold.

In the middle of one of the side walls there is a door, and on each side of the door a window, which is but too often minus several panes at least, their places being occupied with rags. One half of the interior of many of these cottages is boarded or walled off, so as to divide the house into two little rooms. One of these rooms is the living room, the other is a bed-room, in which sleep the whole family, parents, and daughters. It is by no means rare for the two sexes to sleep not only in the same bed-room but in the same bed.

Many of the cottages are two stories in height, with one room on the ground floor, and one above. Some have two small bed-rooms, in one of which the parents sleep, while all the sons and daughters sleep in the other.

Scarcely any cottages have more than two bed-rooms, and very few have more than one.

Even of the few new cottages which are being built, none have more than two bed-rooms, while many have not more than one. Their walls are better built than those of the older cottages, and their roofs are slate instead of thatch; but these are in general the only improvement on the old and general style of cottages.

The sites of the new cottages are at least as wretched as those of the old.

One singular thing is, that this state of things has existed so long, that the poor have sunk below complaining, and that the landlords and richer classes are quite surprised, if you talk to them of the miserable condition of the peasants' cottages. They have learned to think it a necessary state of things, and ridicule the idea of its being the result of a system of defective legislation. Many go much further, and boldly maintain, that it is better that the peasants should not be educated, as education would make them thoroughly discontented with their present position in life. I pray God it may. When it has so done, there will be a chance of reformation; but at present they are below even discontent.

Another singular thing is to hear people talk about the *picturesque* cottages of the English peasants, forgetting, or not caring to remember, that the thatched roofs, old, moss-covered, low, and crooked walls, and dilapidated chimneys, may, indeed, give them an old and quaint appearance, but that they at the same time render them scarcely fit habitations for our cattle, and certainly incapable of being compared to the well-built stables of the landlord's horses.

The following remarkable extracts, selected from various sources of the highest authority, will show the miserable condition of the cottages and dwellings of the peasantry in other parts of England and Wales.

I offer these extracts only as specimens, which I could multiply indefinitely, if my space would allow, of a state of things which exists more or less in every county in England, and as proofs of the wretched way in which the cottages of our peasantry are built; of the miserable lodging and accommodation afforded by them to their poor inmates; of the wretched and unhealthy sites, which are often chosen for them by agents and persons, who do not care where or how the peasants are lodged; of the want of drainage, ventilation, water supply, and privies, which distinguishes most of them; and of the sickness and shocking moral degradation caused by this miserable and lamentable state of things.

If any one should desire to see more of such sad and disgusting details, as those collected in the following pages, I beg to refer him to the Report on the Employment of Women in Agriculture, published by Government, in 1843; to Mr. Chadwick's very able Reports on the Sanitary Condition of the Labouring Population; to the Reports of the Welsh Commissioners; to the Reports of the Poor Law Commission; to the columns of "The Times"; and to the remarkable and exceedingly able letters published in the "Morning Chronicle" in the autumn of 1849.

The first series of extracts will show the present condition of the peasants' houses in the south-western counties—Wiltshire, Dorsetshire, Devonshire, Gloucestershire, Somersetshire, and Cornwall.

Mr. Alfred Austin, Special Assistant Poor Law Commissioner, in reporting upon the condition of the peasants' cottages in the counties of Wilts, Dorset, Devon, and Somerset, says:—*

"The want of sufficient accommodation seems universal. Cottages generally have only two bed-rooms (with very rare exceptions); a great many have only one. The consequence is, that it is very often extremely difficult, if not impossible, *to divide a family, so that grown-up persons of different sexes, brothers and sisters, fathers and daughters, do not sleep in the same room. Three or four persons not unfrequently sleep in the same bed.* In a few instances I found that two families—neighbours—arranged, so that the females of both families slept together in one cottage, and the males in the other; but such an arrangement is very rare, and in the gene-

* See Report on the Employment of Women in Agriculture.

rality of cottages, I believe, that the only attempt that is or that can be made to separate beds, with occupants of different sexes, and necessarily placed close together, from the smallness of the rooms, is an old shawl, or some article of dress, suspended as a curtain between them.

"At Stourpain, a village near Blandford, I measured a bed-room in a cottage, consisting of two rooms, the bed-room in question up stairs, and a room on the ground floor, in which the family lived during the day. The room was 10 feet square, not reckoning the two small recesses by the sides of the chimney, about 18 inches deep. The roof was of thatch, the middle of the chamber being about 7 feet high. Opposite the fire-place was a small window, about 15 inches square, the only one in the room."

Three beds were crammed into this little room. There was no curtain or separation between the beds.

One bed contained the father and mother, a little boy, and an infant.

The second bed contained *three* daughters, the two eldest, twins, aged twenty years each, and the other aged seven.

The third bed was occupied by *four* sons, aged respectively seventeen, fifteen, fourteen, and ten.

Mr. Austin says,—"This, I was told, was not an extraordinary case; but that, more or less, every bed-room in the village was crowded with inmates of both sexes and of various ages, and that such a state of things was caused by the want of cottages.

"It is impossible not to be struck, in visiting the dwellings of the agricultural labourers, with the general want of new cottages, notwithstanding the universal increase of population. Everywhere the cottages are old, and frequently in a state of decay, and are con sequently ill adapted for their increased number of inmates of late years. The floor of the room in which the family live during the day is always of stone in these counties, and wet or damp through the winter months, being frequently lower than the soil outside. The situation of the cottage is often extremely bad, no attention having been paid at the time of its building to facilities for draining. Cottages are frequently erected on a dead level, so that water cannot escape; and sometimes on spots lower than the surrounding ground."

With reference to the subject of lodging, Mr. Phelps, an agent of the Marquis of Lansdowne, says*:—

"I was engaged in taking the late census in Bremhill parish; and, in one case in Studley, I found twenty-nine people living under one roof; amongst them were married men and women, and young people of nearly all ages. In Studley, it is not at all uncommon *for a whole family to sleep in the same room. The number of bastards in that place is very great;* the number of unmarried women is greater than that in the neighbouring places. I don't think this state of things is attributable to the women working in the fields, but rather to the want of proper accommodation in the cottages."

Mr. Austin says again,—"The morality of the agricultural labourer is a subject, to which my inquiry did not extend, nor had I sufficient opportunities of making any satisfactory inquiry respecting it; but certain things forced themselves upon my attention, and, amongst others, the consequences of the want of accommodation in their dwellings for sleeping. The sleeping of boys and girls, young men and young

* Report on the Employment of Women in Agriculture.

women, in the same room, in beds almost touching one another, *must have the effect of breaking down the great barriers between the sexes*,—the sense of modesty and decency on the part of women, and respect for the other sex on the part of men. The consequences of the want of proper accommodation for sleeping in the cottages are seen in the early licentiousness of the rural districts, *licentiousness which has not always respected the family relationship*.

"It appeared to me, that, generally, the accommodation for sleeping is such as necessarily to create an early and illicit familiarity between the sexes; *for universally in the villages, where the cottages are the most crowded, there are the greatest number of illegitimate children, and also the greatest depravity of manners generally*."

The Rev. J. Guthrie, vicar of Colne, Wiltshire, says*:—

"The want of good cottages, where the members of a family can live separately, is a great cause of demoralisation. When grown up members of the same family are continually occupying the same room, modesty, and delicacy, and sense of shame, are soon put to flight. When these are absent, and dirt and disorder take their place, a gradual declension in good morals and character succeeds, and the whole family sink perceptibly to a lower grade in character and conduct."

The Hon. and Rev. S. Godolphin Osborne, rector of Bryanston-cum-Durweston, Dorsetshire, says†:—

"The children of the agricultural labourer, for the most part, sleep in the same room with his wife and himself; and whatever attempts at decency may be made,—and I have seen many most ingenious and praiseworthy attempts—still, there is the fact of the old

* Report on the Employment of Women in Agriculture. † Ibid.

and young, married and unmarried, of both sexes, all herded together in one and the same sleeping apartment. Within this last year, I saw in a room about 13 feet square, three beds; on the first, lay the mother, a widow, dying of consumption; on the second, two unmarried daughters, one eighteen years of age, the other twelve; on the third, a young married couple, whom I myself had married two days before! A married woman, of thorough good character, told me a few weeks ago, that on her confinement, so crowded with children is her one room, they are obliged to put her on the floor in the middle of the room, that they may pay her the requisite attention! She spoke of this, as, to her, the most painful part of that her hour of trial. I do not choose to put on paper the disgusting scenes that I have known to occur from this promiscuous mingling of the sexes together. Seeing, however, to what the mind of the young female is exposed from her very childhood, I have long ceased to wonder at the other wise seeming precocious licentiousness of conversation, which may be heard in every field, where many of the young are at work together."

The Rev. H. Austen, curate of Pimperne, Dorset, says* :—

"The poor people have to struggle with the want of proper accommodation in their dwellings, which, I fear, is too general in our rural districts. A man and his wife, with a large family of children, have, in most cases, only two bed-rooms."

Mr. M. Fisher, of Blandford, Dorset, says† :—

"I think, generally, the habits of the people are worse, and the manners of the women especially, where

* Report on the Employment of Women in Agriculture.

† Ibid.

the accommodation of the cottages is bad. Milton Abbas, I think, is a place, where the character of the population is decidedly inferior. On the average at the late census, *there were thirty-six persons in each separate house.* The houses there are all built on one plan, each containing two dwellings with four rooms. In most of these dwellings there are two families, that is to say, on the average, A FAMILY OF NINE TO EVERY TWO ROOMS. Stourpain is another village, where the population is very thick, the cottages comparatively few, and in a miserable state, and the people crowded together. In that village, there are more bastard children than in any other village of the same size in the union of Winterborne. Kingston is another village, where there is a similar want of accommodation, and where you may see open stagnant drains, pools, and filth of all descriptions; and the character of the people is similar to these external appearances.

"Throughout the whole union, there appears to me to be a great want of cottages; very few have been built for many years, whilst the population has gone on increasing. The villages are overflowing, which produces great demoralisation; the surplus, and that generally the very worst characters, come to Blandford, owing to a great many new houses having been built within the last few years."

H. N. Tilsey, Esq., of North Petherton, Somersetshire, surgeon, and one of the medical officers of the Bridgewater union, says:—*

"There is a great want of cottage accommodation on many farms, so that the labourers are driven to the villages, and often congregate to the injury of their morals, many of them resorting to the beer-shop, who would,

* See Report on the Employment of Women in Agriculture.

under a different system, be better members of society. What cottages there are, are generally badly arranged, badly ventilated, and badly drained; occasionally, all ages and sexes sleeping in one common room. As a class, these labourers—men, women, and children—although, perhaps, sufficiently skilled in all matters relating to their own particular calling, manifest the most complete and perfect ignorance of all that regards school instruction."

Mr. Gilbert, formerly Assistant Poor Law Commissioner for Devonshire and Cornwall, gives the following, as an instance of the common condition of the dwellings of the labouring classes :—*

"In Tiverton, in Cornwall, there is a large district, from which I find numerous applications were made for relief to the board of guardians, in consequence of illness from fever.

"One cause of disease is to be found in the state of the cottages.

"Many are built on the ground, without flooring, or against a damp hill.

"Some have neither windows nor doors sufficient to keep out the weather, or to let in the rays of the sun, or supply the means of ventilation; and in others the roof is so constructed or so worn, as not to be weather-tight.

"The thatch roof is frequently saturated with wet, rotten, and in a state of decay, giving out malaria, as other decaying vegetable matter."

The state of the dwellings of many of the agricultural labourers in Dorset, where the deaths from the four classes of disease bear a similar proportion to those in Devon, is described in the return of Mr. John Fox, the

* See Report on Sanitary Condition of the Labouring Population.

medical officer of the Cerne union in Dorsetshire, who, remarking upon some cases of disease among the poor whom he had attended, says :—*

"*I have often seen the springs bursting through the mud floor of some of the cottages, and little channels cut from the centre, under the doorways, to carry off the water, whilst the door has been removed from its hinges for the children to put their feet on whilst employed in making buttons. It is not surprising that fever, and scrofula in all its forms, prevail under such circumstances.

"It is somewhat singular that seven cases of typhus occurred in one village, heretofore famed for the health and general cleanliness of its inhabitants and cottages. The first five cases occurred in one family, in a detached house on high and dry ground, and free from accumulations of vegetable and animal matter. The cottage was originally built for a school-room, and consists of one room only, about 18 feet by 10 feet, and 9 feet high. About one-third part was partitioned off by boards, reaching to within 3 feet of the roof; and *in this small space were three beds, in which six persons slept.* Had there been two bed-rooms attached to this one day-room, these cases of typhus would not have occurred.

"Most of the cottages are of the worst description, some mere mud hovels, and situated in low and damp places, with cesspools or accumulations of filth close to the doors.

"The mud floors of many are much below the level of the road, and in wet seasons are little better than so much clay.

"In many of the cottages, also, where synochus pre-

* See Report on Sanitary Condition, &c.

vailed, the beds stood on the ground-floor, which was damp three parts of the year; scarcely one had a fire-place in the bed-room; and one had a single small pane of glass stuck in the mud wall, as its only window, with a large heap of wet and dirty potatoes in one corner. Persons living in such cottages are generally very poor, very dirty, and usually in rags, *living almost wholly on bread and potatoes, scarcely ever tasting animal food*, and consequently highly susceptible of disease, and very unable to contend with it. I am sure, if such persons were placed in good, comfortable, clean cottages, the improvement in themselves and children would soon be visible, and the exceptions would only be found in a few of the poorest and most wretched, who perhaps have been born in a mud hovel, and had lived in one the first thirty years of their lives.

"In my district, *I do not think there is one cottage to be found consisting of a day-room, three bed-rooms, scullery, pantry, and convenient receptacles for refuse and for fuel, in the occupation of a labourer.*"

The tenor of much information respecting the condition of many of the labouring classes in Somerset, is exhibited in the Sanitary Report of Mr. James Gane, the medical officer of the Axbridge Union, in Somersetshire, who states* that,—

"The situation of this district, where the diseases therein-mentioned prevail, is a perfect flat called the South Marsh, in the main road between Bristol and Bridgewater. There are numerous dykes or ditches for the purpose of drainage. The cottages of the poor are mostly of a bad description. The walls are frequently made of mud. They are often situated close to the dykes, where the water, for the most part, is in

* See Report on Sanitary Condition, &c.

a state of stagnation. *Oftentimes there is not more than one room for the whole family;* sometimes two, one above the other; with the really poor, *the latter is seldom to be met with* (unless it should happen now and then in a parish where a poor-house was built a short time before the formation of the union). A pigsty, where the inmates are capable of keeping a pig, is frequently attached to the dwelling, and in the heat of summer produces a stench quite intolerable: the want of space, however, prevents it being otherwise. The ordinary houses of the poor peasants (those mentioned above being detached cottages), in most of the parishes in this district, are of a much worse description, several large families existing under the same roof, and *each family occupying only one room*, and having but one entrance door to the dwelling. Here filth and poverty go hand in hand, without any restriction, and under no control; the accumulation of filth being attributable to the want of proper receptacles for refuse. Owing to the indolent and filthy disposition of the inhabitants, in no instance have such places been provided.

"The floors are seldom or never scrubbed, and the parish authorities pay so little attention to these houses, that the walls never get white-limed from one end of the year to the other. The windows are kept air-tight by the stuffing of some old garments; and every article for use is kept in the same room. *The necessary is close to the building*, where all have access, and produces a most intolerable nuisance. In a locality naturally engendering malaria, the diseases with which the poor are for the most part afflicted are fevers, such as are stated in this Report, which sometimes run into a low typhoid state. The neighbourhood in general is considered in as good a state of drainage as it will admit of.

"The occurrence of disease among the poor population, is for the most part at spring and autumn. At those times agues and fevers prevail. Small-pox and scarlet fever are met with at all seasons of the year, but prevail as epidemics, the former in spring and summer, and the latter about autumn or the beginning of winter. I attribute the prevalence of diseases of an epidemic character, which exist so much more among the poor than among the rich, to be owing to the want of better accommodation as residences (their dwellings, instead of being built of solid materials, are complete shells of mud on a spot of waste land, the most swampy in the parish —this is to be met with almost everywhere in rural districts); to the want of better clothing, better food, and of more attention paid to the cleanliness of their dwellings; and to the being so congregated together. The health of persons, even where a large family is, and where superior cottage accommodation is afforded to them, is much better generally than others less advantageously situated. The influence over their habits will also be very beneficial; they will be less likely to run to a beer-house with their last penny.

"The comforts of a home, after the toils of the day, keep them by their own fireside; they become better contented, less liable to disease, make better husbands, better fathers, better neighbours, and better friends with each other. There is a subject, which I wish particularly to press on the attention of the commissioners, —*the existence throughout the country, and in every parish, of low lodging-houses, where persons of the lowest grade of society, beggars, thieves, and such-like, take up a temporary abode in passing from one part of the kingdom to the other, bringing with them the seeds of infectious diseases, and oftentimes the actual disease itself, into a neighbourhood previously in a comparative state of health.*"

The following extract from the report of Mr. Aaron Little, the medical officer of the Chippenham Union, in Wiltshire, affords a specimen of the frequent condition of rural villages which have apparently the most advantageous sites*: "—

"The parish of Colerne, which, upon a cursory view, any person (unacquainted with its peculiarities) would pronounce to be the most healthy village in England, is, in fact, the most unhealthy. From its commanding position, being situated upon a high hill, it has an appearance of health and cheerfulness, which delight the eye of the traveller, who commands a view of it from the great western road; but this impression is immediately removed on entering at any point of the town.

"The filth, dilapidated buildings, the squalid appearance of the majority of the lower orders, have a sickening effect upon the stranger, who first visits this place. During three years' attendance among the poor of this district, I have never known the small-pox, scarlatina, or the typhus fever to be absent. The situation is damp, and the buildings unhealthy, and the inhabitants themselves inclined to be of dirty habits. There is also a great want of drainage."

During the latter part of 1849, some very remarkable and exceedingly able letters were published in the "Morning Chronicle," describing the condition of the cottages of the peasantry in different parts of England. I might crowd my pages with extracts from these letters, all proving the truth of the description I have given above of the cottages of our peasantry. It is impossible for me to do more than make one or two

* Report on Sanitary Condition, &c.

extracts from them, to show how the condition of the cottages of the peasantry is *deteriorating*. I must refer my readers to these remarkable letters for further details. They will well repay the most careful study.

The correspondent of the "Morning Chronicle," describing the condition of the labourers in Devonshire, Somersetshire, Cornwall, and Dorsetshire, says:—

"Devon and Somerset have long been classed in the unenviable category of counties presenting the agricultural labourer in his most deplorable circumstances. With Dorset and Wilts, they are generally regarded as exhibiting the unfavourable, whilst Lincolnshire exhibits the favourable, extreme in the labourer's condition.

"In traversing both counties, more especially Devonshire, I was particularly struck with the utter absence of new cottages. Along the highways and byways their absence is observable; and not only this, but in many places there are abundant evidences that cottages, which a few years ago were tenanted, are now, if not altogether untenantable, going rapidly into decay. Many are so rickety and ruined, that to inhabit them any longer is impossible; whilst, as regards others, the process of demolition or decomposition has only commenced, confining the wretched tenants, who had formerly two rooms, to the only apartment which remains, and which they can with difficulty keep together. In search of these, one has not to go into remote and sequestered parts, where things are done which would not be exposed in the neighbourhood of the highways. I have seen specimens of cottages in this state along the line from Exeter to Honiton, and in the district traversed by the high-road to London. . . . . . . .

"Not only are no new cottages being erected to meet

the exigencies of an increasing population, but old ones, instead of being kept in repair, are suffered to crumble to pieces, if, indeed, decay is not aided by more active means. In a parish between Honiton and the coast, a great part of which is owned by Sir Edward Elton, this process of cottage clearing seems to be a marked feature in proprietary policy. On Sir Edward Elton's property I am told, that the average rate of decay or demolition is about six cottages per annum. As each cottage would contain a family of seven on the average, the proprietor thus clears his estate of about forty-two poor persons each year, unless they can find room in their neighbour's hovels, which can, in most cases, be but ill spared. By this means this estate, and others similarly dealt with, will, by and by, become eased of one incumbrance, at least, which presses upon them—a large and unemployed population.

"Whilst in many parts of Devon and Somerset the process of the demolition of cottages has been going on far more rapidly, than that of building new ones, the population of the two counties has been fast increasing. 'We don't find room for them,' said a farmer with whom I conversed on this subject, 'and they are drafted off to other places.' But they are not thus drafted off in all cases, and the real effect of the demolition of cottages is to reduce, if possible, to a still lower point of wretchedness the physical condition of the labourer. The clergyman of one of the parishes of Devon pointed out to me an addition which had recently been made to the parish church. As it stood, the church was but a small one, but the addition made to it was larger than the original edifice. 'Why was the addition made?' I asked. 'Because the population of the parish has increased,' was the reply. This answer was obvious, and I had anticipated it; but I wished to obtain it, in order to base upon it another question. 'How comes it,' I inquired, 'that if the population has increased so as to require so large an addition to be made to the church, there is not a single new cottage to be found in your parish?' 'That is difficult to say,' he answered. 'It does not appear to me,' I added, 'that there is a cottage in your whole parish, which has been built within the last fifty years.' 'They all seem to be of that age, at least,' he replied, 'and many much older.' 'And when was the addition made to the church?' I inquired. 'Within the last twenty years,' said he. This simple story speaks for itself. The population of the parish in question has largely increased, but the house accommodation has not increased in the slightest degree to meet the exigencies of a growing population.

"It is evident that the new comers were not drafted off elsewhere as fast as they came, otherwise the church might have remained of its original dimensions. The truth, of course, is, that most of them stayed in the parish, every cottage in it becoming more and more crowded with inmates every year. The consequences of this, both in a moral and a physical point of view, are shocking to contemplate. And this is the process which is going on in more parishes than one in the counties of Devon and Somerset. WHILST POPULATION IS INCREASING WITHIN THEM, NOT ONLY IS HOUSE ACCOMMODATION NOT INCREASING, BUT IT IS ACTUALLY DIMINISHING.

"The points in Devon, at which I more particularly inspected the dwellings of the poor, were, in the south, in the neighbourhood of Exeter, along the line between that city and Exmouth, in the direction of Totness, and throughout a great part of the union of Kingsbridge; in the vicinity of Axminster, between that town and Honiton, and between Honiton and Sidmouth; and in the north, around Barnstaple, and along the more northerly part of the Vale of the Torridge. In Somerset I examined them with some care in the neighbourhood of Minehead and Dunster in the north-west; near Bridgewater, in the centre; and about Wells, Chewton, Mendip, &c., in the north-eastern part of the county. *In the great majority of instances I found the condition of the cottages to be deplorably bad.* It is not to be denied that I encountered some, and even many, exceptions. At many points there were cottages to be found well situated and commodious, but they were exceptions to the general character of the peasants' dwellings.

"It is impossible fully to estimate the wretchedness to which the inmates of the hovels, which meet the eye at all points, are exposed, without a close personal inspection of them. We are accustomed to associate with the idea of a country village, or with a cottage situated in a winding vale, or hanging upon the side of a rich and fertile slope, nothing but health, contentment, and happiness. A rural dwelling of this class, with its heavy thatch and embowering trees, makes such a nice pencil sketch, that we are naturally inclined to think it as neat and comfortable as it appears. But to know it aright, it must be turned inside out, and its realities exposed to the gaze of the observer. Could the internal be always given with the external view, it would moderate our enthusiasm for the little sketches, which work so early and so powerfully upon our fancies, and which are suggestive of nothing but contentment and happiness. How often does the cot, which looks so attractive and romantic upon paper, conceal an amount of wretchedness, filth, squalor, disease, privation, and frequently of immorality, which, when exposed in their reality, are perfectly appalling! And as to health, nowhere, perhaps, is the pure air of heaven more tainted than in the neighbourhood of these rustic dwellings. You will encounter odours in a country village, which it would be difficult to match in Westminster or St. Giles's. Indeed, the most sickening and offensive, that I ever came in contact with, had nestled themselves on the summit of Beacon Hill, in the neighbourhood of Bath. It is high time that people divested themselves of the false impressions too generally entertained of the character of our rural cottages. They are chiefly drawn from descriptions which at one time may have suited the reality, when the condition of the agricultural labourer was much better than it is now; for that it was much better than at present, is evident from the information derived from a variety of valuable sources. To go a considerable way back: We find Fortescue alluding to their condition in his day, as one of great comfort and happiness; inasmuch as they lived chiefly upon butcher meat, of which they had plenty, and had abundance of good ale, with which to accompany it at their meals. In regard to their diet, at least, their condition now seems the very reverse of what it was then; and as it is impossible that they could have fallen back so much in this important element of their physical condition, without having all the others deteriorated in proportion, it is fair to infer that their house accommodation was better formerly than now. It was better in this, if in no other respect—that fewer people were to be found under one and the same roof, a state of things much more favourable to health, cleanliness, and good morals than that which now prevails. We must, therefore, judge of the labourer's condition, not from past descriptions of it, but from the sad realities of the present hour."

In another letter the same gentleman writes:—

"But bad as are the tenements usually occupied by the poor, they are not, except in rare cases, quite so revolting in their character, and in the scenes to which they give rise, as are some tenements, which have a claim to be regarded in the light of public buildings. These are the parish houses, which are scattered in considerable numbers over the southern and western districts. They are the houses, in which the poor were accommodated previously to the erection of the union workhouses. In many cases, since the workhouses came into use, these parish houses have been sold, and the proceeds applied to defraying, *pro tanta*, the expense of building the workhouses. But in others, the overseers will not part with them, keeping them for the purpose of letting, and thus deriving a profit from them. They are generally let at a lower rent than ordinary cottages, and thus become the resort of those in the most wretched circumstances, who crowd into them by dozens, and fill up almost every crevice of them with lodgers. One of these I saw on the borders of Devonshire and Cornwall, and not far from Launceston. It consisted of two houses, containing between them four rooms. In each room was a family, who used it both night and day. The lower rooms were about 12 feet square. In one of them were a man, and his wife, and five children; in the other were a man, and his wife and eight children. In this latter, there were but two beds—the father, and mother, and two children occupying one, and the other six being huddled together in the remaining bed. They lay 'head and foot,' as they termed it—that is to say, *three with their heads at the top, and three with them at the foot of the bed!* The eldest girl was between *fifteen* and *sixteen*, and the eldest boy between *fourteen* and *fifteen*. The closeness of this room was overpowering. The beds were necessarily large, and occupied most of the floor; indeed, when the whole family was assembled, several of the children were placed upon the beds to keep them out of the way. In this way the beds may be said to have never been cold. How can health be retained or morals preserved under such circumstances as these?"

And in another letter the same gentleman describes some of the cottages he has been visiting, thus:—

"The cabin is so rude and uncouth, that it has less the appearance of having been built, than of having been suddenly thrown up out of the ground. The length is not above 15 feet, its width between 10 and 12. The wall, which has sunk at different points, and seems bedewed with a cold sweat, is composed of a species of imperfect sandstone, which is fast crumbling to decay. It is so low, that your very face is almost on a level with the heavy thatched roof, which covers it, and which seems to be pressing it into the earth. The thatch is thickly encrusted with a bright green vegetation, which, together with the appearance of the trees and the mason-work around, well attests the prevailing humidity of the atmosphere. In front, it presents to the eye a door, with one window below, and another window—a smaller one—in the thatch above. The door is awry from the sinking of the wall; the glass in the window above is unbroken, but the lower one is here and there stuffed with rags, which keep out both the air and the sunshine. You approach the doorway through the mud, over some loose stones, which rock under your feet in using them. You have to stoop for admission, and cautiously look around, ere you fairly trust yourself within. There are but two rooms in the house, one below and the other above." The sleeping accommodations "are gained by means of a few greasy and rickety steps, which lead through a species of hatchway in the ceiling. *Yes, there is but one room, and yet we counted nine in the family!* And such a room! The small window in the roof admits just light enough to enable you to discern its character and dimensions. The rafters, which are all exposed, spring from the very floor, so that it is only in the very centre of the apartment, that you have any chance of standing erect. The thatch oozes through the wood-work, which supports it, the whole being begrimed with smoke and dust, and replete with vermin. But, perhaps, the climax of misery in this respect, in the district, is to be found in the village of Taversey, about a mile distant from Thame. One house was pointed out to me there with four rooms; each room occupied by a separate family, some of the families being very numerous. It was a two-story house, covered with tiles. There was no communication between the upper and lower stories, the former being approached from the outside by a flight of stone steps, which rose over the door leading into the latter. One of the families counted eight or ten, of both sexes, some of whom had attained maturity. The immorality to which their domestic condition gives rise I shall have occasion hereafter to refer to."

The correspondent of "The Morning Chronicle" traces very powerfully the enormous evils, which spring from the present shameful condition of the cottages of the peasants. He says, in one of his letters:—"Wherever I went, I found the uncertainty of work and the want of cottage accommodation the two great subjects of complaint. I was told by some of the more respectable people in Corfe, that if there were twenty new cottages built in the town, they would be readily occupied. So great is the want of room, that many of the labourers themselves would go to the expense of building, if the opportunity of so doing were given them.

. . . . . . . . . . .

"But if the cottages are so much in demand, it may be asked, why, if the landlords will not build them, others, who are neither labourers nor landlords, do not do so? There could not be a more profitable investment of capital, when the rents are regularly paid, and many would so invest, if it were in their power to do so. But cottages cannot be built in the air, although their foundations are sometimes laid in water. Those who would willingly invest their money in building them cannot get the land on which to build them. *All the land about Wareham is so strictly settled as scarcely to admit of this.* If one of the most respectable inhabitants of Wareham wanted to build himself a house, it is questionable if he could get the land. Not that the landlords would in all cases refuse it, but that in many cases they cannot part with it. A rather ludicrous instance of this occurred a short time ago. A firm in Wareham had negotiated with one of the neighbouring proprietors for a lease of a certain piece of land for some works, which were to be carried on upon it; but when the agreement came to be carried out, the proprietor found, that he had so strictly tied up the land, that he could not give the lease.

"This scarcity of cottages is a complicated evil. It sometimes drives families to the workhouse, who would otherwise not be there; and, at others, serves to keep them perpetually on the parish, after distress has once thrown them upon it. In the Wareham workhouse, for instance, was a woman with her six children, her husband being at the time at work, and in receipt of wages, but staying with his mother, because he could not procure a cottage for himself and family. The woman herself evidently felt her situation very much. She and the whole family would leave the workhouse if a cottage could be procured. Again, take the case of a man whose family is thrown into distress from a temporary suspension of his employment. On applying for relief, he is told by the guardians, that they can do nothing for him, unless he comes into the workhouse. To this he has many objections, one of which is, that he has his cottage and his furniture—poor and scanty though it be, it is his own; and if he goes into the house, his little establishment will be broken up, without the least chance of his recovering it, when he comes out again. But the guardians are inflexible, and he must either starve or comply with the requirements of the law. At last he enters the house, and his little establishment is broken up. Sometimes afterwards he hears of employment, and leaves. But his cottage is now occupied by others, or it has in the meantime altogether disappeared. He cannot find another in which to shelter his family, and has to return to the workhouse. He is thus converted into what he never meant to become—a pauper; and being so, he makes up his mind to make the most of his pauperism. The chances are, that he never makes another effort to retrieve himself, but remains with his family a permanent charge upon the rates. This is not an imaginary sketch of the pauper's progress, but one drawn to me as true in but too many instances, by one who had been for years the relieving officer of a district not far from Wareham."

The "Morning Chronicle" of Nov. 30, 1849, in an exceedingly able article, after reviewing the reports of its correspondents, says,—

"In Sutton Courtney, for example, near Abingdon (Berks), many of the houses were found by our correspondent to contain but *two* rooms, and in one instance we are told that 'ten of a family slept together,' in a room twelve feet square, and containing three beds. The family consisted of the father and mother, young children, and girls and boys growing up to maturity, all huddled together without the smallest regard to decency. In Devonshire, on the high London road, we learn that 'many cottages are so rickety and ruined, that to inhabit them any longer is impossible.' 'One in particular,' adds our correspondent, 'struck my attention. The upper part of one of the end walls was entirely away, exposing the crazy anatomy of the roof, and laying the whole of what used to form the sleeping apartment of the family bare to every tempest that swept around their miserable house.' The family in this cottage consisted of seven. They had been obliged to sleep in the lower room, which was about sixteen feet square, and this was the sole and common dwelling place, for all purposes, of these seven persons. It had a mouldering brick floor, and the rain trickled through the rotten beams of the bulging ceiling. They had lived two years in this place and under these circumstances. At Axminster, our correspondent says, 'In one hovel with two rooms I found no fewer than eleven people; the sleeping apartment was up stairs, as usual, directly under the thatch.' This family consisted of the father, the mother, and nine children. The eldest was a girl of sixteen, the next a girl of fifteen, the third a boy of fourteen. Yet not the smallest reserve or decency could be maintained. A large tattered shawl hung between the beds of the parents and of the children *in summer*, was usually taken down in winter, to make an additional covering for the children. Need we speak of the demoralizing influence of such a mode of life?

"The cottages at Southleigh, in Devon, are, if possible, even worse. One house, which our correspondent visited, was almost a ruin. It had continued in that state for ten years. The floor was of mud, dipping near the fire-place into a deep hollow, which was constantly filled with water. There were five in the family,—a young man of twenty-one, a girl of eighteen, and another girl of about thirteen, with the father and mother, all sleeping together up stairs. And what a sleeping room! 'In places it seemed falling in. To ventilation it was an utter stranger. The crazy floor shook and creaked under me as I paced it.' Yet the rent was 1*s*. a week; the same sum, for which apartments that may be called luxurious in comparison may be had in the model lodging-houses. And here sat a girl weaving that beautiful Honiton lace, which our peeresses wear on Court days. Cottage after cottage at Southleigh presented the same characteristics. Clay floors, low ceilings letting in the rain, no ventilation; two rooms, one above and one below; gutters running through the lower room to let off the water; unglazed window-frames, now boarded up, and now uncovered to the elements, the boarding going for fire-wood; the inmates disabled by rheumatism, ague, and typhus; broad, stagnant, open ditches close to the doors; heaps of abominations piled round the dwellings; such are the main features of Southleigh; and it is in these worse than pig-styes that one of the most beautiful fabrics that luxury demands or art supplies is fashioned. The parish houses are still worse. 'One of these, on the borders of Devonshire and Cornwall, and not far from Launceston, consisted of two houses containing between them four rooms. In each room lived a family night and day, the space being about twelve feet square. In one were a man and his wife and eight children; the father, mother, and two children lay in one bed, the remaining six were huddled 'head and foot' (three at the top and three at the foot) in the other bed. The eldest girl was between fifteen and sixteen, the eldest boy between fourteen and fifteen.' Is it not horrible to think of men and women being brought up in this foul, brutish manner in civilized and Christian England! The lowest of savages are not worse cared for than these children of a luxurious and refined country.

"Liskeard, in Cornwall, is no better off. 'One case,' we read, 'which may be given as an illustration of the state of things in Liskeard, was, that of a man and his wife who had a miner lodging with them, all three occupying the same bedroom at night. A poor widow looking out for a lodger, and anxious to consult delicacy, so far as the wretched necessities of her lot permitted, placed her inmate (a miner) up-stairs to sleep, while she occupied the lower room, through which, however, the man had to pass every morning before she left her bed. In another house 'three men occupied one bed.' In general 'there were two beds in the lodgers' rooms, and sometimes both had two occupants.'

"The disclosures contained in our correspondent's letter of the 17th inst. are, perhaps, the worst of all. That letter details the condition of the labourers in the parish of St. Martin's, which for filth, immorality, and misery, surpasses everything previously described. To extract one specimen worse than the others would be impossible. They are all so bad, that there are no discriminating *degrees* of evil. Illegitimate children swarming about; men and women living almost indiscriminately together; unmarried women confined in the same apartment, in which nine other human beings are stowed away. Such is the moral state of things, to which physical wretchedness has reduced the population of St. Martin's. Here, as in many parts of Wiltshire and Dorsetshire, the most debasing influences seem to have been collected together in one full tide, as if to show how low a portion of a civilized and refined people can be sunk by poverty and neglect."

In some letters on the condition of the peasantry of Dorsetshire, published in the "Times" in June, 1846, by a gentleman, who was sent down, in order to obtain information, it is said,

"Another fruitful source of misery, as well as immorality, is the great inadequacy of the number and size of the houses to the number of the population, and the consequently crowded state of their habitations, which in Dorsetshire generally, and in Stourpain particularly, afford the most limited accommodation. It is by no means an uncommon thing for the whole family to sleep in the same room, without the slightest regard to age or sex, and without a curtain or the slightest attempt at separation between the beds. In one instance, which came under my notice, a family consisting of nine persons occupied three beds in the same bedroom, which was the only one the house afforded. The eldest daughter was twenty-three years of age, the eldest son twenty-one. The bedroom was ten feet square, not reckoning two small recesses by the side of the chimney, about eighteen inches deep. In some few instances, I have seen most ingenious and laudable attempts to effect a barrier between the sexes; but in general, there does not appear to exist any anxiety on the subject; and indeed, in most instances, the size and form of the rooms and the number of beds required for accommodation of the family render all such attempts futile. It will be easily imagined, that the great and promiscuous herding together of young people of both sexes is productive of the most demoralizing effects."

"In case of a death occurring in a family, should there be but one bed-room, which is, I think, generally the case, the inmates of the house are compelled to pass their nights in the same room with the corpse, until the time of burial."

"I could produce instances of the most frightful depravity, which, it must be evident, is the inevitable consequence of this disgusting and indiscriminate herding together of so many persons into one common and confined sleeping apartment; but I prefer suppressing them, more especially as they may be easily imagined."

"The atmosphere of these houses, and especially of the sleeping apartments, to an unpractised nose, is almost insupportable. It is, perhaps, worthy of remark, that dishes, plates, and other articles of crockery seem almost unknown. There is, however, the less need for them, *as grist bread forms the principal, and, I believe, the only kind of food that falls to the labourer's lot.* In no single instance did I observe meat of any kind during my progress through the parish. The furniture is such as may be expected from the description I have given of the place—a rickety table and two or three foundered chairs generally forming the extent of the upholstery."

7*

It is said that this is the condition throughout the greater part of the counties of Dorsetshire, Wiltshire, and Gloucestershire. Another letter, inserted in the "Times" of the 29th of June 1846, and signed "A Country Rector," says, "The misery," described above, "I am afraid is not confined to that county (Dorsetshire): if you go to Devonshire, Wiltshire, and the hill country of *Gloucestershire*, you will find him (the peasant) at the point of starvation."

The Hon. and Rev. S. G. Osborne, in writing of one of the parishes of Dorsetshire, viz. that of Hilton, which he inspected personally, in company with the vicar of the parish, describes the degradation of the inhabitants and the wretchedness of the houses as something almost incredible. He says, "I despair of giving you any faint idea of the manner these people are pigged together within their dwellings;" and this parish "closely adjoins the park of Milton Abbey, the beautiful seat of the Earl of Portarlington."

"In the first cottage, a man and his wife live with two children, a son of his by a former marriage, a daughter of hers by a former marriage; this son is married; but owing to want of room, cannot sleep with his own wife and children, who are living in another part of the parish, but sleeps in a small room, the only other bed of which is occupied by the grown girl, the daughter of the woman. They pay the parish 30*s.* a year rent.

"In one compartment of the large building were dwelling a man, his wife, and five children; five of them had had the fever; the man died of it. With some difficulty, we ascended to a bed-room of this cottage: no one by pen can describe it. You get into it by a sort of ladder; when in it, you find it impossible to stand upright anywhere but in the direct centre, for the roof slopes down to the floor at an acute angle; three beds are so placed as to make the base of so many triangles, of which the sides of the roof are the lateral lines; you must cross the first to get at the second, the second to reach the third; the floor is as rotten as possible, full of holes, through one of which the husband's leg had gone on one occasion. I ventured to ask how they got a corpse out of such a place. I found 'they had him down stairs to die;' there he was seven weeks, and then they took him dead to the churchyard."

"The floors of some of the down-stairs rooms are of mud, in pits or holes in many places; where mended at all, it is done with the rough stone of the country. The parish officers regularly, when they can get it, take rent even of the pauper tenants, with the exception of some few."

"Behind these buildings, is a space between them and a broad ditch, varying, perhaps, from twelve to fourteen feet in width; in the said space, in the case of the first two cottages, occupied partly by some out-houses, rank grass is growing, amongst which is ample evidence of every possible abomination. The ditch is full to overflowing of black sewer filth; the first two cottages have a partitioned portion of a common privy built over this ditch; the other portion, belonging to the larger building, being the only accommodation of the sort for nearly one hundred souls." . . .

"That this accommodation is not sufficient, or that it is too repulsive for even this sort of population, we had an overpowering proof at almost every step in this back-yard. I defy contradiction to the fact, that the night-soil is overflowing in a downward direction to wards the houses, and this well accounted for the sickening stench of some of the sleeping-places. In front of these parish dwellings, across the road, there is also a ditch, as might be expected, full of decaying vegetable and other matter, cast from these houses. The one well, from which for every purpose all the water used must be drawn, is so placed that it is next to impossible, but at times some of the rain must, after washing the filth in the road and ditch, pass into it. The clergyman told me at times the water was not drinkable. The stench produced from all these causes is so great, that in hot weather, he also informed me, he is obliged to close his vicarage windows, some 200 yards off; for it is unbearable."

"I was shown two cottages belonging to the noble proprietor of the estate. The filth here accumulated was such as defies all powers of description I possess."*

We need not and shall not wonder, if we find that the amount of crime in counties, where the peasants are in such a horrible social condition, is alarmingly and terribly increasing. The "Times" of the 30th of November, 1849, shows the terrible increase of crime in the last few years in Dorsetshire. The "Times" says:—"We yesterday published, in a very short compass, some grave particulars of the unfortunate county of Dorset. It is not simply the old story of wages inadequate for life, hovels unfit for habitation, and misery and sin alternately claiming our pity and our disgust. This state of things is so normal, and we really believe so immemorial in that notorious county, that we should rather deaden, than excite the anxiety of the public by

* See Mr. Osborne's letter, published in the "Times" of the 26th of October, 1848.

a thrice-told tale. What compels our attention just now is a sudden, rapid, and, we fear, a forced aggravation of these evils, measured by the infallible test of crime. Dorsetshire is fast sinking into a slough of wretchedness, which threatens the peace and morality of the kingdom at large. The total number of convictions which

"In 1846 was 798, and
"In 1847 was 821, mounted up,
"In 1848, to 950;

"and up to the special general session, last Tuesday," (Dec. 1849) "for less than eleven months of the present year, to the astonishing number of 1193, being at the rate of 1300 for the whole year! Unless something is done to stop this flood of crime, or the tide happily turns of itself, the county will have more than *doubled* its convictions within four years! Nor is it possible for us to take refuge in the thought that the increase is in petty offences. In no respect is it a light thing for a poor creature to be sent to gaol, whatever be the offence. He has broken the laws of his country, and forfeited his character. His name and his morals are alike tainted with the gaol. He is degraded and corrupted. If his spirit be not crushed, it is exasperated into perpetual hostility to wealth and power. . . .

"It is, then, no light affair that a rural county, the abode of an ancient and respectable aristocracy, somewhat removed from the popular influences of the age, with a population of 175,043 by the late census, should produce in four years near 4000 convictions, being at the rate of one conviction in that period for every sixty persons, or every twelve householders."

The next series of extracts will show the condition of the houses of the peasants in the south-eastern counties, viz. Kent, Surrey, and Sussex.

Mr. Vaughan, special Assistant Poor Law Commissioner for the counties of Kent, Surrey, and Sussex, says:—*

"The undivided state of the large families, acting upon the scantiness of house-room and general poverty or high rent, often crowds them together in their sleeping apartments, so as seriously to infringe on the decencies which guard female morals."

Mr. Hart, a professional gentleman at Reigate, says:—*

"The great difficulty is to say, at what age brothers and sisters do not sleep together in the same apartment; but *generally until they leave home, be that at ever so late a period. Many cottages have but one room, and the whole family sleep in one bed.* I have often, when taking the examination of a sick man with a magistrate, an occasion, which has more often taken me into a cottage than any other, observed upon this, and I consider its effects most demoralising."

Mr. Vaughan says:—

"In the neighbourhood of Cuckfield in Sussex, it is said to be common for children of both sexes to use the same sleeping-room and bed up to the age of twelve and even fourteen.

"The Rev. W. Sankie, curate of Farnham in Surrey, mentioned a case within his own knowledge, where two sisters and a brother, *all above fourteen*, habitually slept together. The admission of strangers, too, into the cottager's home produces an effect of a kind sometimes occasionally the same. Where a family is admitted, the same evil is increased. Where the letting of a room to a whole family is prohibited, as in some cases by the owner of the house, and a single lodger

* See Report on the Employment of Women in Agriculture.

only is allowed, the danger strikes more directly at the chastity of the family."

Mr. Rammell, a farmer on a large scale, living at Sturry near Canterbury, says* :—

"Cottage rent is very high. Cottages with two rooms are sometimes let for 1*s.* 6*d.* a-week without a garden; sometimes, though not commonly, for 2*s.*; 2*s.* 6*d.* and 3*s.* are paid for four room cottages. It is common for persons in roomy cottages to let off a room for a stranger. The benefit of an airy abode is thus lost; and other evils follow from the intimacy between a stranger and the grown-up daughters."

The next series of extracts shows the condition of the peasants' houses in Buckinghamshire, Bedfordshire, Hertfordshire, Norfolk, Suffolk, and Essex.

Mr. Parker observes, that the construction of the cottages in Buckinghamshire is frequently unwholesome† :—

"The improper materials, of which cottages are built, and their defective construction, are also the frequent cause of the serious indisposition of the inmates. The cottages at Waddeston, and some of the surrounding parishes in the vale of Aylesbury, are constructed of mud, with earth floors and thatched roofs. The vegetable substances mixed with the mud to make it bind rapidly decompose, leaving the wall porous. The earth of the floor is full of vegetable matter, and from there being nothing to cut off its contact with the surrounding mould, it is peculiarly liable to damp. The floor is frequently charged with animal matter, thrown upon it by the inmates, and this rapidly decomposes by the alternate action of heat and moisture. Thatch placed in

* See Report on the Employment of Women in Agriculture.

† Report on the Sanitary Condition of the Labouring Population.

contact with such walls, speedily decays, yielding a gas of the most deleterious quality. Fever of every type and diarrhœa are endemic diseases in the parish and neighbourhood."

Mr. William Blower, the surgeon of the Bedford union, in Bedfordshire, states *:—

"Throughout the whole of this district there is a great want of 'superior cottage accommodation.' *Most of the residences of the labourers are thickly inhabited*, and many of them are damp, low, cold, smoky, and comfortless. These circumstances occasion the inmates to be sickly in the winter season; but I have not observed them to generate typhus, the prevailing form of disease being principally catarrhal, such as colds, coughs, inflammation of the eyes, dysentery, rheumatism, &c. However, when any contagious or epidemic malaria occurs, *the cases generally are more numerous*."

Mr. Weale reports instances of the condition of large proportions of the agricultural population in the counties of Bedford, Northampton, and Warwick. The medical officer of the Woburn union in Bedfordshire states, in respect to Toddington, that—

"In this town fever prevailed during the last year, and, from the state of the dwellings of the persons I called on, this could not be wondered at. *Very few of the cottages were furnished with privies that could be used*, and contiguous to almost every door a dung heap was raised, on which every species of filth was accumulated, either for the purpose of being used in the garden allotments of the cottagers, or to be disposed of for manure. Scarcely any cottage was provided with a pantry, and I found the provisions generally kept in the bed-rooms. *In several instances I found whole fa-*

* See Report on Sanitary Condition of the Labouring Population.

*milies, comprising adult and infant children with their parents, sleeping in one room.*"

The medical officer of the Ampthill union in Bedfordshire, states*:—

"Typhus fever has existed for the last three or four months in the parish of Flitwick, and although the number of deaths has not been considerable, as compared with the progress of the disease, new cases have occurred as those under treatment became convalescent, and several are still suffering under this malady. The cottages, in which it first appeared (and to which it has been almost exclusively confined), are of the most wretched description: a stagnant pond is in the immediate vicinity, and none of the tenements have drains; rubbish is thrown within a few yards of the dwellings, and there is no doubt but in damp foggy weather, and also during the heat of the summer, the exhalations arising from those heaps of filth must generate disease, and the obnoxious effluvia tend to spread contagion where it always exists. It appears that *most of the cottages alluded to were erected for election purposes, and have since been allowed to decay;* the roofs are repaired with turf dug in the neighbourhood, and the walls repaired with prepared clay without the addition of lime washing. Contagious disease has not been remarkable within the union in any other spot than the one alluded to."

Messrs. Smith and Moore, the medical officers of the Bishop Stortford union, in Hertfordshire, state*:—

"We have always found the smallest and most slightly built houses the seats of the lowest forms of disease; and, although during the last year no epidemic or infectious disease here prevailed, it is but just to

* See Report on the Sanitary Condition of the Labouring Population.

state, that generally speaking *the cottages of labourers in this district are small, badly protected from both extremes of weather, badly drained, and low in the ground.*"

The Rev. Henry Worsley, late Michel Scholar of Queen's College, Oxford, and rector of Easton in Suffolk, writing of the *progressive deterioration* in the character of the peasants' cottages, say, "Another important consideration is, *the alteration for the worse in the dwelling houses of the poor.* A cottage erected in the last century will be generally found to be commodious and roomy; very different in the supply of comforts and conveniences from the hovels, which are now ordinarily appropriated to the labouring class. At the present day, the narrowness of the poor man's cabin (the fact found to be almost universally true, that however numerous the inmates may be, *one small bedroom is deemed sufficient to accommodate all,*) implies so much domestic discomfort, that the natural impulse of the mind is to fly from misery at home to the village beer-shop. Besides this effect on the father, mother, or both, ruinous in itself to family peace, the congregating of so many into one sleeping apartment, *very frequently of two whole families or even more,* is destructive of all sense of modesty. The condition of the poor in regard to house accommodation, thus described, is well nigh general; it is common to the agricultural and manufacturing parts. During the present century we have been building dwellings for the poor, as if we were running up styes for pigs." *

Mr. Twisleton, late Poor Law Commissioner for Ireland, and a gentleman of very great experience in all social questions, and in everything relating to the social condition of the poorer classes, in his Report upon the

* Essay on Juvenile Depravity, 36.

sanitary condition of the labouring population of Norfolk and Suffolk, speaks thus of these cottages. He says, "Although they may be sufficiently commodious for a man and wife and very young children, they are manifestly uncomfortable, and the having only *one* bedroom is even indecent for a man and wife and large growing family; *but I have seen many instances where a man and his wife and six children of different sexes have slept together in one room, on three and sometimes only two beds.* The annoyance of thus herding together must be almost insufferable, and several mothers of families among the labourers have spoken to me with great propriety and feeling against the practice, saying, 'that it is not respectable or decent, and that it is hardly bearable;' 'that such a thing is not right for a Christian body in a Christian land;' and they have used other expressions of a similar import. In order to diminish the evil, they have recourse to various expedients, such as putting curtains to the beds, or dividing the room into two parts, by pinning old counterpanes together, and sometimes by cutting up, and sewing together, old gowns, and stretching them across the room; all of which schemes are attended with the inconvenience, that in a crowded apartment, where pure air is a scarce luxury, they have a tendency to check still more its healthful circulation."

In describing the condition of the agricultural labourers of Norfolk and Suffolk, the able author of the Letters on Rural Districts, published in the "Morning Chronicle," says:—

"The food of the labourer and his family is principally bread, potatoes, and frequently, in Norfolk, the Norfolk dumpling, which consists simply of the dough of which the bread is made, the difference between bread and dumpling being merely, that the one is boiled, while the other is baked. In the neighbourhood of Fakenham I met with a family, whose food was chiefly bread and turnips, and I was informed, that this was a very general diet with the people about there. *In none of the cottages, that I have visited in either of the three counties, have I ever seen such a thing as a piece of fresh butcher's meat. That it may be had occasionally, there can be no doubt, but it is certainly at very rare and long intervals.* When meat of any kind is purchased, it is mostly bacon or salt pork, and the labourer invariably finds it more economical to purchase that kind of food than fresh meat,—the high price, which they have to pay for any little piece, that they may want, being quite sufficient to deter them from its purchase. While at Bury, I was informed by a butcher, who carries on a somewhat extensive business, that the 'shins' and 'stickings' of beef, which he was in the habit of selling in the town for 1½*d.* per pound, he could sell on Saturday to the poor for 5*d.*, 'bone and all,' when it was cut up in pieces of about two or three pounds weight. About Swaffham, Yarmouth, and Lowestoft, red herrings and salt fish will be found occasionally to enter into the dietary table of the labourer. In one cottage, which I visited, I found the woman busily employed in chopping up some pieces of fat pork, which she was about to mix up with some cold potatoes and flour, for dumplings, by way of 'a treat for the children, because it was Mary's birth-day.' The prices, which the poor people have to pay for their grocery, such as tea, sugar, and coffee, are enormous. When in Norwich, I obtained several samples of sugar at 3½*d.* and 4*d.* and 5*d.* per lb., and compared them, in several places, which I visited, with the sugar, for which the poor people had paid at the rate of 5*d.* and 6*d.* per lb., and, according to the opinion of the poor people themselves, my sample at 3½*d.* was as good as their fivepenny, and my fourpenny better than their sixpenny, while my fivepenny was fit for the squire.

"The cottage accommodation of the labourer is in many parts of Norfolk lamentably deficient. A few praiseworthy efforts have been made on the part of some of the landed proprietors to remedy the evil, but their exertions have by no means kept pace with the wants of the population.

. . . . . . . . . . . .

"*Not only is there a great amount of unwillingness, on the part of the proprietors generally, to build cottages for the labourers, but in too many instances there is an evident desire to destroy or pull down numbers of those that at present exist.* In the neighbourhood of Norwich, the extent to which the destruction of cottage property has been carried on was, in the words of my informant, 'fearful and disgraceful.' In Drayton parish, fourteen cottages have been pulled down within the last few years, and none have been erected in their stead. In the Horsted Hundred, twenty-five of the cottages have been ordered to be destroyed. At Long Sutton, Pulham, Wackton, and various other parishes, the destruction has also been carried on to a great extent, though I was not able to learn the exact number, which had been destroyed. I was informed of the case of a large landed proprietor in the vicinity of Norwich, some of whose property being required by the railway company, *it was expressly stipulated in the sale, that no cottages whatsoever should be built upon any portion of the ground.* In point of fact, it is impossible to obtain a piece of ground, for building purposes, in any of the villages within eight or ten miles of Norwich. *Many of the estates have been entirely cleared of tenantry.* To such an extent has the system been carried on, that there are at present in Norwich not less than 500 agricultural labourers, who have to walk to their work distances varying from three to seven miles. Every expedient to prevent the labourer obtaining a settlement in the rural parishes is resorted to by the occupiers. In Wackton parish, one of the modes of removing the paupers was, to set a number of persons, principally weavers, who had some claim on the parish, and who, in all probability, had never had a spade in their hands before, to dig up a common in the middle of January, the snow at the time lying upon the ground several inches deep. The poor wretches were told, that they must dig a certain portion of the common before they could obtain any relief. The first thing, which they did, was to dig in the snow what they called 'the grave' of the magistrate, who had given the order. So far as the experiment was concerned, it was perfectly successful; for after two or three days the greater portion of the persons left their employment, and contrived to settle themselves, by one means or other, in the city of Norwich, or in some of the surrounding open parishes. The effect of this conduct, in addition to the injury inflicted upon the paupers, has been most materially to enhance the rates of the adjoining parishes. In Long Sutton, for instance, a number of small cottages have been built; they are crowded by the evicted of the other parishes, and the rates are 6*s.* in the pound, while in the parish of St. Michael, which adjoins it, and where the cottages have been pulled down, the rates are only 2*s.* 6*d.* in the pound. This system is not, however, confined to Norwich; for it has been carried on to a great extent in the neighbourhood of Castle Acre, which is an open parish, the consequence being, that whilst Castle Acre is overstocked with inhabitants, and the cottages there are densely crowded, there are not in the surrounding parishes anything like sufficient hands to cultivate the land. It is owing to this excess of labourers in one district, and the great want of them in the neighbouring parishes, that the custom has sprung up within the last few years, of employing the people in what are termed 'gangs,'—a system which, there can be no doubt whatever, is attended with a considerable amount of evil to the persons employed."

Speaking of the state of the cottages in Essex, the same able writer says:—

"In the rural districts of Essex, many of the cottages are exceedingly bad; but in the northern and western part of the county this is peculiarly the case. Along the whole line of country from Castle Hedingham to Clavering, there is an almost continuous succession of bad cottages. Among the worst of these might be mentioned those in the neighbourhood of Sible Hedingham, Weathersfield, Bardfield, Wicken, and Clavering. Great numbers of these cottages are situated in low and damp situations, and their heavy and grass-covered thatches appear, as if they had almost crushed the buildings down into the earth. Little or no light can ever find its way into the wretched little windows, many of which are more than half stopped up with rags and pieces of paper. In point of fact, there are many of them which, but for the possession of a chimney, would be nothing superior to many of the most wretched cabins, which I have witnessed in Tipperary and many other parts of Ireland. At Manningtree, there are also a considerable number of wretched one-room cottages, and those which are larger are generally tenanted by as many families as there are rooms. In some cases, the number of families exceeds that of the rooms. It is customary in Manningtree to rate every one of the lodgers in such a house. In one case, of a house with three rooms, the persons living in the lower room, consisting of a husband and wife, and three grown-up children, were rated at 1*l.* 5*s.* The second compartment, occupied by a man and his wife, and one son, was rated at 1*l.* The occupiers of the third room, who consisted of a man and his wife, and five children, were rated at 15*s.*, the poor-rates being 6*s.* in the pound for the year. There are also some wretched holes situated upon Back-hill, where the amount of rates enforced averages about 3*d.* to each house."

The same gentleman describes the effects of the want of more and better cottages in the following manner:—

"One species of immorality, which is peculiarly prevalent in Norfolk and Suffolk, is that of bastardy. With the exception of Hereford and Cumberland, there are no counties, in which the per centage of bastardy is so high as it is in Norfolk—being there 53·1 per cent. above the average of England and Wales; in Suffolk it is 27 per cent. above, and in Essex 19·1 per cent. below the average. In the two first-named counties, and even in the latter one, though not to the same extent, *there appears to be a perfect want of decency among the people.* 'The immorality of the young women,' said the rector of one parish to me, 'is literally horrible, and I regret to say it is on the increase in a most extraordinary degree. When I first came to the town, the mother of a bastard child used to be ashamed to show herself. The case is now quite altered; no person seems to think anything at all of it. When I first came to the town, there was no such thing as a common prostitute in it; now there is an enormous number of them. When I am called upon to see a woman confined with an illegitimate child, I endeavour to impress upon her the enormity of the offence; and there are no cases, in which I receive more insult from those I visit, than from such persons. They generally say they'll get on as well, after all that's said about it; and if they never do anything worse than that, they shall get to Heaven as well as other people.' Another clergyman stated to me, that he never recollected an instance of his having married a woman, who was not either pregnant at the time of her marriage, or had had one or more children before her marriage. Again, a third clergyman told me, that he went to baptize the illegitimate child of one woman, who was thirty-five years of age, and it was absolutely impossible for him to convince her that what she had done was wrong. 'There appears,' said he, 'to be among the lower orders a perfect deadness of all moral feeling upon this subject.' Many of the cases of this kind, which have come under my knowledge, evince such horrible depravity, that I dare not attempt to lay them before the reader. Speaking to the wife of a respectable labourer on the subject, who had seven children, one of whom was then confined with an illegitimate child, she excused her daughter's conduct by saying, 'What was the poor girl to do; the chaps say, that they won't marry 'em first, and then the girls give way. I did the same myself with my husband.' There was one case in Cossey, in Norfolk, in which the woman told me, without a blush crimsoning her cheek, that her daughter and self had each had a child by a sweep, who lodged with them, and who promised to marry the daughter. The cottage in which these persons slept consisted of but one room, and there were two other lodgers who occupied beds in the same room; in one of which 'a young woman occasionally slept with the young man she was keeping company with.' The other lodger was an old woman of seventy-four years of age. To such an extent is prostitution carried on in Norwich, that out of the 656 licensed public-houses and beer-shops in the city, there are not less than 220, which are known to the police as common brothels. And although the authorities have the power of withholding the licenses, nothing is done to put a stop to the dreadful vice. 'At Bury,' said one of the guardians of the poor to me, 'there is, I believe, a larger amount of prostitution, in proportion to the size of the place, than is to be found in any town or city in England.' Harwich appears to be remarkably free from this vice. 'There are not,' I was informed by the police, 'more than six prostitutes in the town, and there is not a single brothel.'

Mr. Harding, medical officer of the Epping union, in Essex, says*:—

"The state of some of the dwellings of the poor is most deplorable, as it regards their health, and also in a moral point of view. As it relates to the former, *many of their cottages are neither wind nor water-tight.*

"It has often fallen to my lot to be called on to attend a labour, where the wet has been running down the walls, and where light was to be distinguished through the roof; and this in the winter season, with no fireplace in the room. As it relates to the latter, in my opinion, *a great want of accommodation for bed-rooms often occurs, so that you may frequently find the father, mother, and children all sleeping in the same apartment,*

* See Report on the Sanitary Condition of the Labouring Population.

*and in some instances children who have attained the age of sixteen or seventeen years, and of both sexes; and if a death occurs in the house, let the person die of a most contagious disease, they must either sleep in the same room, or take their repose in the room they live in*, which most frequently is a stone or brick floor, which must be detrimental to health."

Mr. Chadwick says:—

"The reports from the great majority of the new unions present evidence of the severe over-crowding of the cottages of the rural districts and the tenements occupied by the working classes in the towns.

"The evidence received from every part of the country, from rural districts as well as from towns, attests, that the dwellings of large numbers of the labouring population are over-crowded, and that the *over-crowding in many districts is increased.*"

Mr. T. P. J. Grantham, medical officer of the Sleaford union, in reference to the typhus fever in the family of an agricultural labourer, gives the following instance of the over-crowding, which is frequent in the rural districts:—

"The domestic economy in this house was deplorable; *eight persons slept in a small ill-ventilated apartment, with scarcely any bed-clothing.* The smell arising from the want of cleanliness, and the dirty clothes of the children being allowed to accumulate, was most intolerable. Considering the situation of the house, its filthy state, and the vitiated air which must have been respired over and over again by eight individuals sleeping in one confined apartment, it is surprising that this family should have been afflicted with fever, and that of a malignant type. The mother and one child fell victims to it in a very short time."

The following extract from a communication from the clerk to the Ampthill union, Bedfordshire, pourtrays the effects of this over-crowding on the morals of the population:—*

"*A large proportion of the cottages in the union are very miserable places, small and inconvenient, in which it is impossible to keep up even the common decencies of life.* I will refer to one instance, with which I am well acquainted. A man, his wife, and family, consisting in all of eleven individuals, resided in a cottage containing only two rooms.

"The man, his wife, and four, and sometimes five, children, slept in one of the rooms and in one bed—some at the foot, others at the top; one, a girl about fourteen, another, a girl about twelve, the rest younger. The other part of the family slept in one bed in the keeping room, that is, the room in which their cooking, washing, and eating were performed. How could it be otherwise with this family, than that they should be sunk into a most deplorable state of degradation and depravity? This, it may be said, is an extreme case; but there are many similar, and *a very great number that make near approaches to it.* To pursue a further account of this family, the man is reported to be a good labourer. The cottage he held was recently pulled down, and being unable to procure another, he was forced to come into the workhouse. After being in a short time, they left again, to try to get a house, but again they failed. The man then absconded, and the family returned to the workhouse. The eldest, a female, has had a bastard child; and another younger, also a female, but grown up, has recently been sentenced to transportation for stealing in a dwelling-house. The

* See Report on the Sanitary Condition of the Labouring Population.

family, when they came in, were observed to be of grossly filthy habits and of disgusting behaviour. I am glad to say, however, that their general conduct and appearance is very much improved since they have been inmates of the workhouse. I, without scruple, express my opinion that their degraded moral state *is mainly attributable to the wretched way, in which they have lived and herded together, as previously described.* I have been thus particular in my account of this family, *knowing it to be a type of many others.*"

The relieving officer of the Leighton Buzzard union states that in Leighton—

"There are a number of cottages without sleeping-rooms separate from the day-rooms, and frequently *three or four families are found occupying the same bed-room, and young men and women promiscuously sleeping in the same apartment.*"

Mr. Blick, the medical officer of the Bicester union, states that—

"The residences of the poor in that part of the district are most wretched, the majority *consisting of only one room below and one above, in which a family of eight or ten (upon an average I should say five) live and sleep.* In one of these rooms I have witnessed a father and mother, three grown-up sons, a daughter, and a child, lying at the same time with typhus fever. But few of the adjacent residents escaped the infection."

Mr. L. O. Fox, the medical officer of the Romsey union, states*—

"There is not only a great want of cottages, but also of room, in those which now stand. In the parish of Mottisfont, *I have known fourteen individuals of one*

* Report on the Sanitary Condition of the Labouring Population.

*family sleeping together in a small room, the mother being in labour at the time, and in the adjoining room seven other people sleeping, making twenty-one persons, in a space which ought to have been occupied by six persons at most.* Here are the young woman and young man of eighteen or twenty years of age, lying alongside of the father and mother, and the latter actually in labour! It will be asked—What is the condition of the inmates? Just such as might be expected."

The next series of extracts show the condition of the houses of the peasants in the northern counties of England. The following extracts are only a repetition of the same sad description with respect to other parts of the northern counties.

Sir F. H. Doyle, speaking of the cottages of the peasantry of Northumberland, says:—

"The ordinary cottages *contain but one room*, perhaps 17 feet by 15 feet. In point of construction and ventilation there is nothing to be said for them; but as the Northumbrians are, *in spite of everything*, a healthy and vigorous race of men, such inconveniences do not amount to a crying evil; but when we find that a whole family,—father and mother, and children of both sexes and of all ages—live together, *and have to sleep together in one and the same room*, any degree of indelicacy and unchastity ceases to surprise, and the only wonder is, that the women should behave as well as they do."

Mr. W. Weatherill, clerk of the Gainsborough union, says:—

"The cottages contain occasionally one room only, generally two, though it not unfrequently occurs, that there is only one bed-room; where there are two, there are two lower rooms, and two bed-rooms. Their being crowded together at night, without any reference to sex, has unquestionably an influence in weakening, if not destroying, the modesty of the female sex."

Dr. Gilly, Canon of Durham, in an appeal on behalf of the border peasantry, describes their dwellings as built of rubble and unhewn stones, loosely cemented; and from age or from badness of the materials, the walls look as if they could scarcely hold together. "The chinks gape in so many places as to admit blasts of wind :—

"The chimneys have lost half their original height, and lean on the roof with fearful gravitation. The rafters are evidently rotten and displaced; and the thatch yawning to admit the wind and wet in some parts, and in all parts utterly unfit for the original purpose of giving protection from the weather, looks more like the top of a dunghill than of a cottage.

"Such is the interior; and when the hind comes to take possession, he finds it no better than a shed. The wet, if it happens to rain, is making a puddle in the earth floor. (This earth floor, by-the-bye, is one of the causes to which Erasmus ascribed the frequent recurrence of epidemic sickness among the cotters of England more than 300 years ago. It is not only cold and wet, but contains the aggregate filth of years from the time of first being used, the refuse and droppings of meals, decayed animal and vegetable matter of all kinds, which has been cast upon it from the mouth and stomach; these are all mixed together, and exude from it.) Window-frame there is none. There is neither oven, nor copper, nor grate, nor shelf, nor fixture of any kind. All these things he has to bring with him, besides his ordinary articles of furniture. Imagine the trouble, the inconvenience, and the expense, which the poor fellow and his wife have to encounter, before they can put this shell of a hut into anything like a habitable form.

"This year I saw a family of eight,—husband, wife, two sons and four daughters,—who were in utter discomfort and in despair of putting themselves in a decent condition three or four weeks after they had come into one of these hovels.

"In vain did they try to stop up the crannies, and to fill up the holes in the floor, and to arrange their furniture in tolerably decent order, and to keep out the weather. Alas! what will they not suffer in the winter.

"There will be no fireside enjoyment for them. They may huddle together for warmth, and heap coals on the fire; but they will have chilly beds and a damp hearthstone; and the cold wind will sweep through the roof and window, and the crazy door-place, in spite of all their endeavours to exclude it.

"The general character of the best of the old-fashioned hinds' cottages is bad at the best. They have to bring everything with them, partitions, window-frames, fixtures of all kinds, grates, and a substitute for ceiling; for they are, as I have already called them, mere sheds. They have no byre for their cows, nor styes for their pigs, nor pumps, nor wells,—nothing to promote cleanliness or comfort.

"The average size of these sheds is about 24 feet by 16 feet; they are dark and unwholesome. Their windows do not open, and many of them are not larger than 20 inches by 16, and into this place are crowded eight, ten, or twelve persons.

"How they lie down to rest, how they sleep, how

they can preserve common decency, how unutterable horrors are avoided, is beyond all conception. The case is aggravated, when there is a young woman to be lodged in this confined space, who is not a member of the family, but is hired to do the field-work, for which every hind is bound to provide a female. It shocks every feeling of propriety to think, that in one room, and within such a space as I have been describing, civilised beings should be herded together without the decent separation of age and sex. So long as the agricultural system in this district requires the hind to find room for a fellow-servant of the other sex in his cabin, the least that morality and decency can demand is, that he should have a second apartment, where the unmarried female, and those of a tender age, should sleep apart from him and his wife. Last Whitsuntide, when the annual lettings were taking place, a hind, who had lived one year in the hovel he was about to quit, called to say—farewell, and to thank me for some trifling kindness I had been able to show him. He was a fine, tall man, of about forty-five, a fair specimen of the frank, sensible, well-spoken, well-informed Northumbrian peasantry; of that peasantry, of which a militia regiment was composed, which so amazed the Londoners (when it was garrisoned in the capital many years ago) by the size, the noble deportment, the soldier-like bearing, and the good conduct of the men.

"I thought this a good opportunity of asking some questions. Where was he going, and how would he dispose of his large family (eleven in number)? He told me, that they were to inhabit one of these hind's cottages, whose narrow dimensions were less than 24 feet by 15, and that the eleven would only have three beds to sleep on; that he himself, his wife, a daughter of 6, and a boy of 4 years old, would sleep in one bed; *that a daughter of* 18, *a son of* 12, *a son of* 10, *and a daughter of* 8 *have a second bed*, and a third would receive his three sons of the age of 20, 16, and 14. Pray, said I, do you not think that this is a very improper way of disposing of your family? Yes, certainly, was the answer; it is very improper in a christian point of view; but what can we do until they build us better houses?"

The next series of extracts are taken from the reports of Mr. Lingen, the Commissioner who was sent by Government, in 1848, to examine the state of education in the counties of Carmarthen, Glamorgan, and Pembroke.

Mr. Lingen is a Fellow of Balliol College, Oxford, and assistant secretary of the Privy Council on Education; he is a very able and highly accomplished man, and his report is a very remarkable one in every respect, and is well worthy of study.

He describes the social state, habits, and houses of the peasants of the above-mentioned counties as follows:—

"I am about to enter on one of the most painful subjects of my inquiry. It is a disgusting fact, that out of 692 schools I found 364, or 52·6 per cent. utterly unprovided with privies. But it is not schools that stand alone in this respect; they are but instances of the general neglect."

Here are facts.

(See Report, p. 233.)

"The whole row of houses (part of the main street) in which this school is held, varying in rent from 10*l.* to 15*l.* a year, had not a single, not even a common privy. The inhabitants resorted to a hedge-side in a field adjoining at the back, wholly unsheltered from sight."

(See Report, p. 304.)

"The vast majority of houses have no privies. Where there is such a thing, it is a mere hole in the ground, with no drainage. This is the case nearly all over Wales; but in a dense population the consequences of such neglect are more loathsomely and degradingly apparent. . . . . I was assured by people, whose houses look into fields or open spaces at the back of rows and streets, that persons of every age and sex are constantly to be seen exposed in them.

"And here is an expedient to supply the deficiency."

(See Report, 241.)

"The school, as usual, possessed no privy, and the master informed me, that the churchyard is generally used by the poor of the town as a privy; few of them possessing at home any convenience of that nature.

"The peasant girls proceed from homes and domestic habits like the following to service in a farmhouse.

(See Report, p. 243, 4.)

"The floor was of mud; on the right hand of the door, on entering, ran a partition of wattles so far towards the opposite wall, as just to leave room to turn round it into the other division. At the end of the passage thus formed, was an old chest, and on turning round the end of the partition a cupboard bed occupied one whole side of the inner room. Close to it was the hearth. The remaining furniture consisted of two shapeless stools, a few inches high, another of the same sort a little higher, and an old dresser, or something like one. The chimney, which descended from the roof over the hearth like a bonnet or umbrella, was made of plastered wattles. A heavy shower must have put the fire out and deluged the hut, the orifice of the chimney was so large. The floor was perfectly hard and dry, though very uneven. The cottage was smoke-dried into a feeling of comfortable warmth. The ceiling, or what came between one's head and the thatch, was some poles laid from wall to wall, and on these poles was strewed a little loose brushwood."

Appendix, p. 229. (Evidence of Rev. J. Pugh):—

"In their habits, the labouring classes are particularly dirty. This arises, in great measure, no doubt, from their poverty and the low rate of wages which, until lately, they have been in the habit of receiving, so that it was quite impossible for them to have decent clothes or convenient houses. Pigs and poultry are frequently allowed to come inside. The flooring is generally bare earth, not even prepared with lime. There are rarely any privies. Neither light nor ventilation is well provided for. There are not usually more than two rooms. Cupboard beds are those most commonly used, which are shut up as soon as the occupant quits them, and never opened again until night. The use of linen, until lately, either by day or night, was almost unknown; it is now, however, coming more into fashion among the young people.

"I also heard, from the master of the union workhouse at Haverfordwest, that the paupers were excessively filthy in their habits.

"In the farm-houses, separation and decency are not better attended to than must have been the case in such homes, *and the natural bar which consanguinity opposes to vice is removed.*"

Ibid, p. 217.—(Evidence of John Jones, Esq.):—

"Immorality exists between the sexes to a considerable extent, chiefly among farm-servants. The main cause is, perhaps, the imperfect arrangements in the older farm-houses, which leave the sexes too much together, and this even at night.

"Captain Napier, the superintendent of police in Glamorganshire, to whom, by the kindness of the Marquis of Bute, I was introduced, strongly confirmed this statement in a conversation which I had with him, saying that he had known servants of different sexes put to sleep in the same room.

"But it is not merely among inmates of the same farm-houses that evil arises; there are several other causes producing similar effects."

Ibid, p. 394. :—

"The system of bundling, or, at any rate, something analogous to it, prevails extensively. The unmarried men servants in the farms range the country at night; and it is a known and tolerated practice, that they are admitted by the women servants at the houses to which they come. I heard the most revolting anecdotes of the gross and almost bestial indelicacy, with which sexual intercourse takes place on these occasions."

Ibid, p. 234. (Evidence of Mr. W. Rees) :—

"The farmers connive at young people meeting in their houses after the family has retired to rest."

Appendix, p. 282. (Evidence of Messrs. Roberts, Glantowi) :—

"The male farm-servants sleep in the out-buildings, and keep what hours they please; the women ask leave to go out in the evening, and then the men meet them at the public-houses, of which there are fourteen in the town here (among a population of 736), and eight between here and Llandilo, a distance of 6½ miles. In this way much immorality takes place."

Ibid, p. 254 (note of a conversation) :—

"Such are some of the circumstances under which

the early life of a Welsh peasant girl is passed. So far from wondering at what is said of them, viz., that they are almost universally unchaste, the wonder would be if they were otherwise. Their offences, however, arise rather from the absence of all checks, than from the deliberate infringement of them, and betoken, therefore, much less depravity than the same conduct in persons more favourably situated."

Ibid, p. 217. (Evidence of John Johnes, Esq.) :—

"In cases where marriage would be out of the question, from the superior rank of the man, the women would not generally listen to proposals of an immoral kind.

"The first breach of chastity with a woman in the lower class is almost always under a promise of marriage."

Ibid, p. 237. (Mr. David Owen) :—

"The peasantry are generally very poor, and possess few comforts; but they are economical, and more cleanly than a stranger would think. The woman has the entire management of the house, and this she generally does well. She can generally sew and knit, and is very industrious.

"But families like these are ill prepared for the change of life to which the mining districts expose them on their immigration.

"At the top of a valley forming a *cul-de-sac*, suppose some 5000 or 6000 people collected and nearly cut off from the rest of the world. This is their domestic economy."

Appendix, pp. 304. and 351. :—

"The works have increased faster than adequate accommodation for those employed in them could be provided. The houses are all over-crowded. They are commonly of two stories, and comprise four or five rooms; the fifth, however (where there is one), is seldom more than a pantry. *The average number of the inhabitants is said to be nearly twelve to each house.* I entered upwards of a dozen at random, and found the average to be quite as great as this. The houses are often in the hands of middlemen: in such cases the rents are usually higher than when they belong to the company. Rent ranges from 8*l.* to 10*l.* per annum.

"The tenant makes it up by the payments of his lodgers. The cottages are expensively furnished."

Evidence respecting the mining and manufacturing populations (Rev. John Griffith, vicar of Aberdare), p. 489.:—

"Nothing can be lower, I would say more degrading, than the character in which the women stand relative to the men. The men and women, married as well as single, live in the same house, *and sleep in the same room.* The men do not hesitate to wash themselves naked before the women; on the other hand, the women do not hesitate to change their under garments before the men. Promiscuous intercourse is most common, is thought of as nothing, and the women do not lose caste by it."

Mr. Symonds, another of the commissioners, says of the peasantry of Brecknockshire, Cardiganshire, and Radnorshire:—

"The people of my district are almost universally poor. In some parts of it wages are probably lower than in any part of Great Britain. The evidence of the witnesses, numbered 22, 23, 1, 47, and 48, fully confirmed by other statements, exhibits much poverty, but little amended in other parts of the counties on which I report. *The farmers themselves are very much impoverished, and live no better than English cottagers in prosperous agricultural counties.*

"The cottages in which the people dwell are miserable in the extreme in nearly every part of the country in Cardiganshire, and every part of Brecknockshire and Radnorshire, except the east. I have myself visited many of the dwellings of the poor, and my assistants have done so likewise, and the results of some of these observations are stated in the notes in the Appendix on Tregaron, Llanfihangel, Rhidithon, Bequildy, &c. *I believe the Welsh cottages to be very little, if at all, superior to the Irish huts in the country districts.*

"Brick chimneys are very unusual in these cottages; those which exist are usually in the shape of large cones, the top being of basket-work. *In very few cottages is there more than one room*, which serves the purposes of living and sleeping. A large dresser and shelves usually form the partition between the two, and where there are separate beds for the family a curtain or low board is (if it exists) the only division with no regular partition. And this state of things very generally prevails, even where there is some little attention paid to cleanliness; but the cottages and bed are frequently filthy. The people are always very dirty. In all the counties the cottages are generally destitute of necessary outbuildings, including even those belonging to the farmers; and both in Cardiganshire and Radnorshire, except near the border of England, the pigs and poultry have free run of the joint dwelling and sleeping rooms.

"As an exemplification of this I may perhaps venture to cite a note I took of the small town of Tregaron in Cardiganshire.

"The extreme filthiness of the habits of the poor, though observable every where, is as striking in this place, if not more so, than elsewhere; inasmuch as in a town it might be expected that a little more of the outward observances of cleanliness and decency would be met with.

"Dung heaps abound in the lanes and streets. There seemed seldom to be more than one room for living and sleeping in; generally in a state of indescribable disorder, and dirty to an excess. The pigs and poultry form a usual part of the family. In walking down a lane, which forms one of the principal entrances to the town, I saw a huge sow go up to a door (the lower half of which was shut) and put her fore paws on the top of it, and begin shaking it. A woman with a child in her arms rushed across the road from the other side of the way, and immediately opened the door, and the animal walked into the house, grunting as if she was offended at the delay, the woman following and closing the door behind her. Even the churchyard gives evidence of the absence of necessary outbuildings in the town, and several were covered with half-washed linen hanging to dry. This church and churchyard stand on a rocky eminence in the centre of the town, forming, therefore, a very conspicuous object in the place."

"The evidence numbered 1. 22. 47, and 48, will further develop the prevalent disregard of cleanliness and domestic comfort.

"The mining population exists exclusively in the extreme south and south-east border of Brecknockshire. It is congregated chiefly at Brynmaur in the parish of Llanelly and at Beaufort in Llangattock, Llangymder, at Vainor, and at Ystrad Cynlais. The characteristics, so well known and often described of mining districts, prevail in the former of these places, if possible with still less than the usual attention to cleanliness and comfort.

"The evidence given me of the immoral character of the people, with a few exceptions, tells us the same tale. The Welsh are peculiarly exempt from the guilt of great crimes. There are few districts in Europe where murders, burglaries, personal violence, rapes, forgeries, or any felonies on a *large scale*, are so rare. On the other hand, there are perhaps few countries, *where the standard of minor morals is lower*. Petty thefts, lying, cozening, every species of chicanery, drunkenness (where the means exist), and idleness prevail to a great extent among the least educated part of the community, who scarcely regard them in the light of sins. There is another very painful feature in the laxity of morals, voluntarily attested by some of those who have given evidence. I refer to the alleged want of chastity in the women. If this be so, it is sufficient to account for all other immoralities; for each generation will derive its moral tone, in a great degree, from the influences imparted by the mothers who reared them. Where these influences are corrupted at their very source, it is in vain to expect virtue in the offspring. The want of chastity results frequently from the practice of bundling, or courtship on beds, during the night,—a practice still widely prevailing.

"*It results also from the revolting habit of herding married and unmarried people of both sexes, often unconnected by relationship, in the same sleeping rooms, and often in adjoining beds without partition or curtain.* Natural modesty is utterly suppressed by this vile practice, and delicacy alike in men and women is destroyed in its very germ. These practices obtain in the classes immediately above as well as among the labouring people.

"The several features in the moral condition of the

people will derive illustration from the following evidence :—

"In Brecknockshire the Reverend Edward Williams, Independent minister at Builth, says,—

"'The house accommodation is not good in the country. They often have only two rooms, one for the kitchen and one for sleeping. *The whole family sleep in one room, without any division of sexes in most cases.* I have known cases in farm-houses where the same system existed as to farm servants, but not in the better classes of farmhouses.'

"As regards morality in that district, Mr. Williams speaks more favourably than most persons; he says,—

"'The general character of the villagers is pretty fair as to honesty and also as to chastity. Cases of bastardy are not uncommon, but promiscuous intercourse does not usually occur. These cases are chiefly among farm servants.

"'They are tolerably fair as to truth, and they are generally industrious.

"'This town (Builth) is very bad as to drunkenness. In the country they are pretty fair as to that.

"'The observance of the Sabbath is better in Breconshire than in Radnorshire, and good in the former. Radnorshire is very much neglected, and attendance at places of worship not good. The clergy generally reside at their livings just in this neighbourhood.

"'The country people are generally peaceably disposed, they are free from gambling, but they are not very cleanly in their habits.'

"The Reverend David Charles, the principal of the College at Treveca, says,—

"'The morals of this part of the country are certainly

very defective, owing to the system of drinking cyder, &c. so prevalent here. Drunkenness is the common sin of both farmers and their servants. Seldom do we meet farm servants returning from any considerable distance with their master's waggon or cart, but that we find them intoxicated, while it is quite lamentable to witness the number of drunken farmers returning from market on Saturdays. In harvest-time this practice is still more prevalent. There is also, among the class mentioned, very little attention paid to the observance of the Sabbath.'

"The Reverend R. Harrison, the incumbent of Builth, says:—

"'The Welsh are very dirty. I found a house in Builth, where, in the bed-room down stairs, I found two pigs in one corner, and two children ill with the scarlet fever in the other. The dung-hills are placed in the front of the houses in some parts of the town.'

"The Reverend Richard Lumley, Calvinistic Methodist minister at Builth, says:—

"'The country-people are anything but cleanly in their habits. It is not uncommon for the *whole family among labourers to sleep in the same room, without any distinction of sexes;* and *I have lately witnessed instances of the same habit among the classes immediately above them.*'

"The Reverend James Morgan, vicar of Talgarth, says:—

"The standard of morality is certainly low. Illegitimate children are by no means rare, and pregnancy before marriage is of common occurrence. It scarcely seems to be considered a sin, or even a disgrace, for a woman to be in the family-way by the man, to whom she is engaged to be married.

"'Drunkenness is but too prevalent, particularly on fair-days and other similar occasions.'

"Edward W. Seymour, Esq., a magistrate of Crickhowel, speaking of the mining district, says:—

"'The vices of lying, thieving, swearing, and drunkenness, and *the vastly increasing crime of illicit intercourse between the sexes*, prevail to a great extent, and these are by no means confined to the uneducated. Of their disregard of common decency, I have an instance, among many, which have come to my knowledge, in a case, which was brought before me only the other day, wherein it appeared, that a young girl of sixteen, going on a visit to her sister (a married woman), was actually placed by her for many nights together in the same bedroom (without even a curtain between them), in which lay a young labouring man (a lodger and a stranger), which man was brought before me on a charge of stealing; the parties, with the exception of the lodger, being to all appearances respectable, intelligent, and above the common order among the lower classes. Upon my expostulating with them on the impropriety of their subjecting a female under their protection to such indecency, the parties seemed rather astonished at the remark than sensible of their error.'

"The Reverend J. Hughes, curate of Llanelly, a mining parish, says:—

"'. . . . Their dwellings are almost universally destitute of those conveniences, which are necessary to the health and comfort of mankind, and from the practice of the males stripping to wash themselves in the presence of the females, the usual barriers between the sexes are done away with, and the result is shown in the frequency of illicit intercourse.

" 'Drunkenness is also prevalent, although not to so great an extent as formerly.'

" The Reverend W. L. Bevan, vicar of Hay, says:—

" 'Drunkenness and illegitimacy are the prevailing vices of the neighbourhood. Very many of the poorer classes are ruined by indulgence in the first, while the second is considered a very venial offence. A promise of marriage on the part of a man seems to legitimatise the whole affair in the eyes of the parties themselves, as well as in the estimation of their friends.'

" The Reverend James Denning, curate of St. Mary's, Brecknock, says:—

" 'The poor seem ignorant on most subjects, except how to cheat and speak evil of each other. They appear not to have an idea what the comforts of life are. There are at least 2000 persons living in this town in a state of the greatest filth, and to all appearance they enjoy their filth and idleness, for they make no effort to get rid of it. From my experience of Ireland, I think there is a great similarity between the lower orders of Welsh and Irish,—both are dirty, indolent, bigoted, and contented.'

" 'The Reverend Mr. Griffiths, the principal of the college, says:—

" Generally speaking, our calendars are not remarkable for their number of gross crimes; in fact, I believe quite the reverse. I am afraid, however, that social and domestic moralities are very low among us.

" 'The number of illegitimate children, when compared with England, is astounding.'

" The Reverend D. Parry, of Llywell, thinks that—

" 'The morals of a great number are defective in respect of chastity, truth-telling, and veneration for God's sacred name. In proof of which, suffice it to allude to the number of illegitimate children in the country,—to the little reliance that can be placed on what is often said or spoken, provided the individual have some bias or interest in the matter,—and to the frequent abuse of God's holy name in the common intercourse and transactions of life. These are facts well known to all observant minds, and loudly calling for some means of reformation.'

"In Cardiganshire, the morals and habits of the people are not much better.

"The Very Reverend the Dean of St. David's says of many of the young persons in Sunday schools, that they are—

"'Not only grossly ignorant on every other subject, but also grossly immoral. Many of these girls have bastard children, but this generally exists without promiscuous intercourse. Drunkenness is very general, especially at the fairs. I think there cannot be a doubt that education, accompanied by religious instruction, would materially improve this state of things; and I think people would go to good schools if they existed.'

"Thomas Williams, Esq., clerk to the magistrates at Lampeter, and superintendent of the Independent Sunday school, says:—

"'I do not think the moral state of the people low; but for want of education, they practise a great deal of low cunning. Generally speaking, they are honest. Bastardy cases are, however, very common. The women used to be ashamed of being in the family-way, but are not now. The promiscuous intercourse is carried on to a very great degree.'

"The Reverend L. H. Davies, of Troedey Raur, says:—

"'They (the young people) often meet at evening

schools in private houses, and this tends to immoralities between the young persons of both sexes, who frequently spend the night afterwards in the hay-lofts together. So prevalent is want of chastity among the females, that although I promised to return the marriage fee to all couples, whose first child should be born after nine months from the marriage, only one in six years entitled themselves to claim it. Most of them were in the family-way. It is said to be a customary matter for them to have intercourse together, on condition that they should marry if the woman becomes pregnant; but the marriage by no means always takes place. Morals are generally at a low ebb, but want of chastity is the giant sin of Wales. I believe that the best remedy for the want of morals and of education, is that of the establishment of good schools, such as I have described.'

"Richard Williams, Esq., M.D. and coroner, says:—

"'The youth of both sexes are very unchaste, and do not consider promiscuous intercourse any disgrace, which is chiefly owing to the want of proper education; to the ancient practice of bundling or courting in bed, still prevalent; TO THE CONSTRUCTION OF THEIR DWELLINGS; and to the bad example of their parents.

"'The morals of the poor are generally indifferent. They are not disposed to commit atrocious crimes, but are addicted to petty thefts and prevarication. In justice I should say, that many strangers have informed me the lower classes of Wales are far superior to those of the same class in other parts of the kingdom.'

"W. O. Brigstocke, Esq., magistrate of Blaenpant, says:—

"'Morals generally very bad, intercourse between the sexes previous to marriage being very general.

Misconduct after marriage is of rare occurrence. Drunkenness is a very common vice, especially on market or fair days.'

"In Radnorshire, the morals of the people are of a very low standard.

"The Archdeacon Venables, chairman of quarter sessions, says:—

"'Their morals are at a very low ebb. An acknowledged thief is almost as well thought of, and as much employed, as better characters, by the lower orders.'

"The Reverend W. D. West, curate of Presteigne, says:—

"'There is a great laxity in the prevalent notions on the subject of sexual intercourse.' And he cites an instance which will be found in his evidence. He adds—

"'Sexual lusts and drunkenness (which last I omitted above) being the popular vices, education, not mere instruction, might counteract them by creating other tastes.'

"Sir William Cockburn, Bart., of New Radnor, a magistrate, says:—

"'In one crime, of bastardy, I fear that the people of this country are pre-eminent. As magistrates and individuals we have done our best to discourage this vice, but the remedy is yet to be found.'

"The Reverend R. Lister Venables, vicar of Clyro, and a magistrate, says:—

"'Crimes of violence are almost unknown, such as burglary, forcible robbery, or the use of the knife. Common assaults are frequent, usually arising from drunken quarrels. Petty thefts are not particularly numerous. Poultry stealing and sheep stealing prevail to a considerable extent. There is no rural police, and the parish constables are for the most part utterly useless, except for serving summonses, &c. Sheep and poultry stealers therefore very frequently escape with impunity.

" 'Drunkenness prevails to a lamentable extent, not so much among the lower class, who are restrained by their poverty, as among those who are in better circumstances. Every market or fair day affords too much proof of this assertion. Unchastity in the woman is, I am sorry to say, a great stain upon our people. The number of bastard children is very great, as is shown by the application of young women for admission into the workhouse to be confined, and by the application to magistrates in petty sessions for orders of affiliation. In hearing these cases, it is impossible not to remark how unconscious of shame both the young woman and her parents often appear to be. In the majority of cases where an order of affiliation is sought, marriage was promised, or the expectation of it held out. The cases are usually cases of bonâ fide seduction. Those who enter the workhouse to be confined are generally girls of known bad character. I believe that in the rural districts few professed prostitutes would be found.'

"The Rev. John Price, rector of Bledfa, and a magistrate, says:—

"Drunkenness is rare in this neighbourhood, and the poorer classes are really honest, quiet, and industrious; the prevailing vice of the country is a disregard for chastity, a breach of which is considered neither a sin nor a crime. Apparently there is no disgrace attached to it; the women who have had two or three illegitimate children are as frequently selected by the young men for their wives as those of virtuous conduct. But after marriage the women are generally well conducted.

" 'Probably the chief causes of this disregard to modesty and chastity *may be referred, first, to the want of room in small farm-houses and cottages. Grown up sons and daughters, and men and female sevrants, generally sleep in the same room.* Secondly, to the bad habit of holding meetings at dissenting chapels and farm-houses after night, where the youth of both sexes attend from a distance for the purpose of walking home together. As a magistrate, I can safely report that, in the investigation of numerous cases of bastardy, I have found most of them to be referred to the opportunities of meeting above mentioned.'

" Francis Phillips, Esq., of Abbey-cum-hir, Radnorshire, says:—

" 'Crime of a serious character is not of frequent occurrence; but bastardy, which is scarcely considered a crime or disgrace, is very prevalent with young women. Those who afterwards marry generally become industrious and domestic, but they have little idea of cleanliness and comfort. The very high price of coal leads to pilfering of wood, &c.'

" Such appear to be the prevailing vices throughout my district, with the exception of the town of Brecknock, and the hill district in the hundred of Crickhowel, where the mining district commences, and of which I shall presently have occasion to speak.

" In Brecknock and Builth a graver character of vice prevails than in the country.

" Mr. Thomas Davies, of Llangattock, for many years the agent of the Duke of Beaufort, says:—

" I fear in too many instances they have not much idea of the obligation of an oath when examined as witnesses. Such I know was the opinion of the late Mr. Baron Gurney, which he attributed to the want of religious education. The morals of the people are of a very low standard. In fact, immorality prevails rather from the want of a sense of moral obligation than from a forgetfulness or violation of recognised duties. I am confident that, as regards mendacity, there is frequently no real consciousness that it is sinful, so habitual is disregard for truth whenever interest prompts falsehood.

" 'The whole people are kept back by their immoralities and low tone of principle. A Bristol merchant, who endeavours to deal with the Welsh to some extent in a line of business, which throws him into communication with many of the country people, told me that his efforts to continue a commerce with them, which would be mutually profitable, were they even commonly trustworthy, are wholly frustrated by their inveterate faithlessness to their bargains, the moment they see the possibility of gaining a penny by breaking them. The astute ingenuity exercised in obtaining a minute advantage, or excusing themselves from an error, and escaping the effects of it, is remarkably great. Their want of morality is, *however, entirely owing to their total want of mental cultivation, and the very great deficiency of all means of moral training.* They are not taught better, and have at present little means of improvement.

"The morals of the population congregated at and near Byrnmaur and Beaufort are deplorably low. Drnnkenness, blasphemy, indecency, sexual vices, and lawlessness widely prevail there. This district was one of the chief sources of Chartism. One of the main bodies of the mob who marched upon Newport congregated at, and issued from thence; they took the chapels by storm, and forced many reluctant men to join them. Byrnmaur contains 5000 people, nearly all of whom are of the lowest class, and with the exception of one or two shopkeepers exclusively so. Nearly every family in it is in the employment of Mr. Baily, the iron master, whose works are at Nant-y-glo, in the adjoining parish, in Monmouthshire.

"The town reeks with dirt; there are no lamps or effective drainage; and although so many years have elapsed since the Chartist outbreak, not the slightest step has been taken to improve the mental or moral condition of the violent and vicious community. Neither church nor school have been established by those, who employ the people or own the land; and the only step that has been taken for their benefit is that of establishing within a week or two of this time a police station. It is exclusively owing to the Dissenters that instruction of any kind is given to the place. By their unaided efforts, an inferior school and six chapels have been built, and imperfect as their means of ameliorating the morals of the people are, their efforts have not been unattended with benefit. There is a visible improvement in the conduct of the people, according to the statement of Mr. Kershaw (No. 6.), but it is still lamentably bad, and their neglected state cannot be deemed otherwise than perilous to the tranquillity of the neighbourhood. I ought to state that the people of this place are not wholly Welsh.

"A large portion of them are strangers, and not unfrequently outcasts from distant places, in England, Ireland, and Scotland.

"I felt it my duty to take especial means of verifying the statements, which poured in upon me, with respect to this dangerous and degraded population; and in addition to the evidence already cited of Mr. Seymour (an active magistrate of this district), I beg to present to your lordships the following evidence from the Reverend Richard Davies, of Courty Gollen, a beneficed clergyman and magistrate of the highest respectability, who, in answer to my request that he would as a magistrate of the district state facts, which would illustrate the condition of Byrnmaur, favoured me with the following evidence respecting it:—

"'It has long been a matter of deep regret and sorrow to those who are responsible for the peace, good conduct, and well-being of society, to witness the degraded and corrupt state of what is generally termed the hilly district, more especially the locality designated as Byrnmaur. It has been the painful duty of the furnisher of this information, to bring the sad and lamentable state of this district more immediately before the view of the magistracy of the county. It afforded a frightful picture of the consequences, that a want of education necessarily entails, and the fearful result of masses being brought together, without an adequate provision made for leading their minds to higher and better things, to subject them to the guidance of religious tuition, and thus pave the way for their becoming loyal subjects, peaceable citizens, a contented, well disposed, and orderly community. The elements necessary to produce this wished for result are not in Byrnmaur. Let us refer to statistical details as our guide and index. There are 5000 inhabitants in Byrnmaur, and fifty new houses are added at a moderate computation yearly.

"'There are already nineteen licensed public-houses and thirty-eight beer houses. No church or chapel of the established religion nearer than two miles. Six meeting houses, of comparatively small dimensions, with some schools attached to them, but far from affording an antidote to the great amount of evil, that a vast increasing population, without responsible guides and pastors, must inevitably give rise to. One half of the criminal cases, that are entered upon the pages of our petty sessions record, come from and may be traced to the densely populated Byrnmaur. The scenes that the magistrates are compelled to witness, and which I can personally vouch for, baffle all description and outrage every feeling of propriety. Oaths and profane language are apparently familiar to persons of all ages; even children lisp out the foul expressions they hear, and seem perfectly accustomed to every epithet that the most evil mind could suggest.' "

Speaking of the mining population of Monmouthshire, Mr. Symons says :—

"Evil in every shape is rampant in this district; demoralisation is everywhere dominant, and all good influences are comparatively powerless. They drink to the most brutal excess, especially on occasions, which I will endeavour presently to describe, which are designed for the purpose. They have little regard to modesty or the truth ; and even the young children in the streets, who can scarcely articulate, give utterance to imprecations. The bodies and habits of the people are almost as dirty, as the towns and houses of the swarthy region, in which they swarm. The whole district, with the exception of Newport, teems with crime, and all the slatternly accompaniments of animal power and moral disorder, with scarcely a ray of mental or spiritual intelligence. The people are savage in their manner, and mimic the repulsive rudeness of those in authority over them. The whole district and population partake of the iron character of its produce; everything centres in and ministers to the idolatry of profit; physical strength is the object of esteem, and gain their chief god. There are, of course, even in this black domain, some individual exceptions, but the general picture can only be drawn with truth in the colours I am constrained to use.

"Even the physical condition of the people seems almost as if contrived, for the double purpose of their degradation and the employers' profit. Some of the works are surrounded by homes built by the companies, without the slightest attention to comfort, health, or decency, or any other consideration, than that of realising the largest amount of rent from the smallest amount of outlay. I went into several of this class of houses in the north part of my district and examined them from top to bottom. *Men, women, and children, of all sexes and ages, are stowed away in the bed-rooms without any curtains or partitions, it being no uncommon thing for nine or ten people, not belonging to the same family, to sleep together in this manner in one room.* In one instance, I found three men sleeping in a sort of a dungeon, which was about 9 feet by 6 in dimensions, without any light or air except through a hole in the wall not a foot square, which opened into another room occupied by some women. The houses are many of them so constructed, that each story is let off to different tenants. The necessary out-buildings in most cases do not exist at all. An immense rent, in comparison to the accommodation, is paid to the company or master for these miserable places. Heaps of rubbish lie about in the streets, although coal is close at hand. Tram-roads intersect and run along the streets of these places, which contain about 30,000 inhabitants. Nevertheless, these places are little worse than others, and in some respects superior to Byrnmaur, which I described in my last report. In many cases, the iron companies have merely a lease of the estate, and have no other interest, than that of making the most they can out of it. In some places I heard of beds being so scarce, that they were perpetually occupied, one gang or set of men turning in as the others turned out; they work every eight hours consecutively, and the beds have never time to cool. I need hardly say that fever ensued, and the practice was then forbidden by the employers."

I select the next series of extracts from the Report of Mr. Johnson, a barrister, who was sent by Government into *North Wales*, in 1847, to examine the state of the schools there. He gives a lamentable description of the social condition of the people of that part of our island.

I visited and inspected a great part of North Wales and the Isle of Anglesey myself, in the summer of 1849. Nothing can be more miserable and disgraceful, than the condition of the greater part of the cottages in those parts. They are low hovels of one story in height, divided into one or at most two rooms. These have generally only two windows, often only little apertures in the walls, filled up with glass. The roofs are so low, that I was not able to stand upright in them, if I kept my hat upon my head. Many of them have no grate or fire-place, but only a hearth with an open chimney above it. They are generally miserably built, the lumps of stone of which the walls are formed being often merely piled one upon another, the interstices being filled up with mortar. Many of the cottages have only one little window, measuring about eight inches square. I have seen quantities of such hovels within a few yards of the park gates of great landowners in that country; and, as a general rule, I should say, that the larger the estate in North Wales or the island of Anglesey, the worse invariably is the condition of the peasantry. I do not wish to draw attention to individuals, nor to appear to be personal in my remarks, or I could specify particular parts of the country, where any one might obtain as much evidence of the truth of this statement as he could desire. The contrast between the condition of the Welsh and Swiss or Saxon peasantry is very remarkable.

Mr. Johnson says:—

"The social defects of the agricultural districts of the counties of Merioneth, Montgomery, and a considerable portion of those of Carnarvon and Denbigh is illustrated by the following evidence, relating to the parishes of Talyllyn and Llanfihangel, in the county of Merioneth:—

"I visited many cottages in Talyllyn, and the adjoining parish of Llanfihangel. The house accommodation is wretched. The cottages are formed of a few loose fragments of rock and shale piled together, without mortar or whitewash. The floors are of earth, the roofs are wattled, and *many of these hovels have no window.* They comprise one room, in which all the family sleep. This is in some cases separated from the rest of the hut by wisps of straw, forming an imperfect screen.

"The social and moral depravity of the pauper population in the towns is illustrated by the following evidence of Mr. William Williams, Chemist, of Carnarvon:—

"'There is a great amount of extreme poverty, filth, and misery in Carnarvon, for the most part owing to immorality and ignorance. I can mention three places in particular in this town, of Glanymor, Tanallt, and Smithfield, *where many families have only one room to live in, 9 feet square, with an earthen floor, and the ventilation dreadfully bad.*

"'These rooms have but one window of a foot square, which is always closed. With the exception of some who are aged, sick, or widows, the poverty in Carnarvon is generally owing to the depravity of the people. Wages are good here. Owing to the railways, 2*s.* 6*d.* is now paid where 1*s.* 6*d.* would formerly have been paid. Able-bodied men can always get work, if they are disposed, and at good wages. *But the people crowd into the towns from the country roand*, in order to be lodged in these filthy houses, and to beg. Carnarvon is full of such people. Rates are now 1*s.* where they used to be but 4*d.*

"'The chief vice in this town is drunkenness. Many who earn 20*s.*, some of them 26*s.* a week, bring home 5*s.*, some only 3*s.*, to their families; the rest is spent in the public-house. Their families cannot attend a place of worship or a school, either on Sunday or week-day. They have no clothes. Ragged schools would do great good among these people. The two which have been set on foot by the Methodists have already done a great deal of good; the children attend them with very little clothing.'"

Upon the same subject, the Rev. William Williams, Independent minister, said :—

"'In Carnarvon, if you go beyond the different religious circles, you will find scarcely a single young man, who does not devote himself to smoking and drinking, and things that are worse. They are beastly in their habits in this town.'

"Evidence to the same effect might be adduced respecting Bangor, and other large towns in North Wales.

"Mr. Joshua Williams, schoolmaster, Llandwrog, stated:—

"'There are a great many all round the schools who are of an age for instruction. They are anxious for it, both parents and children. But they are very poor; the majority are labourers with very large families, many of them eight or nine children. A great many are too poor to pay for instruction—too poor to pay for clothes, and shoes, or clogs for their feet, in order to send them to school. I have to teach many for nothing.

"'The cottages are very, very poor. *One bed-room for three or four beds, and the beds of straw very bare. Very often all the family sleep in the same room. Grown up children among them of both sexes. This has a bad effect; very bad on their health and morals.*'

"But the lowest form of social degradation and moral depravity is met with in the mining districts, and is found to grow worse in approaching the English border. These districts extend from Llangollen through the parishes of Ruabon and Wrexham to the point of Air, at the north-eastern extremity of Flintshire.

"The following evidence was taken from personal inspection of the district:—

"I visited Rhosllanerchrugog, Sunday, January 13. It is situated midway between Ruabon and Wrexham, and is a place of great importance, owing to the vast number of operatives, who are employed upon the extensive coal mines, with which the district abounds. I visited the Sunday schools of several religious denominations, which were filled with persons of all ages, respectably dressed and well conducted. I then visited many cottages in different parts of the village.

"Some of these consist of a single room, from 9

to 12 feet square; others have, in addition, a sort of a lean-to, forming a separate place to sleep in. They are in general void of furniture; but in some I *found a bed, which is made to accommodate double numbers, by arranging the occupants feet to feet.* The roofs are wattled, sometimes plastered over with mortar, sometimes bare; others are of straw, and full of large holes open to the sky, which are frequently the only means for admitting light. Each of these hovels contains, on an average, a family of six children, with their parents. If they comprise two rooms, the parents sleep in one, and the children in the other; if there is but one room, all sleep together. In either case, the young people sleep together in the same confined room, regardless of age and sex. I observed one cottage unusually neat and clean; it contained a father and mother, well and neatly dressed, a son eighteen years old, and a daughter aged twenty: *all these sleep together in the same room*, which is about 9 or 10 feet square. Next door live two idiots, a brother and sister. In several other cottages I observed the inmates well, and even expensively, clothed, and the tables were supplied with food—bacon, &c.

"Yet in these, the families were crowded in the same unseemly manner, *the father, mother, and six children all sleeping together.*

"The existence of the evils above mentioned was less surprising than the remonstrances addressed to me by persons of high religious profession in the neighbourhood, representing the injustice of apprehending immoral results from habits of promiscuous intercourse. Nothing could more forcibly illustrate the imperfect nature of indigenous civilisation, when it is isolated and unaided.

"The following is a Report of Mr. John James, assistant:—

"'January 20.—I went, in company with the Rev. P. M. Richards, the officiating minister of the district, to visit some of the houses of the colliers at Rhosllanerchrugog; and though I have seen St. Giles's, Cow Cross, Wapping, and other places in the metropolis, where the houses of the poor are unfit to live in, I never beheld anything to equal some of the cottages at Rhosllanerchrugog, as regards confinement, filth, and utter unfitness for human abode.

"'Cottage No. 1. consists of one low room, about 12 feet square, containing an old man, perfectly black with dirt, lying on a bed of rags and filth. In the same cottage lives his son, who is in a consumption.

"'No. 2. consists of one small room, dirty, and so close that the atmosphere was insupportable. The floor was alternately of mud and stone. In the centre an idiot was seated on a stool; her mother, an old woman, seventy or eighty years of age, was lying on a filthy bed beside her, reduced to a skeleton by disease. The room was without an article of what would be called furniture.

"'No. 3. contains only one room, in which live a man and his two idiot children, both about twenty years old.

"'No. 4., a cottage of one room, contains a father and mother, their daughter and her husband, occupying two beds placed close together, the room being very small. The beds were filthy, the furniture miserable, and the ventilation bad.

"'No. 5., a cottage of one room, inhabited by two adult sisters and their two adult brothers. All occupy the same bed, which may be enlarged a little, but is still the same bed. The room is low-roofed and ill-ventilated.

"'None of these houses had a necessary, anywhere near them, nor did I see such a thing in the whole village.

"'The Rev. Mr. Richards and Mr. William Jones, of Llanerchrugog, informed me, that houses of this description are frequent in this place; that they are for the most part built by the poor people themselves, an acknowledgment of from *7s.* to *15s.* per annum being paid to the landlord as ground-rent; that fever is very common in this district, although the village is well situated, and naturally very salubrious; that morals are exceedingly low; that there is a man in the district who notoriously lives in a state of incest with his own daughter, and that this is not an isolated case.

"'Superstition is said to be very common among the poor of this neighbourhood. There was recently a woman in the village, who gained her livelihood by conjuring, and there is now a pretended conjuror at Wrexham, to whom scores of people are said to go annually from Rhosllanerchrugog.—John James, Assistant.'

"As the influence of the Welsh Sunday-schools decreases, the moral degradation of the inhabitants is more apparent. This is observable on approaching the English border.

"The following evidence relates to the town of Flint:—

"The streets of the town are filthy; the houses are wretchedly built, and in worse repair; and the people are squalid and in rags. I visited several cottages in the town. A small house, 10 or 12 feet square, with a chamber above, accommodates, on an average, two parents, six children, and six lodgers. The floors are of earth, and in wretched condition. There is no room for furniture, and the interiors are filthy and unwholesome. I saw other cottages of 9 feet square, with no other room adjoining. These generally contain a husband and wife, with infants and a lodger. I visited a parish almshouse of this description, containing nine people, a father, mother, and seven children.

"There was one bed for the parents, and another for the seven children, both placed in the only room which the house contained. The eldest boy was sixteen years old, the eldest girl fifteen. The character of the inhabitants is degraded in respect of turbulence, intemperance, and debauchery.

"The prevailing vice of the neighbourhood is drunkenness, which is rendered more flagrant and pernicious from the prevalence of the old Welsh custom of keeping merry nights. A week previous to my visit, a murder had been committed by a party (as was supposed) who had been thus engaged in revelry. The clergyman informed me that fornication also is common in the town and neighbourhood; but that in Flintshire, as in England, it assumes the form of promiscuous debauchery, and is not a recognised systematic institution as in other counties of North Wales. The female population are ignorant of economy and of all kinds of domestic industry; in consequence of which, and of the general improvidence and intemperance of the men, the social condition of Flint is almost as degraded as at Rhosllanerchrugog (Ruabon).

"In the adjoining district of Bagillt, in some of the collieries the men are paid every Saturday, and do not return to their work until the following Tuesday or Wednesday.

"In Bagillt, and in the adjoining town of Flint, the

old Welsh custom of keeping a merry night (noswaith-lawen) is still prevalent, and, being generally reserved for a Saturday, is protracted to the following Sunday, during which drinking never ceases. This custom is represented by the clergy and others as involving the most pernicious consequences.

"I saw two men stripped and fighting in the main street of Bagillt, with a ring of men, women, and children around them. There are no policemen in the township. The women are represented as being, for the most part, ignorant of housewifery and domestic economy. The girls are very early sent to service, but marry as early as eighteen, and have large families. Women are not employed in or about the mines, but spend most of their time in cockling, or gathering cockles on the beach. They have low ideas of domestic comfort, living in small cottages, dirty and ill-ventilated, and at night are crowded together in the same room, and sometimes in the same bed, without regard to age or sex.

"In the district of St. Matthew, in the parish of Hawarden, where the inhabitants are exclusively English, the Rev. J. P. Foulkes, the officiating minister, states that—

"'The state of morals is degraded in respect of drunkenness, profanity, dishonesty, and incontinence; that the latter vice is increasing so rapidly as to render it difficult to find a cottage where some female of the family has not been *enceinte* before marriage.'

"But there is one vice which is flagrant throughout North Wales, and remains unchecked by any instruments of civilisation.

"It has obtained for a long time as the peculiar vice of the principality, but its existence has almost ceased to be considered as an evil; and the custom of Wales is said to justify the barbarous practices which precede the rite of marriage. Upon this subject it is unnecessary to add more than the following evidence.

"The Rev. William Jones, Vicar of Nevin:—

"'Want of chastity is flagrant. This vice is not confined to the poor.

"'In England, farmers' daughters are respectable; in Wales, they are in the constant habit of being courted in bed. In the case of domestic servants, the vice is universal. I have had the greatest difficulty in keeping my own servants from practising it. It became necessary to secure their chamber windows with bars to prevent them from admitting men. I am told by my parishioners, that unless I allow the practice, I shall very soon have no servants at all, and that it will be impossible to get any.'

"The Rev. St. George Armstrong Williams, incumbent of Demo, states:—

"'The want of chastity is the besetting evil of this country, but especially of this district of Lleyn. In the relieving officer's books, out of twenty-nine births, I counted twelve illegitimate. This was in one quarter of a year. Our workhouse is completely filled with the mothers of illegitimate children, and the children themselves. What is worse, the parents do not see the evil of it. They say their daughters have been unfortunate, and maintain their illegitimate grandchildren as if they were legitimate. In my parish, Llannor, in one house, there is a woman with five illegitimate children, and these by different fathers; her sister had four children, all illegitimate. Another in the same village had four, also by different fathers. In this parish of Llannor, there are no means of education for the female children of the poor. These low morals I attribute entirely to the want of education.'

"The fullest evidence on this subject was given by the Reverend J. W. Trevor, chaplain to the Lord Bishop of Bangor:—

"'It is difficult as it is mortifying, to describe in proper terms the disgraceful state of the common people in Wales in the intercourse of the sexes, but it is important that the truth should be known. I believe the proportion of illegitimate children to the population in Anglesey (with only one exception, and that is in Wales), exceeds that in any other county in the kingdom. The fact is enough to prove the moral degradation of our common people. But I must draw your notice more particularly to some details on this subject, which will show you at once, what I want to make known, that the moral principles of the Welsh people are totally corrupt and abandoned in this respect,—that no restraints or penalties of law can cure or even check the evil, until by appliances of better education and more general civilisation, they are taught to regard their present custom with a sense of shame and decency. I put out of consideration now any higher motives, for they are not to be looked for at present. *While the sexes continue to herd like beasts, it were idle to expect they can be restrained by religion or conscience.* I assert with confidence, as an undeniable fact, that fornication is not regarded as a vice, scarcely as a frailty, by the common people in Wales. It is considered as a matter of course, as the regular conventional process towards marriage.

"'It is avowed, defended, and laughed at, without scruple, or shame, or concealment by both sexes alike. And what, if, as it often happens, the man prove faithless, and marriage does not ensue, and yet a child is to be born. Then comes the affair of affiliation, and with it, as the law now requires, all the filthy disclosure in open court of the obscenities which preceded it. I will state some facts, as they came under my own cog nisance as a magistrate; and you will bear in mind, they are heard by the public of all ages and both sexes. A young girl was brought to swear that she sat by the fire, while her widowed mother was in bed with her paramour in the same room, and this she did on several occasions. Another swears, that she stood by in open day-light, and in the open air, while the deed was perpetrated, which made her friend the mother of a bastard. A man lay in bed with two women, night after night for months together; and one of the women swore to the required fact.

"'Both parents, or either of them, came forward to prove the parentage of their daughter's bastard—wit nesses often to the very act. I might multiply such instances to prove the utter disregard of common natural decency and shame among the people. This evidence was given (with but few exceptions it is always given) without the slightest reluctance or modesty, and with a levity and confidence of manner, which prove the parties to be quite callous and lost to all sense of shame. When I have attempted at the union board to persuade the guardians to build a workhouse (we have none in Anglesey), and used as an argument, that it would check the increase of bastardy, which is a mon strous charge on our poor-rates, as well as a disgrace to our community; they quite scouted the notion of its being any disgrace, and they maintained that the custom of Wales justified the practice. In fact, the guardians, who are almost all country farmers, are so familiarised to this iniquity, and have so long partaken in it, that they are totally incapable of any right feeling on the subject. They absolutely encourage the practice: they hire their servants, agreeing to their stipulation for freedom of access for this purpose at stated times, or, it may be, whenever they please. The boys and girls in farm-houses are brought up from childhood with these filthy practices ever before their eyes and ears, and, of course, on the first temptation, they fall into the same course themselves. In short, in this matter, even in a greater degree than the other which I have noticed, the minds of our common people are become thoroughly and universally depraved and brutalised. To meet this appalling evil, *the present system of education in Wales is utterly powerless.*'"

I have endeavoured, in the preceding pages, to represent, as dispassionately as possible, the social condition of a great part of the poor of England and Wales in this the *nineteenth* century. I have quoted the statements and statistics of government officers or eminent individuals on every branch of my inquiry. From those statements and statistics it is only too evident that the social degradation and misery of our labouring classes is appalling.

We have become so accustomed to this sad and disgraceful social state, that people talk in England of "pauperism being a *necessity*;" of "the Bible teaching us so;" of its being "the dream of enthusiasts to hope to change this order of things;" and of the "necessity of submitting to the dispensations of Providence." Impious assertions! Happily, each year since 1820 has been more and more belying this insane reasoning, and every year henceforward will still further belie it.

Since the foreign governments began to educate all the children of their poor, and since they first enabled the peasants to purchase land, *by refusing to allow proprietors to tie up their estates after their deaths, or to prevent their successors selling the fee*, the poor of many of the European countries have been steadily emerging from pauperism. The more their intelligence is developed by means of the liberal systems of education, which are in force in those countries, the higher will they henceforward rise in the scale of humanity and of social prosperity.

Not much more than a quarter of a century has elapsed, since the governments of modern Europe commenced anything like an effective effort to educate the children of their poor; not half a century has elapsed, since the peasants of foreign countries first found themselves enabled, after the long continuance of the feudal system, to purchase land; and yet, in the short time, which has elapsed, since these great changes in the middle-age system of legislation, great results, as I have already shown, have been obtained. When the present system of general education and division of land among the peasants has worked for another half century, the world will look back with astonishment on the degradation to which the poorer classes have been so long subjected, by imperfect legislation.

But what are the principal causes of the pauperism, misery, and crime, which distinguish so unhappily the condition of a great part of our poor? They are the following:—

1. The great and continued neglect of the intellectual training of the poorer classes.
2. The neglect of their religious education.
3. The game laws.

4. The system of laws which affect land.
5. The gin-palaces.
6. The want of classification in our prisons.

Let us briefly consider each of them.

## 1. *The Neglect of the Intellectual Training of the Poorer Classes.**

About ONE HALF of our poor can neither read nor write, have never been in any school, and know little, or positively nothing, of the doctrines of the Christian religion, of moral duties, or of any higher pleasures, than beer or spirit drinking and the grossest sensual indulgence. Even of the small shopkeeping and farmer classes, there are great numbers, who can neither read nor write, and who have never entered even a Sunday school. It is a very common thing for even farmers, who are members of the union boards of guardians in the midland and eastern counties of England, to sign their names with a cross, from being unable to write.

None of all this class can ever search the Scriptures for themselves; few of them care to give their children any instruction, as they have never experienced the benefits of instruction themselves; scarcely any of them are sensible enough to even desire to improve their condition in life; scarcely any of them ever enter into a place of public worship, or ever come into contact with a religious minister; none of them understand anything of the phenomena of nature around them, of the thoughts and wishes of their age, of their own

* These statements are the results of an examination of the Reports published by the Committee of Council on Education, of those of the Welsh Commissioners, of the Journals of the Statistical Society, and of personal inquiry in various parts of England.

situation here, or of the mysterious change before them. They live precisely like brutes, to gratify, as far as their means allow, the appetites of their uncultivated bodies, and then die, to go they have never thought, cared, or wondered whither.

All this must seem exaggeration to those, who have not examined for themselves the reports of the Inspectors of Schools, or those of the Welsh Commissioners, or those of the visitors, chaplains, inspectors, and governors of our prisons, or those of the City Missionaries, *or the admirable letters published in the* "Times" and "Chronicle." But those persons, who have examined these reports, will know, that I have understated the deep ignorance of our poorer classes.

The reports, to which I allude, disclose a degree of ignorance, which must be quite incredible to all who have not given their attention to the study of these facts. I might fill volumes with quotations confirmatory of my statements, but as my space does not allow me to do more than state the fact, I am obliged to refer my readers to these reports for proof of the universal truth of what I have affirmed.

If these poor creatures commit what the more intelligent classes call "crimes against society,"—if they are improvident and immoral,—if they have no love for the society which has left, if it has not made, them thus degraded,—and if they punish that society by burdening it with vice and pauperism, is it a matter of great surprise?

Brought up in the darkness of barbarism, they have no idea, that it is possible for them to attain any higher condition; they are not even sentient enough to desire, with any strength of feeling, to change their situation; they are not intelligent enough to be perseveringly discontented; they are not sensible to what we call the voice of conscience; they do not understand the necessity of avoiding crime, beyond the mere fear of the police and a gaol; they do not in the least comprehend, that what is the interest of society is their own also; they do not in the least understand the meaning, necessity, or effect of the laws; they have unclear, indefinite, and undefinable ideas of all around them; they eat, drink, breed, work, and die; and while they pass through their brute-like existence here, the richer and more intelligent classes are obliged to guard them with police and standing armies, and to cover the land with prisons, cages, and all kinds of receptacles for those, who in their thoughtlessness or misery disturb the quiet and happiness of their more intelligent, and, consequently, more moral and prosperous neighbours, by plunder, assault, or any other deed, which law is obliged, for the sake of the existence of society, to designate a "crime," although most of those who commit it do not in the least comprehend its criminality.

It is to this totally uneducated class, and to the class of those, who can only read and write very imperfectly, as Mr. Porter shows in the statistics I have quoted above, that the greatest part of our criminals belong. The majority of all our criminals have received no education, and cannot read or write at all; or have received so wretched an education, as only to be able to read or write very imperfectly. Scarcely any of the inmates of our prisons have received even a decent education. And yet, in the presence of such facts as these, 1850 years have passed since the birth of Jesus Christ, and scarcely anything worthy of mention has yet been done for the education of the English poor!

The very able correspondent of the "Morning Chronicle," in one of his letters on the condition of the peasants in the rural districts of England, published on December 1st, 1849, says:—

"Taking the adult class of agricultural labourers, it is almost impossible to exaggerate the ignorance in which they live, and move, and have their being. As they work in the fields, the external world has some hold upon them through the medium of their senses; but to all the higher exercises of intellect, they are perfect strangers. You cannot address one of them, without being at once painfully struck with the intellectual darkness which enshrouds him. There is in general neither speculation in his eyes nor intelligence in his countenance. The whole expression is more that of an animal than of a man. He is wanting, too, in the erect and independent bearing of a man. When you accost him, if he is not insolent—which he seldom is—he is timid and shrinking; his whole manner showing that he feels himself at a distance from you greater than should separate any two classes of men. He is often doubtful when you address, and suspicious when you question him; he is seemingly oppressed with the *interview, whilst it lasts, and obviously* relieved, when it is over. These are the traits, which I can affirm them to possess as a class, after having come in contact with many hundreds of farm-labourers. They belong to a generation, for whose intellectual culture little or nothing was done. As a class, they have no amusements beyond the indulgence of sense. In nine cases out of ten, recreation is associated in their minds with nothing higher than sensuality. I have frequently asked clergymen and others, if they often find the adult peasant reading for his own or others' amusement? The invariable answer is, that such a sight is seldom or never witnessed. In the first place, *the great bulk of them cannot read.* In the next, a large proportion of those who can, do so with too much difficulty to admit of the exercise being an amusement to them. Again, few of those who can read with comparative ease have the taste for doing so. It is but justice to them to say, that many of those who cannot read have bitterly regretted, in my hearing, their inability to do so. I shall never forget the tone, in which an old woman in Cornwall intimated to me what a confort it would now be to her, could she only read her Bible in her lonely hours.

"Education has advanced him but little beyond the position which he occupied in the days of William the Norman. The farm-labourer has scarcely participated at all in the improvement of his brethren. As he was generations gone by, so he is now—a physical scandal, a moral enigma, an intellectual cataleptic.

"Let it not be said, that this picture is too strongly drawn. *The subject is one, which does not admit of exaggeration.* Did space permit, or could any good purpose be served by it, I could adduce instances, almost innumerable, of the profound ignorance in which this class of British subjects is steeped. There is scarcely a field in the agricultural districts, which does not exhibit a living illustration of it. Search any county throughout the south and west, and the examples start up around you in hundreds. I have found it so in all those, which I have traversed—from Salisbury to the Land's-end—from Portland-bill to Oxford—in the vale of the Torridge, and in the vale of Aylesbury—by the Thames, the Severn, the Frome, the Stour, the Exe, the Camel, and the Plym. Where all is bad, it is sometimes difficult to point out the worst."

But what is the intelligence of the *partially instructed*

*half* of our poorer classes? It is miserable. They can, perhaps, read and write, and they know something of the Scriptures; but that is all that the greatest part of even the instructed half understand. A few, but these are very few, are well educated, and know something of physical and political science, of the relations of their own nation with foreign nations, and of those truths of political economy, which all educated persons admit and understand, although often without knowing that they do so. But by far the greatest part of this partially instructed moiety know nothing of geography, nothing of the history of their country, nothing of science, nothing of the natural phenomena around them, nothing of political or of economical science, nothing of the history of the world, nothing of the relations of their own country with foreign countries, nothing of the necessity of having laws, and nothing of the laws by which they are governed; in short, the greatest part of even this partially instructed moiety of the poor have few ideas, beyond the most vulgar and crude notions of God and the devil, of heaven and hell, of everlasting happiness and everlasting burning; of our Lord Jesus, the sacrifice of an enraged Deity; and of those unpractical theories of equality, universal happiness, fraternity, and present oppression, which demagogues pour forth for their own selfish ends.

What is the character of the education which the majority of those poor children who go to school receive? Most of them are instructed either by poor ignorant women, who just know how to read, write, and cipher; or by poor men of the lowest attainments, who have taken to school-management, because they are fit for nothing else. A great part of the very best-built and endowed schools have no seats inside them;

no separate rooms for the different classes; only one teacher for each school; no maps; very few books; and no apparatus for instruction. The poor children, all of them young,—for few remain at school beyond the age of ten,—are obliged to stand in many of these schools nearly the whole day, and are, in this fatiguing position, obliged, by the threat of a flogging, to learn the most beautiful passages of the Scriptures by heart! Do my readers think that these passages, learned amidst such miserable associations, will have any beneficial influence in after life? Do they think that children, who leave school at the age of twelve, even if the school be a good one, can carry away much that will be remembered afterwards to their moral improvement?

I am quite convinced, that our dame schools, and those schools which are unfurnished, where the classes are unseparated, where the teachers are uneducated, and where the children are tortured by being made to stand the greater part of the day, are very much worse than no schools at all.

A poor boy, brought up under the kindly influences of his parents, however rude and unenlightened they may be, is much more likely to turn out a good citizen afterwards, than one who has been taught to hate instruction, the Bible, and moral and religious precepts, by being tortured daily in such wretched schools as those I have mentioned; and yet such schools form the majority of all we have at present established!

But the small number of our schools, and the miserable character of the majority of them, are not the only obstacles to the progress of the education and to the improvement of the social condition of the poor in England. Almost as great an obstacle as the character or small number of the schools, is *the short time during which the children are left in schools.* The educational inspectors complain very much of this fact. It is said that the time during which the children have been left in school has been actually shortened of late years, owing, no doubt, to the increasing poverty of the lower orders.

The Rev. H. Moseley, government inspector of the Midland District, says,* "the general impression amongst those persons, who are likely to be best informed on the subject, is, *that the average age of the children who attend our elementary schools is steadily sinking.* We may be educating more, but they are, I believe, younger children, and stay with us a less time."

Mr. Moseley represents the age at which the majority of the children leave our schools to be about *nine;* Mr. Fletcher, another inspector, represents it at no more than *ten.* In Germany, the children remain in school to the end of their *fourteenth*, and in Switzerland to the end of their *fifteenth*, and often to the end of their *sixteenth* year. So that, not only are our schools and teachers too few in numbers, and incomparably worse than those of foreign countries, but our children only remain in the schools about four years, or less than one-half the period during which every child in Switzerland receives a first-rate education.

The Rev. H. Worsley, rector of Easton, in Suffolk, says:—†

"The low rate of wages for work, especially in the agricultural districts, may be alleged as the reason of the diminished term of a child's continuance at school; in some instances, perhaps, with justice; but the general

* See Minutes of Committee of Education, 1846.

† See his admirable Essay on Juvenile Depravity, p. 14.

conclusion cannot be eluded, that parents place very low value on the education of their children. A very small pecuniary gain, to be derived from their children's labour, immediately outweighs, with the majority, all the benefits of instruction. Such low appreciation of a chief blessing is not confined to agriculture, or to manufacturing districts, but is common to all. The labourer, who can procure for his son employment with a farmer of the most trifling emolument, will at once remove him from school. The practice of what is called corn-keeping in the country districts, in which small boys are mostly employed to defend the newly-sown corn or ripe grain from the attacks of birds, is a serious obstacle to the advance of instruction. During the whole of the Lord's day, the poor little fellow will be stationed in the cornfield, and must, of course, be absent, not only from the Sunday school, but also from church; and he may be thus occupied for months together. After so long an intermission of secular and religious instruction, (for in nine cases out of ten it cannot be supposed that he is taught at home,) the boy returns to the Sunday, perhaps weekly, school, manifestly no whit better in his general conduct for this long cessation from school duties, and with his small stock of previously obtained knowledge almost sheer forgotten."

Owing to these circumstances, the poor education, which we are giving, is rendered all the more imperfect, and ineffectual. The children leave the schools, at nine or ten years of age, with a mere smattering of knowledge, but with nothing more. Now, there is no saying more true than this, "that a little knowledge is a dangerous thing." It would be much safer, and much more expedient for the lower classes themselves, to give them *no* instruction, than to impart to them as little as we are doing by our present system. The miserable instruction, which is being given in our present schools, is positively doing more harm than good, as it is actually tending to increase the criminality of our poorer classes.

The reports of crime, published by government, show, that the number of persons who are committed annually out of the class of poor *who can read and write imperfectly*, *i. e.* who have only received a little miserable instruction for about three years of their life, has INCREASED within the last ten years 7·43 per cent.

Talk of education not having yet done much for our poor!—why, we have scarcely begun anything like education in England. Can you educate a citizen by taking a child of six years of age, and keeping him in such schools as those I have described from his *sixth* to his *tenth* year? Can you educate a child by sending him to a dame school or to a ragged school, or to such a school as any of those I have described above, for *four* years? The supposition is absurd. And yet this is all we attempt in the case of most of even those children who go to school at all.

A good teacher ought to interest his scholars in the beauties of the Scripture history; to make them love the Bible; to teach them to read, write, and cipher, in order that afterwards they may continue their own education; to teach them the history of their own country and its great men, in order to inspire them with patriotism, with a love of their fellow-countrymen, with pride in their nation, and with that respect for high character which would lead them to seek a higher class of leaders, than those who pass off their ignorance and selfishness upon them now; to teach them to sing and chant, in order to provide them with a higher kind of amusement, which might tend to elevate their tastes, their social meetings in after life, and their amusements; and to train them in such habits of cleanliness and neatness, as would make filthy and incommodious houses, such as those I have described above, as intolerable to them, as they are to educated members of the middle classes of society.

I have shown that these ends are being actually attained throughout western Europe. I appeal to my readers, if we have even begun to realise them to any extent in England or Wales.

I am quite convinced, that if our schools and teachers were anything like what they ought to be in character and in numbers, and if our poor were only obliged and enabled to send their children to some school or another from their sixth to their fifteenth year, that by these means alone we should, in twenty years, make our labourers happy and prosperous, and get rid of the greatest part of our pauperism and crime, and of the outlay now required for its suppression.

If democracy should ever invade this country—and the march of events during the last half-century ought to show us that it will be in the midst of us in a few years—the people, among the first laws they will pass, will establish a great system of compulsory and gratuitous education, and will oblige all parents to send their children to school. The most stringent educational regulations that have been ever put in force are those of Switzerland and America.

The reports of the Welsh Commissioners, and of the Educational Inspectors, and the accounts given by teachers, in the manufacturing districts of the north of England, disclose an amount of ignorance among the labouring classes which is almost incredible; and this, be it remembered, exists contemporaneously with the frightful state, which the statistics quoted in this chapter disclose, and with a system of education, which depends for its support upon the efforts of charitable individuals, and upon the paltry sum of 125,000*l.* doled out annually by Government.

Why, in France, every parish is *obliged* by law to build at least one school, and to support a sufficient number of teachers; and, in addition to the enormous annual expenditure of the communes of France, in carrying out the above regulations, the government is now granting about 2,000,000*l.* per annum in order to assist the departments to carry on effectually the education of the people.

### 2. *The Neglect of the religious Education of our Poor.*

I have mentioned this before. I have said that the forms of worship of the English Church, and of the greater part of the dissenting sects, are not imaginative enough to attract an *ignorant* people, and that our labouring classes are much too ignorant to be capable of being attracted by, or of taking pleasure in, the simple and unadorned spirituality of our forms of worship. We must either adorn the spectacle, or we must *educate the people.* If we neglect to do one of these things, we must rest contented to see the poor of our towns remain as at present—outside the places of national or public worship, and uninterested in the religious worship and ceremonies, because their minds cannot understand them, and because their feelings are not excited by them.

In the towns, too, as I have shown, the English clergy require assistance, and the English Church requires another grade of workmen. We want a class of clergy, who could enter *daily* into the lowest haunts without disgust, and with whom the poor could converse *daily* without shyness or fear, and to whom they might relate their troubles without difficulty, and with a certainty of being understood, and of meeting with sympathy.

The greatest part of the poor of our towns are now never visited by a religious minister, or are visited so seldom that the minister always enters as a stranger. Even when the poor man is visited by a clergyman, it is by a man of so strangely different a rank of life, that the poor man knows his clergyman cannot comprehend the peculiar wants or difficulties of his life. The clergyman is, therefore, received with shyness, and with the constraint, which the visit of a great and wealthy man always inspires in the house of a poor and humble one. As the operatives in Lancashire are in the habit of saying, "there is no church in England for the poor; there is only a church for the rich."

How seldom, too, in the course of a year, are the poor of the cellars, garrets, or lodging-houses of the towns visited by any religious minister! How often are these poor creatures never visited at all! And yet how else is religion to be spread among the masses of our town poor? Sermons will not do it. Constant personal intercourse between the ministers of the Church and the poor can alone succeed in effecting this result. That intercourse, under the existing state of things, is often quite impossible. The number of clergy is too small. The social rank of the clergy is too much removed above that of the poor. Another class of clergy is required. Most of the town churches, too, are virtually closed to the poor. Go into the churches and see how little room is reserved for the poor. It is as if the churches were built exclusively for the rich; and as if the English Church thought it was of much less importance, that the poor should enjoy the consolations of religious worship, than that the rich should do so. In the Roman churches there are no closed pews and reserved places. In their churches, all men are treated as equals in the presence of their God. In the Roman churches, the poor are welcomed with an eagerness, which seems to say,—the church was meant especially for such as you; and in the Roman Church, many of the priests are chosen from the body of the poor, in order that the ministers of religious consolation may be able the better to understand the religious wants of their poor brethren.

Let the English Church take warning. In these democratic days we want institutions for the poor; and especially do we want religious institutions for the poor; and it is partly because we have in our towns no church, no religious ministers, and no effective religious ministration for the masses of the poor, that they are still in so wretched a condition.

The absence of the poorer classes from our churches has been often remarked by foreigners. Amongst many others, M. Leon Faucher, lately a minister of state in France, says:—

"Place yourself on a Sunday in the midst of Briggate Street, in Leeds; of Mosley Street, in Manchester; or of Lord Street, or Dale Street, in Liverpool; what are the families whom you see walking to the churches silently and gravely? It is not possible to deceive oneself; *they belong almost exclusively to the middle classes.* The operatives remain on their door-steps, where they collect in groups until, the services in the churches being concluded, the taverns will open. Religion is presented to them with so sombre an aspect, and with such hard features,—she affects so well not to appeal either to the senses, or to the imagination, or to the heart,—that it ought not to be a matter of surprise if she remain the patrimony and the privilege of the rich." *

### 3. *The Game Laws.*

There can be no doubt whatsoever, that these laws are one of the chief causes of the demoralisation of the peasant classes.

I am far removed from any desire to see our country gentry deprived of their healthy sports. I believe that our system of sports is productive of certain good results. It promotes the health and mental activity of our legislators, of our professional men, and of our gentry. It draws away from the towns to the healthy pursuits of a country life, many who would otherwise seldom seek the change. It often brings the landlords into connection with their tenantry, in a kindly and familiar manner, and tends to interest them in their welfare in at least some small degree. It promotes the friendly, useful, and healthy intercourse of people of the richer classes, who often are drawn together by the plea of sporting; and it mingles together gentlemen of the highest intellectual culture, and of the most extended political views, with others, who have spent their whole life in the country, and who are often men of the lowest intellectual culture, and of the most narrow and prejudiced views on questions of national expedience.

* Etudes sur l'Angleterre, tome première.

Such are some of the good effects of the system. Now let us look at the other side of the picture.

No crimes are so much on the increase, and none are tending to degrade the moral condition of the peasants more, than offences against the game laws.

The following table will give an idea of the singular manner in which the numbers of these offences have been increasing of late years.

| Years. | Proportions of Convictions for Offences against the Game Laws to every 100,000 Individuals. |
|---|---|
| 1839 | 33·5 |
| 1840 | 33·2 |
| 1841 | 36·8 |
| 1842 | 46·1 |
| 1843 | 54·8 |

"The great increase of late years in poaching, is a striking feature in rural crime. In the three years from 1827 to 1830, no fewer than 8,502 persons were convicted under the game laws. The increase since that period has been startling. In 1843 the committals for this offence amounted to 4,529. In 1844–45, and up to May 1846, that is, during a period of eighteen months, the convictions were 11,372, which gives an average of 4,834 per annum."*

The peasants, who have no amusements, no gardens, no farms, and no chance of getting any, are irresistibly tempted to begin poaching. They cannot learn to regard a hare, a pheasant, or a partridge as the property of any particular person. They know, that the property in them is subject to perpetual change, at the will of the creature itself. One day it is the property of Squire Walters, and the next day of Squire Wyndham. Where

* See Rev. H. Worsley's Essay on Juvenile Depravity.

it will be the following day no one knows. The sport of snaring them is a much greater pleasure and temptation to the poor, than the sport of shooting them is to the rich. The sport is immensely increased by the danger and the consequences of detection, and by the mode in which it is carried on. It is as exciting as smuggling. In the dark and stormy nights the young peasants venture by twos and threes into the strictly watched and solitary enclosures of their landlords; they are in constant risk of being discovered by the gamekeepers, and of being torn from their homes and consigned to gaol; they are tempted by the excitement of the enterprise, and by the desire to add something to the miserably scanty fare of their families. The poor fellows have no other amusement, and therefore take to this dangerous sport with the greater zest.

But what are the consequences of detection? Here comes the enormous evil resulting from these laws.

If detected, the young peasant, who is very often a man, who has never committed any other crime or offence against the laws; who has only yielded to the same kind of impulse as that which makes his landlord love sport; who has, in short, only done that, which we should all do without the least remorse, were we in his position; this poor fellow, who had no other amusement in which he could indulge, and who has been goaded on by misery and destitution, is caught by a gamekeeper, is carried off to the tribunal of the petty sessions, where his own landlord, who is interested in his punishment, or where some other neighbouring landlord, who is equally interested in his punishment, for the sake of his own sport, is sitting as judge! Before such an unfair tribunal the poor fellow is placed. *No jury is allowed him.* He is tried, judged, condemned, and sentenced by the landlords themselves, and is by them sent off to the county gaol, there to spend one, two, or six months, and often a whole year, in company with felons and criminals of the worst possible character. There he becomes inured to the contemplation of vice of all kinds, and of all degrees. There he gradually loses all horror of it; and thence he returns, hardened in villany, and prepared for the commission of deeds, from which he would have shrunk when he entered.

During the time of his incarceration, his poor wife and family are driven to the workhouse in order to escape starvation; their household goods are all sold up; their independence of character is ruined; and the happiness of a whole family is often destroyed for ever. This is no fanciful picture. It is an occurrence of every day in the rural districts. About 5000 such committals take place every year in England and Wales!

An old baronet, himself a landed proprietor, and one of the greatest sportsmen of Norfolk, once said to me,—"If nothing else is done, I am convinced, that the jurisdiction in cases of offences against the game laws ought to be taken out of the hands of the landlords. It is very wrong, that those who are so strongly interested in punishing should be allowed to be the judges in cases of this description. I have constantly seen the most shameful injustice and cruelty practised by the magistrates in cases of this nature. Many times have I been obliged to interfere to protect a poor fellow, who had never done any other wrong in his lifetime, but who was being sentenced, for a trifling offence against the game laws, more severely than if he were a common felon."

For my own part I am convinced, as I have already observed, that these laws, as at present constituted, are demoralising our poor to an incalculable extent, and that they are capable of being easily altered, without depriving the landlords of their sport. I think two changes might be very advantageously introduced.

1. *All jurisdiction in matters of offences ought to be taken from the landlords themselves, and ought to be transferred to some impartial tribunal, as for instance that of the County Courts.* It is really monstrous, that the magistrates, who are nearly all of them sportsmen and game preservers, should be allowed to be judges in cases of offences against the game laws; and it is still more monstrous, that they should be allowed to exercise summary jurisdiction in cases of this description, and that they should be empowered to judge and sentence the offender, without the intervention of any jury, and according to the unfettered will of their own necessarily biassed minds. Such a system is opposed to the spirit of our constitution, and to every principle of civil liberty and impartial justice.

2. *The punishment, in cases of offences against the game laws, ought to be changed at once from imprisonment to a fine.* No judge should be allowed to imprison for poaching, except in cases of a *third* conviction; but only to award a fine of not more than 1*l.* for the first offence, and 3*l.* for the second. The fines ought to be levied, not by the landlord, but by an officer of the court. The court ought to be empowered to enable the officer to distrain, in case the fine is not paid within a certain time.

The punishments, which the landlords are now enabled to adjudge at petty sessions, for offences against these laws, are shamefully and ridiculously excessive. I will enumerate a few of them:—

1. Any person, by night, unlawfully taking or de-

stroying any game or rabbits, in any land, whether open or inclosed, or on any public road, highway, or path, on the sides thereof, or at the openings, outlets, or gates from any such land into any such public road, highway, or path, or by night unlawfully entering or being on any land, whether open or inclosed, with any gun, net, or other instrument, for the purpose of taking or destroying game, may be punished by the landlord-magistrates at petty sessions, without the intervention of a jury—

For first offence, with three months' imprisonment with hard labour, and at the expiration thereof may be required to find sureties, himself in 10*l.*, and two sureties in 5*l.* each, or one in 10*l.*, not so to offend again for one year; and in case of not being able to find sureties, as is often the case, the poor fellow may be sent back to his felon associates in the gaol for six calendar months longer.

For a second offence, he may be imprisoned *a whole year*, and sureties to double the former amount may be required.

2. Where game has been killed out of season, the offender may be sentenced, in the same manner as above, to pay 1*l.* a head for every head of game so killed, and in default of payment, may be imprisoned for two or three calendar months.

3. Any person selling game without a certificate, may be in the same manner sentenced to pay 2*l.* for every head of game so sold, and in default of payment may be imprisoned for two or three calendar months.

4. Any person killing game, without having taken out a certificate, may be in the same manner sentenced to pay 5*l.*, and in default to be imprisoned for two or three calendar months.

5. Any persons taking the eggs of game, without having the right to do so, may be in the same manner fined 5*s*. per egg, and in default imprisoned for two or three calendar months.

6. Any person entering land in the day-time, in search of game, may be in the same manner fined 2*l*., and in default of payment imprisoned for two or three calendar months.

7. Any person killing game upon land, which he occupies himself, but upon which some other person has reserved the right of shooting, may be, in the same manner, fined 2*l*., and in addition 1*l*. for every head of game killed or taken, and in default, may be imprisoned for two or three calendar months.

Many of the poor fellows, who are thus imprisoned for the pardonable offence of poaching, return from the gaols with all the shame and dread of a prison destroyed, with all horror of felony too often destroyed also, and with a fatal familiarisation with criminals and crime. They return, to find their families too often in the work-houses, and their household furniture sold. They return, with an injured character, and with a very greatly increased difficulty of obtaining employment. Goaded on by a knowledge of these sad facts, and no longer restrained by their former dread of a prison and of the name of felon, they soon commit some greater crime than that of shooting or snaring a pheasant, and thus add to the sad length of our criminal lists, and to the numerous inmates of our crowded gaols.

### 4. *The System of Laws which affect Land in Great Britain and Ireland.*

I have shown, that these laws have had the effect of gradually annihilating the old English class of yeomen;—that they prevent the small shopkeepers, farmers, and peasants buying land;—that they tend to increase the size of farms, and to diminish their number;—that by acting in this manner they take away from the peasant every chance of rising in the social scale, unless he emigrates either to the manufacturing districts or to the colonies;—that they destroy the strong motives which would otherwise urge him to economise, to keep from excesses of all kinds, to defer his marriage, and to bear patiently present hardship for future good;—that they stimulate the increase of population in a most unhealthy and unnatural manner;—that they deprive the shopkeepers and town-labourers of the healthiest of all recreations, and of the most humanising of all employments;—that they deprive the shopkeepers of what would otherwise be the object and end of their labours, viz., the possibility of purchasing a small estate, and of retiring from the toil of business to the happiness of a rural life;—that they keep great tracts of country out of cultivation, which would otherwise be immediately bought up and cultivated by our peasants, or by our small farmers;—that they tend to accumulate enormous masses of wealth in a few hands, and by so doing to render the competition and toil of all the other classes of society very much more intense and painful;—that they entirely destroy the independence of the peasant, while they render him turbulent and discontented;—that they condemn the peasants to live in wretched hovels, and prevent their getting commodious houses, by preventing their building for themselves;—that they tend to destroy all respect for property among the peasants, and among the labourers of our smaller provincial towns;—that they are considered abroad as the real cause of the degradation of the Irish;—that they have deprived the people of that country of all security of tenure, of all interest in the proper cultivation of the soil, and in the preservation of order or of social tranquillity;—that they tend to drain that country of its wealth for the support of a foreign aristocracy;—that they have subjected the peasantry and farmers of that country to the will of agents, who are left to act according to their own unchecked pleasure;—that they are keeping nearly one-third of the rich soil of that island out of cultivation, while the peasantry are starving;—that they have destroyed almost every trace of manly virtue, independence, and energy in the Irish peasantry;—that they have prevented the introduction of capital into that country;—and that they have been one of the principal causes, if not the principal cause, of the degradation and pauperism of the peasants and labourers of the British Isles.

### 5. *The Gin Palaces.*

As I have before shown, the only amusement or relaxation which the English poor possess, in many parts of the country, is, the frequenting the taverns.

I have shown, that in Western Europe, the amusements of the poor are of a much healthier and a much higher order than those of our poor, and that they consist of musical concerts, village dances, village festivals and sports, gardening, and reading. I have said, that it is a common thing for the labourers of the towns to possess gardens of their own; that the peasants generally possess farms of their own; and that both peasants and town-labourers are educated, and understand music.

But, in England and Wales, generally speaking, the

poor have no other resource for amusement, than the taverns. Generally speaking, the poor do not possess land or gardens; they do not understand music or dancing, while nearly all the old athletic pastimes of the villages are forgotten.

But no people have ever lived without amusements of some kind or other. According as they are in a moral or immoral condition, so will their amusements also be moral or immoral. And, on the other hand, it may be said to be a universal truth, that the character of the amusements of a people will always show the character of the people.

In the case of the English poor, the amusements are of a very degraded character, and what is worse, they are degrading our people more and more.

The streets of our towns are crowded with gaudy, conspicuous buildings, the style of whose architecture has at last gained a name for itself. We call it the "gin-palace style." The interiors of these buildings are intended principally for night-work, though they are, alas! filled throughout the day. The ornaments are such as will produce the greatest effect by the glare of gas-light, and are flaring and disgusting in their painted finery, when the sun shines in upon them, and shows their real character.

In these "palaces," ale, beer, porter, and, more particularly, all kinds of spirits, are sold. These are sometimes drunk by the purchasers in the room where they are sold, and sometimes in an adjoining or upper room.

These wretched resorts are paying so well, that larger and larger sums are spent every year in embellishing them, so that many in London and in the manufacturing districts have attained a singular degree of tawdry splendour.

The beer-houses, which are still more numerous than the gin-palaces, and which are to be found both in the towns and in the villages, differ from the gin-palaces in this respect—that the owners of the former have obtained from the magistrates licences to sell spirits, while the owners of the latter have not been able to obtain such licences, and are, consequently, unable to sell spirits, and are obliged to confine themselves to the sale of beer, ale, and porter.

The gin-palaces and beer-houses of the towns are the places where the prostitutes resort in search of gain or of stimulants. Many of these places are either brothels, or are connected with brothels kept in an adjoining house, and often by the owner of the gin-palace or beer-house.

In the manufacturing districts it is very common for the same house to serve both as drinking house and as brothel, and in the majority of cases the beer-houses are provided with rooms for the use of the prostitutes and their companions. Those who attend the police courts in our towns, and especially in our manufacturing districts, know but too well what infamous scenes are enacted almost every evening in these places.

There can be no doubt whatever that our legislation has *increased* the numbers of these hotbeds of crime and pauperism.*

In the beginning of the revolutionary war the duties on malt were *augmented*, and in 1825 the duties on spirits were *decreased*. It was thus that whisky was substituted for ale as the beverage of the Scotch, and that gin and brandy began to be generally drunk by the English poor.

* Almost the whole of the remainder of this section is taken from Mr. Worsley's and Miss Meteyard's Essays on Juvenile Delinquency.

The consumption of spirits immediately increased in a tremendous proportion. From 4,132,263 gallons, the consumption in 1825, it rose in one year to 8,888,648 gallons; that is, the consumption was *in one year* more than *doubled* by the change; and from that period, with the exception of the year next following, viz. 1827, the consumption has been progressively augmenting.

Since that time the noted beer-shop act has been passed. By that act, any one was enabled to obtain a licence to enable him to sell beer, whether the person desirous of doing so was a person of respectable character or not.

But this was the least of the evils, which were effected by that act. A clause, which was still more injurious, was that which prescribed that the liquor *must be drunk upon the premises of the beer-house*, i. e. either in the beer-house or on a bench just outside the door.

This has the effect in many cases, where the poor would otherwise take the beer home to their own cottages, of forcing the young men who wish to have a little to drink, to sit down and take it in the society of the worst people of the neighbourhood, who always, as a matter of course, spend their leisure in the tavern. I am convinced that nothing can be more injurious in its effects upon the poor than this clause. It may be said to *force* the honest labourers into the society and companionship of the most depraved, and so necessarily to demoralise the young and honest labourers.

The following is the number of gallons of *native* proof spirits, on which duty was paid for home consumption in the United Kingdom, in the undermentioned years:—

| Years. | Gallons. |
|---|---|
| 1843 . . . . | 18,841,890 |
| 1844 . . . . | 20,608,525 |
| 1845 . . . . | 23,122,588 |
| 1846 . . . . | 24,106,697 |

To the above, must be added the number of gallons of foreign and colonial spirits retained for home consumption, as follows:—

| Years. | No. of Gallons of Foreign, &c. Spirits. | No. of Gallons of Home and Foreign Spirits consumed in the United Kingdom. |
|---|---|---|
| 1843 | 3,161,957 | 22,026,289 |
| 1844 | 3,242,606 | 22,042,905 |
| 1845 | 3,549,889 | 26,672,477 |
| 1846 | 4,252,237 | 28,360,934 |

From the above statistics it appears, that the consumption of spirits in the United Kingdom is increasing much more rapidly than the population!

The number of licenses granted to retailers of spirits or beer amounted, in 1845, to 237,345; that is, there was to be found, in 1845, a retailer of beer or spirits in every 115 of the population! Of the beer licenses, 68,086 were for dwellings rated under 20*l.* per annum, and 35,340 were licenses for premises rated under 10*l.* per annum! This shows how large a proportion of the beer-shops are situated in the poorest districts, for the use of the poorest classes.

The valuable return for 1847, issued by the Commissioners of *Metropolitan* Police, shows that 5,307 males and 3,697 females were committed in that year for drunkenness, and that 4,161 males and 3,709 females were committed in the same year for drunken and disorderly conduct in the metropolis alone! Thus the total number of persons committed in the metropolis in 1847 for drunkenness, was 16,847, of which 7,406 were females!

Between the years 1831 and 1843, there were taken into custody by the *metropolitan police* alone for drunkenness and disorderly conduct 482,936 persons, of whom 183,921 were females.

Some idea of the way in which some of our towns are crowded with beer-houses and gin-palaces may be formed from the following facts. A district of London is mentioned in the Twelfth Annual Report of the London City Mission (1847), comprising 400 families, which contains *one* butcher's shop, two bakers' shops, and *seventeen* beer-houses. Another report mentions, that in a *single* street near the docks, there are SIXTY-SEVEN gin-palaces, public-houses, and beer-shops. In a population of about 1,212,000, comprising the most important towns of the manufacturing districts of Yorkshire and Lancashire, there were found to be, in 1846, 14,300 public-houses!

The sum of money, which is frequently given as a premium for the good-will of a public-house doing a good business in London, is from 2000*l.* to 4000*l.**

The total cost of the spirits and beer consumed in the United Kingdom was, in 1843, estimated to amount to 65,000,000*l.*, *i. e.* the sum spent by the British nation in intoxicating liquors is greater by several millions than the whole revenue of the government!

Our judges have, over and over again, remarked in their charges to the grand juries, and in their sentences, that the chief and almost universal causes of nearly all the crimes for which offenders are prosecuted in our courts of justice, are the taverns and gin-palaces. If my

* Report of Commission on Drunkenness, p. 10.

space would allow, I could quote many of these dicta; but the effect of drinking upon the amount of crime is proved still more clearly by the subjoined table.

In 1825, as I have before said, the duty on spirits was lowered from 12*s.* 7*d.* to 7*s.* the imperial gallon; and now mark the effect as shown in the following table:—

| Years. | | Annual Consumption of Spirits in England and Wales. | Poor Rates. | Crime in England and Wales. | Crime in London and Middlesex. |
|---|---|---|---|---|---|
| | | Gallons. | £ | Committed. | Committed. |
| High Duty. | 1823 | 4,225,903 | 5,772,962 | 12,263 | 2,503 |
| | 1824 | 4,880,679 | 5,736,900 | 13,698 | 2,621 |
| | 1825 | 4,132,263 | 5,786,989 | 14,437 | 2,902 |
| Low Duty. | 1826 | 8,888,644 | 5,928,501 | 16,164 | 3,457 |
| | 1827 | 8,005,872 | 6,441,088 | 17,924 | 3,381 |
| | 1828 | 9,311,624 | 6,298,003 | 16,564 | 3,516 |

The above statistics would seem to prove that the amount both of crime and pauperism is dependent in great measure upon the quantity of spirits consumed by the people.

The same fact is proved, wherever the records of the prisons have been well tabulated.

I have already mentioned the fact, that in the towns, the beer-houses and gin-palaces are generally either brothels or the constituted rendezvous of the prostitutes.

The following authorities bear me out in this assertion.

The Rev. H. Worsley, in his admirable report on juvenile depravity,* says, "The beer-shops and gin-palaces are the general centres of meeting, and serve

* See Juvenile Depravity, p. 170.

as 'rendezvous' to vagabonds, thieves, and prostitutes."

The Rev. Mr. Clay, the chaplain of Preston gaol, of whose enlightened efforts in behalf of the poor I cannot sufficiently express my admiration, says, in one of his last reports, "My last year's intercourse with the subjects of my ministry has made me acquainted with practices resorted to in certain beer-houses, which must be mentioned, in order to show what demoralising agencies are added to those already existing in them,—viz. the keeping of prostitutes. From three entirely independent sources, and at different times, I received statements fully confirming each other, which leave no doubt of the extent to which this profligate system is carried on. Sixteen houses in one town, harbouring, or rather maintaining, about fifty-four prostitutes, have been *named* to me. But this is not the full amount of the evil. The neighbourhood of these houses is corrupted. *Women—married women—occupied, to all appearance, with their own proper avocations, at home, hold themselves at the call of the beer-house for the immoral purposes to which I have referred.*"

The evidence of a police magistrate states*,—"A very short time since, I fined a publican the utmost penalty that the law would admit. It was proved that he had thirty thieves and prostitutes in his house at eight o'clock on Sunday morning."

The evidence of Mr. Symons, on the state of Leeds, says†,—"I went, accompanied by Inspector Childs and three police officers, to visit the low places of resort of the working classes of Leeds. We started soon after nine o'clock, and visited about a score of beer and public-houses, and as many lodging-houses. . . . .

* Report on Drunkenness, p. 18. † Juvenile Depravity, p 174.

In the beer-shops there were several mere children; and *in almost all were prostitutes.* In some of these places we found a fiddle or other instrument played: these places were thronged as full as they could hold. In another, dancing was going on in a good-sized room upstairs, where I found a dozen couples performing a country-dance; *the females were all factory girls and prostitutes.* Not one of these dancers, boys or girls, was above twenty or twenty-one years of age, and most of them were sixteen or seventeen."

We have often, and as I think with great reason, cried shame upon France, for granting licenses to the brothels in her towns; but by our present system of licensing beer-houses, we are in reality giving the sanction of law to, and encouraging the establishment of the worst possible species of brothels for the demoralisation of the poorer classes of society.

The present unchecked system of beer-houses is producing greater evils every year. It is destroying the health and deteriorating the physical character of our labouring classes more and more; it is increasing the amount of pauperism and criminality; and it is stimulating political disaffection among the masses of the manufacturing districts, more than almost any other cause.

It is in the taverns, whether beer-houses or gin-palaces, that the lowest of the demagogues instil their doctrines into the minds of the young;—it is in the taverns, that the worst of the political publications are read aloud to gnorant audiences;—it is in the taverns, that the young peasants make friends with the hardened poachers and rick-burners of their neighbourhoods;—it is in the taverns, that the young men and young women of our towns are first habituated to the sight and manners of the prostitutes, and that they lose all horror of their condition;—it is in the taverns, that young boys and girls, of not more than fifteen or sixteen years of age, go to dance and amuse themselves, in company with all the worst frequenters of the place;—and it is in the taverns, that nine out of ten of all the inmates of our crowded gaols are first instructed in crime. Judges, magistrates, and police all agree in earnestly and continually deprecating the present system, and yet it is continued. And why? The only reason is, that it produces a considerable sum towards the expenses of government. It was for this reason that the duty was first lowered. But ought we not all of us to be willing to bear any amount of increased taxation, rather than ruin the moral and physical condition of our poor, for the sake of increasing our revenue, by any amount, however great?

We must do something to check this enormous evil, if we would not see the moral and physical character of our people completely ruined. My own opinion is:—

1. That we ought to give much greater powers to the magistrates to withdraw the licenses from, and to close, any gin-palace or beer-house, the proprietor of which could be convicted of permitting excesses to be committed in his house.

2. That we ought not to allow any beer-house or gin-palace keeper to keep his house open, or to serve out or sell any spirits or beer, after eight o'clock in the evening, or at any time during the Sundays.

3. That in every town a certain number of the police ought to be chosen every week to act specially as inspectors of the taverns, to prevent indecencies or excesses, and see that the law was obeyed.

4. That any tavern-keeper should be deprived of his licence, who was convicted before a magistrate of suffering persons of different sexes to have criminal intercourse in his house, or of knowingly permitting certain indecent practices, not fit to be named here; or of allowing any child, of less than fifteen years of age, to enter the drinking-rooms, and to remain there more than five minutes in the course of any day.

Enactments such as these would put a stop to a great part of the demoralising effects of these wretched rendezvous of the lower orders.

But I do not think we should stop there. My own opinion is, and has always been, that we must sooner or later raise the duty upon spirits again. Such a step would be hailed with joy by millions of the poor themselves, however great an outcry it would raise among the gin-palace keepers.

### 6. *The Want of Classification in our Prisons.*

A good deal has been done of late years to improve our prisons, but a great deal remains to be done.

It is quite possible, and it is very common, for a poor boy or for a poor person of good character to do something, which society is obliged to designate a crime, and to punish severely, although, morally speaking, the person who committed the deed was almost innocent. Now, it is very important, that this class of offenders, and especially the younger portion of them, should be kept from the contamination of thoroughly depraved associates, during the period of their imprisonment. If a young or a comparatively guiltless offender is thrown into the society of abandoned companions in the gaols, the chances are ten to one that he will go out worse than he came in.

Our criminal records and our courts of justice are singular proofs of the truth of this assertion.

Moreover, it is an undeniable fact, that if the poor may only have companions in the gaols, they would often rather be in prison than out, especially during the winter months. It is no punishment, but a decided privilege to most of them. Any one, who will visit the prisons, and converse with the more talkative of the felons, may learn this from their own lips.

We have, in fact, gone from one extreme to another. A few years back the gaols were wretched, filthy, badly ventilated, small, and so miserable, as to be a dreadful punishment even to the poorest of the wretches sent to them. Now, they are large, capacious, well ventilated, well warmed, beautifully cleaned, and well arranged; the food is good, clean, and abundant; the beds are very comfortable; the health of the prisoners is very well attended to; they are very kindly treated; and are lodged *much* better, than they often are before they enter. All this is quite right; *but where is the punishment?* Solely the loss of liberty; and, in exchange for this, they find themselves comfortably housed, well though simply fed, without any labour worth calling hard, without any risk of going to bed supperless, and with plenty of companions.

Is it any wonder, that our criminal records should be full of instances of persons being convicted *three*, *four*, and *five* times, and that the prisoners at our quarter sessions should very often receive their sentence with actually a smile of pleasure?

For three reasons it is becoming absolutely necessary to introduce the separate system into all our prisons, and to do away altogether with the plan of imprisoning persons in company:—

1. To save the younger and more innocent prisoners from being contaminated by associating with the more hardened offenders.

2. To make our gaols a *punishment*, instead of being, as many of them are at present, an actual *premium* for the commission of crime.

3. To save our counties the expense of prosecuting, and committing, and imprisoning the same person *four* or *five* times in the course of as many years, and each successive time for a worse offence than the former one.

In Germany and in America they are substituting solitary confinement for the old plan of confining a number together. Wherever this system has been introduced, it has been found to work well. It keeps the less depraved prisoners from contamination; it makes the prison a real, though still a lenient, punishment; it affords excellent opportunities for the instruction and moral reformation of the prisoners; and, in the long run, it saves expense to the counties, by rendering recommittals and reimprisonments of the same persons much rarer than in those provinces where the prisoners are confined together.

## CHAPTER II.

THE PRESENT STATE OF PRIMARY EDUCATION IN ENGLAND AND WALES.—THE COMMITTEE OF COUNCIL ON EDUCATION.—HOW WE MIGHT PROVIDE SUFFICIENT MEANS FOR THE EDUCATION OF THE PEOPLE.

SINCE the year 1801, the population of England and Wales has nearly DOUBLED. In 1801, the population, inclusive of the army and navy, amounted to only 8,872,980, while at the present time it amounts to nearly 17,000,000, exclusive of the same forces. In 1831, the population, exclusive of the army and navy, amounted to only 13,897,187; so that, in the short space of EIGHTEEN years, it has increased by more than 3,000,000 souls!

We have, within the last four years, freed our trade and commerce from nearly every impediment to their fullest development.

We have repealed the duties on corn, which tended formerly to prevent corn-growing countries from bringing their corn to our markets, in order to exchange it for our manufactured products; we have opened our ports to the ships of all nations, and have invited them all to come and take away our goods; we are rapidly destroying the system of piracy, which has hitherto infested the seas of China and the Eastern Archipelago, and greatly hindered the progress of our commerce in those regions; we are about to open the vast and almost unexplored markets of India by railways, and by the flat-bottomed steam-boats on the great rivers; our people are spreading themselves over all the colonies faster and faster, carrying with them a taste for, and thus forming vast markets for the sale of, English manufactures; the American people are increasing prodigiously in numbers, and the more they increase, so much the more of our products are they demanding; the American corn and cotton growers are beginning to cry out for free trade, in order that they may be able to sell us more of their corn and cotton in exchange for more of our productions; and, lastly, our own people are increasing rapidly in numbers; and as they do so, they also require more and still more from our manufacturing districts. All this must of necessity rapidly and prodigiously develope our commercial and our manufacturing system. It will augment the numbers of our operative population faster and faster, and will enormously swell the size of our manufacturing towns, and the crowd of labourers in the sea-port towns and in the manufacturing and mining districts.

To those who know, from personal experience, what the present state of those districts is, their further growth in their present condition is a terrible alternative. Upon the way in which we legislate for them during the next twenty years, depends the fate of the British Empire.

Times of terrible distress must necessarily recur at regular intervals, owing, partly, to the gluts of foreign and of home markets, produced by the ever-increasing rapidity of production by machines, and partly, also, to the disturbance of the markets by bad harvests, by wars, and by periodical speculations.

But if the population should increase in those districts during the next twenty years, as it inevitably will do, and if no *vast* plan is carried into operation, whereby to raise the moral and religious tone of those districts, it is frightful to contemplate what may be the result in some season of distress of concentrating such a mass of such a people as the present operatives upon so small an area.

I have already shown the condition of the labourers of this country, and the neglected state of the juvenile population of the towns.

What are we doing to remedy this state of things, and to prepare for the future?

I will give a short summary of the present state of primary education in England and Wales, as collected from the reports, of Her Majesty's Inspectors, of the Commissioners of Inquiry in Wales, of the National Society, of the Statistical Society, and of the city mission; from Mr. Redgrave's reports from some very able articles in the North British Review and from numerous personal inquiries in various parts of England and Wales.

1. It has been calculated that there are at the present day, in England and Wales, nearly 8,000,000 persons who cannot read and write.

2. Of all the children in England and Wales, between the ages of five and fourteen, more than the half* are not attending any school.

3. Even of the class of the farmers, there are great numbers who cannot read and write.

* The following table was put into my hands in the autumn of 1849, by the Rev. Charles Richson, clerk in orders of the Cathedral of Manchester, as representing the state of the education of the poor in Manchester in that year. If such is the state of the education of the poor in this town, where so much has been done of late years, it may be comprehended what its state is, in the poorer and less intelligent districts of this country.

4. Even of those children of the poor, who have received some instruction, very few know anything of geography, history, science, music, or drawing. Their instruction in the village schools has hitherto generally consisted of nothing more than a little practice in reading, writing, and Scripture history.

5. Of the teachers, who are officiating in many of the village schools, there are many who cannot read and write correctly, and who know very little of the Bible, which they profess to explain to their scholars.

6. A very great part of our present village and town-schools are managed by poor and miserably instructed dames, who thus seek to make a livelihood, and who literally do no good to the children, except it be keeping them for a certain number of hours in the day out of the dirt and out of worse society.

7. Many of these dame schools are so wretchedly managed, as to do the children a very great deal more harm than good,—by uniting miserable associations with the sacred writings, and with the subjects of the wretched instruction given in these schools.

## MANCHESTER CATHEDRAL AND PARISH CHURCH DISTRICT.

*Return of the Children of the Poor, between the Ages of Three and Fifteen, in the District between Long Millgate and Shudehill, attending Day School or otherwise.*

No. of Families visited, 917.

| No. of Children | | No. of Children attending some Day School. | No. of Children at work. | No. of Children at Home | | No. of Children who have *never* been at Day School, out of Tables A and B. |
|---|---|---|---|---|---|---|
| between 3 & 10 | between 10 & 15 | | | from various excuses except poverty. A | from alleged poverty. B | |
| 1693 | 518 | 754 | 392 | 625 | 440 | * 407 |
| | | 1146 | | 1065 | | |
| Total. 2211 § | | 2211 | | | | * Between 3 & 15 |

§ Many of these go to Sunday School.

8. Very many of our town-schools are held in small and unventilated cellars or garrets, where the health of the children is seriously impaired.

9. If we except only the *worst* part of the dame-schools, we have not even then *one-half* as many school-buildings as we require, for the *present* numbers of our population.

10. By far the greatest part of our school-buildings have only *one* room, in which all the classes are instructed together, in the midst of noise and foul air.

11. Many of our present school-rooms have no forms and no parallel desks,—both of which are to be found in every school-room throughout Western Europe,—and in all such schools the children are kept standing the whole day.

12. Very few of our school-rooms are properly supplied with maps, books, or school apparatus.

13. The majority of our town-schools have no play-grounds; and in all these cases the children are turned out into the streets during the hours of recreation.

14. Scarcely any schools throughout the country have more than *two* class-rooms; the classification of the children is therefore very deficient, and the instruction is thereby much impaired.

15. Very few schools have more than one teacher.

16. Great numbers of parishes and districts throughout England and Wales have no school-room at all, and no place, in which their children can be instructed.

17. Of these latter districts, many are too poor or too careless to raise anything towards the erection of school-buildings, and in none of these cases does the Committee of Council give any assistance.

18. In many other districts, the inhabitants are so divided in religious opinions, that they find it impossible

to act in concert, in providing for the education of their children, and in these cases the Committee of Council renders no assistance.

19. In most of our schools, it is necessary in order to provide salaries for the teacher, and funds for the support of the school, to charge from 2*d.* to 4*d.* a week per head for the instruction of scholars. This absolutely excludes the children of all paupers, and of all poor persons, who cannot afford to pay so much out of their small earnings, whilst throughout the greatest part of Western Europe, the education afforded in the primary schools is quite gratuitous.

20. There is no public provision for the proper payment and maintenance of our teachers, and these latter are therefore generally placed in so very humiliating and dependent a position, as in many cases virtually to prevent any man of ability and education from accepting such an office.

21. A great part of our village teachers are only poor uneducated women, or poor men who are not fit for any other office or employment, and who are themselves miserably educated.*

* To give an idea of the character of the teachers' profession in our country, I append here a remarkable and curious statement taken from Mr. Lingen's very able report on the state of education in South Wales.

"The present average age of teachers is upwards of 40 years; that at which they commenced their vocation upwards of 30; the number trained is 12·5 per cent. of the whole ascertained number; the average period of training is 7·30 months; the average income is 22*l.* 10*s.* 9*d.* per annum; besides which, 16·1 per cent. have a house rent-free. Before adopting their present profession, 6 had been assistants in school, 3 attorneys' clerks, 1 attorney's clerk and sheriff's officer, 1 apprentice to an ironmonger, 1 assistant to a draper, 1 agent, 1 artilleryman, 1 articled clerk, 2 accountants, 1 auctioneer's clerk, 1 actuary in a savings-bank, 3 bookbinders, 1 butler, 1 barber, 1 black-

22. In proportion to our population, we have scarcely one-fourth part as many colleges for the instruction of

smith, 4 bonnet-makers, 2 booksellers, 1 bookkeeper, 15 commercial clerks, 3 colliers, 1 cordwainer, 7 carpenters, 1 compositor, 1 copyist, 3 cabinetmakers, 3 cooks, 1 corndealer, 3 druggists, 42 milliners, 20 domestic servants, 10 drapers, 4 excisemen, 61 farmers, 25 farm-servants, 1 farm-bailiff, 1 fisherman, 2 governesses, 7 grocers, 1 glover, 1 gardener, 177 at home or in school, 1 herald-chaser, 4 housekeepers, 2 hatters, 1 helper in a stable, 8 hucksters or shop-keepers, 1 ironroller, 6 joiners, 1 knitter, 13 labourers, 4 laundresses, 1 limeburner, 1 lay-vicar, 5 ladies' maids, 1 lieutenant R. N., 2 land-surveyors, 22 mariners, 1 millwright, 108 married women, 7 ministers, 1 mechanic, 1 miner, 2 mineral agents, 5 masons, 1 mate, 1 maltster, 1 militia-man, 1 musician, 1 musical-wiredrawer, 2 nurserymaids, 1 night-schoolmaster, 1 publican's wife (separated from her husband), 2 preparing for the church, 1 policeman, 1 pedlar, 1 publican, 1 potter, 1 purser's steward, 1 planter, 2 private tutors, 1 quarryman, 1 reed-thatcher, 28 sempstresses, 1 second master R. N., 4 soldiers, 14 shoe makers, 2 machine-weighers, 1 stonecutter, 1 sergeant of marines, 1 sawyer, 1 surgeon, 1 ship's cook, 7 tailors, 1 tailor and marine, 1 tiler, 17 widows, 4 weavers, and 60 unascertained, or having had no previous occupation.

"In connection with the vocation of teacher, 2 follow that of assistant-overseer of roads, 6 are assistant-overseers of the poor, 1 accountant, 1 assistant parish-clerk, 1 bookbinder, 1 broom and clog-maker, 4 bonnet-makers, 1 sells Berlin wool, 2 are cow-keepers, 3 collectors of taxes, 1 drover (in summer), 12 dress-makers, 1 druggist, 1 farmer, 4 grocers, 3 hucksters or shopkeepers, 1 inspector of weights and measures, 1 knitter, 2 land-surveyors (one of them is also a stone-cutter), 2 lodginghouse keepers, 1 librarian to a mechanics' institute, 16 ministers, 1 master of a workhouse, one matron of a lying-in hospital, 3 mat-makers, 13 preachers, 18 parish or vestry clerks (uniting in some instances the office of sexton), 1 printer and engraver, 1 porter, barber, and layer-out of the dead in a workhouse, 4 publicans, 1 registrar of marriages, 11 sempstresses, 1 shopman (on Saturdays), 8 secretaries to benefit-societies, 1 sexton, 2 shoemakers, 1 tailor, 1 teacher of modern languages, 1 turnpike-man, 1 tobacconist, 1 writing-master in a grammar-school, and 9 are in receipt of parochial relief."

teachers, as any of the countries of Western Europe; and not one-fourth part as many as are necessary for the education of a sufficient number of teachers for our poor.

23. In nearly all the few colleges we have established for the instruction of teachers, the education is very limited and meagre in its character; as these colleges depend upon voluntary aid, and cannot afford to give the students more than a year's or eighteen months' training; while throughout Western Europe the teachers receive *three years'* training in the teachers' colleges at the expense of the government.

24. The colleges we have established are so poor, that they cannot afford to support nearly so large and complete a staff of teachers and professors as are to be found in almost all the teachers' colleges throughout Western Europe.

25. A great part of our schools and teachers are never visited by any public inspector, or by any private person, or committee of persons from the year's beginning to the year's end. In many of these cases, bad teachers are left to do great injury to their scholars unchecked and unheard of, and in many other cases, good and able teachers are left without encouragement or advice, to labour on unknown, disheartened and alone.

26. In most of our schools, owing to the teacher either not having been trained at all, or not having been educated for a long enough time in a college, the methods of teaching are miserable and ridiculous. The noise in the school-rooms is often so great, that it is with difficulty that any individual can make himself heard. The children are often kept standing the greater part of the day, and are wearied beyond en-

durance, so that the lessons, and all the associations connected with the subjects of instruction are rendered hateful ever afterwards. The highest religious subjects are thus often made odious to the children, who during their after life avoid as much as possible recurring to what awakens so many disagreeable recollections. In most of our schools, there is little or no attempt to interest the children in their studies, or to teach them to think or reason. The instruction is mere parrot work. They are taught by rote, and forget again almost as soon as they have left the school.

27. Great numbers of the school-buildings in the more remote country districts are of the most wretched and miserable character.

An idea of some of these may be formed from the following descriptions, selected from the able report of Mr. Lingen on the state of education in South Wales, published in 1848. These are fair specimens of schools, which may be found throughout England and Wales.

Mr. Lingen says: There was no room for making furniture and apparatus separate considerations in most of the schools throughout the remoter districts, exhibiting, as they did, every form of squalid destitution. I subjoin a few instances out of many others perhaps more striking.

Of one school, he says:—

"The furniture consisted of one desk for the master, two longer ones for the pupils, and a few benches, all in a wretched state of repair. The room was not ceiled. In one corner was a heap of spars, the property of the master, for the purpose of thatching his house. In another place was a heap of culm, emptied out on the floor. The floor was boarded, but all the middle of it was in holes."

Of another, he says:—

"The school was held in a miserable room over the stable; it was lighted by two small glazed windows, and was very low; in one corner were a broken bench, some sacks, and a worn-out basket; another corner was boarded off for storing tiles and mortar belonging to the chapel. The furniture consisted of three small square tables, one for the master, two larger ones for the children, and a few benches, all in a wretched state of repair. There were several panes of glass broken in the windows; in one place paper served the place of glass, and in another a slate, to keep out wind and rain; the door was also in a very dilapidated condition. On the beams which crossed the room were a ladder and two large poles."

Of another, he says:—

"The school was held in a room built in a corner of the churchyard; it was an open-roofed room; the floor was of the bare earth, and very uneven; the room was lighted by two small glazed windows, one third of each of which was patched up with boards. The furniture consisted of a small square table for the master, one square table for the pupils, and seven or eight benches, some of which were in good repair, and others very bad. The biers belonging to the church were placed on the beams which ran across the room. At one end of the room was a heap of coal and some rubbish and a worn-out basket, and on one side was a new door leaning against the wall, and intended for the stable belonging to the church. The door of the school-room was in a very bad condition, there being large holes in it, through which cold currents of air were continually flowing."

Of another, he says:—

"This school is held in a dark miserable den under the town-hall; the furniture comprised only a few old benches and tables; in the corner was a litter of broken cups and a bottle; there was a starling of the master's loose in the room, which, by flying about, greatly disturbed the children during my visit."

Of another, he says:—

"In one corner was a heap of culm, in another a bench or two, piled against the wall, and various litter; at the bottom of the room lay a gravestone, on which the master had been chalking the letters which the village mason was to cut as an inscription: on the table lay a jug and pipe."

I might quote endless instances to prove the miserable character and ill effects of the present school-buildings in Carmarthenshire and Pembrokeshire. Indeed, Report after Report is too often only a wearisome repetition of such particulars. It will suffice for me to subjoin a few instances, by way of illustration, taking them almost at hazard.

Of another school, he says:—

"The school was held in a room, part of a dwelling-house; the room was so small that a great many of the scholars were obliged to go into the room above, which they reached by means of a ladder, through a hole in the loft; the room was lighted by one small glazed window, half of which was patched up with boards; it was altogether a wretched place; the furniture consisted of one table, in a miserable condition, and a few broken benches; the floor was in a very bad state, there being several large holes in it, some of them nearly half a foot deep; the room was so dark that the few children whom I heard read were obliged to go to the door, and open it, to have sufficient light."

Of another, he says:—

"This school is held in the mistress's house. I never

shall forget the hot, sickening smell, which struck me on opening the door of that low dark room, in which thirty girls and twenty boys were huddled together. It more nearly resembled the smell of the engine on board a steamer, such as it is felt by a sea-sick voyager on passing near the funnel. Exaggerated as this may appear, I am writing on the evening of the same day on which I visited the school, and I will vouch for the accuracy of what I state. Every thing in the room (*i. e.* a few benches of various heights and sizes, and a couple of tables) was hidden under and overlaid with children."

Of another, he says:—

"This school is held in a ruinous hovel of the most squalid and miserable character; the floor is of bare earth, full of deep holes; the windows are all broken; a tattered partition of lath and plaster divides it into two unequal portions; in the larger were a few wretched benches, and a small desk for the master in one corner; in the lesser was an old door, with the hasp still upon it, laid crossways upon two benches, about half a yard high, to serve for a writing-desk! Such of the scholars as write retire in pairs to this part of the room, and kneel on the ground while they write. On the floor was a heap of loose coal, and a litter of straw, paper, and all kinds of rubbish. The vicar's son informed me that he had seen eighty children in this hut. In summer the heat of it is said to be suffocating; and no wonder."

Of another, he says:—

"In the school-room, which, at six square feet pe. child, is calculated to hold 28 scholars, I found 59 present, and 74 on the books: some of the children are drafted off into the master's dwelling-house."

Of another, he says:—

"The school is held in a room over the stable, which is a very small one. The children were much crowded. There was a very comfortable fire in the room on the day of my visit. Some 10 or 12 of the senior boys were obliged to sit in the adjoining chapel, on account of the smallness of the room. The chapel had no fire in it, and was very cold and uncomfortable."

Of another, he says:—

"The school-room is part of a dwelling-house, on the ground-floor, and the smell arising from so many children being crammed in such a small room was quite overpowering. There was a large fire in the grate at the time. The window was a small one, and was kept closed. The floor, walls, and the room altogether were in bad repair. I observed, after the scholars went out at noon (for there was no seeing anything but children while they were in the room), 1 square table for the master, 2 long tables for the writers and cipherers, 5 benches, and 1 chair."

Of another, he says:—

"This school is kept upstairs in two rooms of the master's house. There is a door to each room from the landing at the top of the stairs, but the master cannot see all the scholars from one room while they are in the other. He generally sits with the elementary classes."

Of another he says:—

"The floor was of the bare earth, very uneven and rather damp. There was a fire in an iron stove placed in the middle of the room. The steam which arose from it was quite insufferable, so much so that I was obliged to keep both door and window open to enable me to breathe. The master remarked that it was 'bad to a stranger, but nothing to those who were used to it.'"

Of another, he says:—

"This school is held in the church. I found the master and four little children ensconced in the chancel, amidst a lumber of old tables, benches, and desks, round a three-legged grate full of burning sticks, with no sort of funnel or chimney for the smoke to escape. It made my eyes smart till I was nearly blinded, and kept covering with ashes the paper on which I was writing. How the master and children bore it with so little apparent inconvenience I cannot tell."

Of another, he says:—

"The day-school (which used to be held in private houses) is now held in an old Independent chapel, no longer used for religious purposes, and rented by the master. There was a raised hearth of brick in the room, with a grate on the top, but no chimney. There was a fire of culm burning on it; the heat and vapour made the room almost insufferable to one coming from the fresh air."

Of another, he says:—

"The floor of the chapel was of earth and lime, very uneven and broken: it contained a few pews, a pulpit, a table, and a couple of desks, with a few benches in use, others being heaped together at one end of the chapel; there was a grate full of culm* in the middle of the chapel, but no chimney."

Of another, he says:—

"The room in which this school is held is a most miserable hut, not fit to shelter cattle in, as the thatched roof would be anything but proof against bad weather. The master said that he often suffered from the rain;

* This is the name of the common fuel in Wales, which is anthracite coal made up into balls with clay. It burns without smoke, but with a glowing vapour like charcoal.

and there were large quantities of straw inside the roof to shelter in some degree himself and pupils."

Of another, he says:—

"The boys' free school was held in a most miserable hovel, lighted by four small windows. The floor was of the bare earth and excessively damp. The door was in a very dilapidated state, and the rain was coming through the thatch when I was in the school-room."

Of others, he says:—

"I am about to enter on one of the most painful subjects of my inquiry. It is a disgusting fact that, out of 692 schools, I found 364, or 52·6 per cent., utterly unprovided with privies."

These are not isolated instances. I could quote hundreds of such descriptions of schools situated in all parts of England and Wales. I have myself seen many which are held in cellars, garrets, chapels, and kitchens, badly warmed, wretchedly ventilated, dirty, unfurnished, dark, damp, and unhealthy. Are the miserable hours spent in these miserable places likely to leave good impressions afterwards? Are they likely to create happy, moral, and healthy ideas and associations in the minds of the children? Are they likely to make the children love what they learned in such scenes and places, and remember it with reverence and with a desire to act upon it afterwards? Are they not much rather likely to make the children hate and shun everything which would remind them of the school and the miserable school-day?

28. By far the greatest majority of the criminals wh are convicted every year in England and Wales, are persons *who have never been educated at all.* Very few persons, who have received even a tolerable education, are found among the great numbers annually committed.

29. Whilst throughout the agricultural districts of Western Europe, the children remain in school until they have completed their fourteenth year, and very often until they have completed their sixteenth year, very few even of those children who go to school at all in our agricultural districts continue to attend school beyond their ninth year; whilst very many do not continue to attend them beyond their eighth year. So that of the children of the poor, who do go to school in England and Wales, the greatest number discontinue their attendance long before they have received anything worthy the name of education.

30. The present system is bearing very unfairly, and very oppressively upon many conscientious and benevolent clergymen in the remote rural districts.

The nation is entirely ignorant of the almost marvellous efforts which some of the clergy are making in the remote rural districts, to provide schools for the poor.

Many poor clergymen, with not 150*l.* of annual income, are out of that small stipend supporting their schools and teachers themselves, wholly unaided either by the public or by their neighbours. How they can do it God only knows, but that many of them, in all parts of the country, do effect this prodigy of self-denial, all the inspectors unanimously attest. These good men receive and expect no public praise as their reward. They are labouring unheard of, and unknown by their fellows, and are looking for their reward to Heaven alone.

But what a disgrace it is to us, as a nation, to impose such a burden upon any of our clergy! What a shame it is, that the small stipend of a religious and benevolent man should be made still smaller, by forcing him to pay, what ought to be borne by the nation at large! And what a precarious means of support for these schools! It is not reasonable to expect, that each succeeding incumbent can or will be equally self-denying; and when one fails to give the accustomed support, such a school must necessarily be closed.

Such is a short summary of the state of education of the poor in England and Wales, as attested by the inspectors of schools, by the government and by the clergy. Whilst foreign countries, by the aid of the central authority, have established such perfect systems, and have accomplished such magnificent results, the system of leaving the education of a nation dependent upon the efforts of charitable individuals finds us, in 1849, in the situation which I have described.

I have shown in Chap. IX. of this work, that, notwithstanding the very large size of the primary schools in the towns of Germany and Switzerland (many of them containing as many as *ten* class-rooms and *ten* teachers, and scarcely any containing fewer than *four* class-rooms), there were:—

*In Prussia*

| | | |
|---|---|---|
| 1 primary school for every | 653 | inhabitants. |
| 1 teacher for every | 522 | " |
| 1 normal college for every | 377,360 | " |

*In Saxony*

| | | |
|---|---|---|
| 1 primary school for every | 900 | inhabitants. |
| 1 teacher for every | 588 | " |
| 1 normal college for every | 214,975 | " |

*In Bavaria*

| | | |
|---|---|---|
| 1 primary school for | 508 | inhabitants. |
| 1 teacher for every | 603 | " |
| 1 normal college for every | 550,000 | " |

*In the Duchy of Baden*

| | | |
|---|---|---|
| 1 primary school for every | 700 | inhabitants. |
| 1 normal college for every | 500,000 | " |

*In Switzerland*

| | | |
|---|---|---|
| 1 teacher for every | 480 | inhabitants. |
| 1 normal college for every | 176,923 | " |

*In France*

| | | |
|---|---|---|
| 1 primary school for every | 568 | inhabitants. |
| 1 teacher for every | 446 | " |
| 1 normal college for every | 356,564 | " |

and that supposing we required fewer schools, fewer teachers, and fewer normal colleges than any other country, and that we should be sufficiently provided if we had

| | | |
|---|---|---|
| 1 primary school for every | 700 | inhabitants. |
| 1 teacher for every | 600 | " |
| 1 normal college for every | 400,000 | " |

we should then require, for our population,

23,581 *large* schools,
26,500 teachers, and
41 normal colleges.

There are four principal defects in our present educational system, which I would here more particularly notice.

I. THE WANT OF NORMAL COLLEGES.

When all the normal colleges in course of erection are completed, there will then be only sixteen in the whole of England and Wales. There are only twelve colleges finished, while at the very lowest computation we require forty-one,—each capable of accommodating one hundred students and six professors,—if we are to have a sufficient supply of educated teachers. We should not even then have so many colleges in proportion to the numbers of our population, as the greater part of Western Europe.

Most of the counties and several of the most populous

dioceses of this country have no normal college at all, and are obliged to content themselves with teachers, who have never received anything worthy the name of education, and who are as fit to manage a school and teach children, as they are to drill and command a regiment. Nearly all these men do their scholars much more harm than good.

The smallness of the numbers of our normal colleges is felt all the more, in consequence of the small number of efficient teachers at present in the primary schools, and of the constant change going on in their ranks, owing to the smallness of their pay, and the abject dependence of their situations.

The great demand for teachers, and the imperfect ideas at present afloat of the character of the education required to make an efficient schoolmaster, are rendering several of the few colleges, which have been founded in this country, quite worthless; for the directors of some of these establishments, imagining that it is better to supply a great number of inefficient teachers than a smaller number of efficient and well-educated instructors, or perhaps ignorant of what ought to be expected from a teacher, permit the young students to leave and undertake the charge of primary schools after a year's, and in some cases after six months' residence! Mr. Coleridge, on the contrary, justly considers that the most important duty of the principal of a normal college is, to form the *habits* and *disposition* of his students, and he is well convinced of the soundness of the conclusion, to which all foreign countries have come, viz. that it is ridiculous to hope to remodel the *habits* of a young man, to inspire him with high and religious aims, and to instruct him sufficiently for the important post of a teacher in the short space of twelve months.

The greater part of the first year's residence at the normal college is always required, for the *preparation* of the student's mind, for what is *afterwards* to be instilled. It is the *second*, and still more the *third* year, which is the most valuable period for the development of his character, and for the education of his mind. If we could have more than this, it would be really advisable, but certainly we ought not to have less.

A long training in the normal college not only makes the future teacher much more efficient, but it ensures his remaining longer at his post; for the more thoroughly the habits of his mind are moulded to his future occupations, and the more thoroughly we habituate him to the peculiar life that is marked out for him, the less capable will he be afterwards of changing his career. To imagine, that we can in *twelve months* not only sufficiently instruct, but also religiously and morally educate a young man,—that in *twelve months*, we can change or remodel the habits of his mind, or instil into him so strong an enthusiasm for his profession, as to make him proof against the temptations to forsake it that will present themselves,—is perfectly absurd. Vehrli of Kreuitzlingen, the Frères Chrétiens of Paris, and those master trainers, the Jesuits, all tell us a very different tale.

It would be much better to turn out fewer and more efficient teachers,—men who would be unwilling afterwards to forsake their posts,—than to send out a set of pedantic young men, who have gained a little knowledge and no new habits in the normal schools, and who will be ready to forsake their profession whenever they can do so with advantage to themselves.

Mr. Coleridge, in an interesting report on the normal school at Stanley Grove, speaking of the plan of training teachers, says, that it "proposes *to form* the character, both generally and with especial reference to the scholastic office. Thus principally, yet at the same time to give them every *appropriate* acquirement,—in fact, a very much larger amount of acquirements (though this be a subordinate end) than could be otherwise commanded. Agreeably to this idea, *youths* only are admitted and are kept in training for a period of time measured by years, not months. The force of habit and association—early and long-continued impressions—favourable influences of many kinds—the daily sight and sound of good—the means and opportunity of discipline, moral, physical, and intellectual—such are the advantages, which in this way it is intended to secure; and to these are added every facility for special instruction. Yet must this statement be received with limitation. The object is indeed to *form* the character; yet, as the institution cannot be open to children or very young boys, a groundwork of good must have been laid beforehand. There must be evident signs of towardness in the youth at his admission; for though much may be done for him afterwards, *much* cannot be undone. It is not a school of correction. The principle of selection, therefore, cannot be dispensed with—it rather stands out with increased force."

It will not be necessary for me to speak of the pretended system of training for six months. The utter fallacy of the idea is self-apparent, and still more when instruction only, without any good domestic training, is given, as in some of our so-called training establishments.

But can we do without normal colleges?—I might just as well ask, can we do without teachers? I see no difference whatsoever between the questions. We can do without them certainly, if we are resolved not to educate the people. We may as well hope to educate the people by means of teachers, who have never been trained, as to educate them without schools. Or, if education consists in merely teaching to read and write, and forcing instruction into the child by means of the ruler and the cane, then we may do without normal colleges. Or, if the profession of a teacher is one, for which *any one* is fitted, and to which *any one* may turn as his last shift in the world for obtaining a decent maintenance, then we may do without normal colleges: or, if it is impossible for a badly organised school to do harm, and most grievous harm, and to demoralise, instead of improving youth, then we may do without normal colleges. In short, if the education of the people is a visionary scheme, on which none but enthusiasts speculate, or, if it is doubtful, whether it will advance the cause of religion, morality, prudence, foresight, and order; or, if it is merely a plaything, wherewith to soothe and gratify the people, then assuredly we have no need of normal colleges. But I think very differently of education combined with good government. I look to Europe, and regard the mighty change, which has, since 1800, been wrought in the character of the Swiss, German, and Dutch people, and the great difference between them and the Italians, and I feel confident, it is no dream to hope and believe, that we might effect the same in our own land, if we adopted similar means. But, so long as we commit the education of the poor to a set of men, as ignorant and low-minded as the majority of our present primary teachers are, so long, instead of advancing, we shall positively retard the moral progress of the people. Mere instruction, unaccompanied with the true development of the mind,—the moral and religious education of the man,—is a positive harm. It awakens his intellect sufficiently to render it a powerful and dangerous auxiliary to his unbridled and to his unruly passions; whilst the religious and humanising influences of his soul remaining dormant, leave him like a vessel with its canvas spread, but without a rudder, on a dark and stormy sea. He is then no longer dull, stupid, and totally without capabilities of reasoning, as the labourers in our agricultural districts, but sufficiently enlightened to indulge, not only the mere sensual appetites and demands of his ill-governed body, but the restless, wild, and rebellious promptings of his scarce-awakened and unreflecting mind.

The establishment of normal colleges is of such great importance, that the efficiency of the education of our poor may be considered wholly ruined, so long as we are unsupplied with them; and the efficiency of the normal colleges themselves is destroyed, so long as we continue to send out teachers from them after a twelvemonth's training.

II. THE WANT OF A CERTAIN AND SUFFICIENT MAINTENANCE AND OF AN HONOURABLE POSITION IN SOCIETY FOR THE TEACHERS.

Let me ask, is there anything, if we consider the *majority* of the existing English schools, without choosing out certain honourable exceptions,—is there anything in the present situation of a village schoolmaster in this country, to tempt a well educated man to engage in such a despised and laborious profession, as long as any hope remains of his earning an independent livelihood by any honest, however humble trade?

Is the pay in the majority of the schools good enough?

—Is the support and encouragement the teacher receives from the rich and powerful sufficient to compensate for the want of good pay?—Is the honour paid to the profession of a teacher in England great enough to make up for all or any of the other disadvantages?—Is the want of education so fully understood by the poor themselves, as to insure the teacher their gratitude at least, for his exertions? Is not the contrary of all these suppositions too true?

The salaries in most cases are miserable, and in very many cases so poor, as to oblige the teacher to follow other occupations in connection with his office, in order to gain a livelihood. The teachers in the schools have therefore in most cases hitherto been men or women of such very miserable education, and so utterly ignorant of the nature of their duties, that the name of "schoolmaster" has almost become a byword and reproach: whilst the importance of their work has been so little understood by either the gentry or the poor, that in many cases, they have received no encouragement from the former, while by the latter they have been almost wholly neglected. I know that of late years a great change has been effected, but still it is to be remembered, as I have before said, that hardly one *half* of the country is properly supplied with schools, and that of this half, there are many schools directed by dames or half-educated men, or which are the private enterprises of vulgar and low-minded men, who having failed in every other attempt to gain an honest livelihood, have turned to school-keeping as to their last resource.

In very many cases, I might perhaps say with truth, in nearly one-half of the schools now in existence, the incomes are too poor to induce any *man* to accept the place of teacher, so that the wives of peasants or common mechanics manage them,—women, who have not had the least previous training, and who have all their domestic concerns to attend to while they conduct the imperfect *instruction* of their classes. What is the character of the education given in these schools? Reading, the poorest and most meagre description of writing, a little arithmetic and the most injudicious and injurious description of religious instruction. Whether I am right or not in setting down this class of schools, as answering the description *of half* our present supply of primary schools, I will not say; but it is notable, that the majority of those established in the agricultural districts are only "dame" schools.

Then how are the salaries of the teachers obtained? Generally, either entirely from the precarious and uncertain pay of the scholars, or partly from this source, and partly from a small yearly sum proceeding, either from the school endowments, or from the voluntary subscriptions of inhabitants of the locality, or from the liberality and exertions of the clergymen.

What is the consequence? Even supposing that the teacher is a well-educated man, which is very rarely the case, he is entirely and wholly dependent on the caprices, either of the clergyman of the parish, or of the local subscriber or subscribers to the school, or of the parents of his scholars. Now, although it is most important that the religious ministers should be *ex officio* inspectors of their schools and of the religious instruction given there, still it does seem to me, that it is putting the teacher into a most invidious position, to subject him to the uncontrolled caprice of any individuals of his locality. What is and what must often be the consequence of such a position? It very often happens, that the teacher of a school, from his previous training, supposing him to have had any, knows very much more about the minor details of school management, than either the clergyman or the inhabitants of the locality. In such cases he very naturally wishes to follow out the directions, which have been given him, by the learned professors of the normal college where he was educated. If the clergyman who has not been educated in pedagogy, should think differently, a dispute often ensues on some point of school management, and either the parish dismisses an able teacher, or the teacher is rendered discontented, and is hindered in the improvement and instruction of his children. As long as his position is one of such dependence on the whims of those about him, his usefulness and contentment must both be lessened. There ought always to be an impartial arbitrator between the teacher and those who object to his method of instruction, &c.; and that arbitrator ought to be well educated in pedagogy, and removed above the influence of personal enmities and personal vexation. Whether this arbitration be vested in the government, or in the school societies in London, it matters little; but it certainly ought to be vested in some person or persons at a distance, who might defend the teachers against unreasonable caprices, and at the same time take care that they performed their duty, and that all sound objections to them were immediately attended to. To leave them in their present position is to cripple their powers of doing good, and to make the profession contemptible in the eyes of every honest, independent, and intelligent man.

In all foreign countries this evil is most carefully guarded against. The teachers cannot be discharged from their situations, unless the central power concurs with the local authorities; but every complaint of the local committees, or of the local clergy, is *immediately* attended to; their causes are investigated by the inspectors, and full redress is afforded for every real grievance. In Germany, as I have shown, the parochial clergy are *ex officio* inspectors of their several schools; and if the teacher neglects his duty, or is guilty of any unbecoming conduct, they have first the right of reprimanding him; and if that reprimand fails in convincing him of the impropriety of his conduct, they can report him to the inspector of the district, who immediately examines into the complaints, and then, if he finds those complaints well founded, he reports to the provincial consistory, which at once dismisses the teacher. In this way, the clergy are insured good teachers, and these latter are defended against the whims and caprices of peevish or ignorant clergy. In France, Holland, Denmark, and Switzerland, the teachers are also most carefully protected from subjection to local influence; whilst in all these countries local influence and local superintendence are considered most necessary adjuncts to the moderating influence of the central power.

If a teacher feels, that his continuance in office depends entirely on the pleasure of people, who are living near him, his independence and honesty are generally diminished; his power of doing good is curtailed; his satisfaction with his work and with his situation is lessened; his own education in a college is in a great measure thrown away, by making others, who have not been so educated, the directors of the instruction given in his schools. It degrades and enervates the teacher to subject him so entirely, as we now do, to the influence of any local authority, which is much oftener exercised in a manner biassed by personal feelings, than that of some person living at a distance. Of course, if we are to employ teachers as uneducated and low-minded as the majority of those employed at the present day, it makes little matter by whom the control of them is exercised; but *if* we are desirous to make the office such, that men, like those educated by Sir James P. Kay Shuttleworth at Battersea, or by Mr Coleridge at Stanley Grove, shall be willing to accept it; and if we are desirous of increasing the efficiency of such men, when they have accepted situations, we must alter this state of things.

Besides this, good salaries ought to be provided for the teachers, independent of the school-pence, or *schulgeld*, as the Germans call it; and the amount of these payments ought to be defined by other authorities than the school-masters, whilst these latter should be interested in the increase of the numbers of their scholars, by being permitted to receive, as additions to their fixed incomes, the school-pence of all their children. At the same time it ought to be provided here, as in France, and Germany, and Holland, that when the parents are really too poor to pay these small sums, their children should be allowed to attend the school free of expense.

But what will be the consequence of our pursuing our present course, of leaving the payment of the teachers entirely dependent on the precarious payments of individuals? Why, so long as we do this, the educated men, who leave our normal colleges, will find scarcely any situations worth their taking; and if they do accept some of the present miserable places, it will be with discontented, and justly discontented minds, and with a resolution to leave as soon as the term of their apprenticeship is ended. For we need not think, that good situations will be wanting to them. There are plenty of warehouses in Lancashire where, with their education, they would be received with joy, and where they would obtain 50*l.*, 80*l.*, or 100*l.* per annum, for work not one-half so laborious as the management of a village school. The difficulty of applying for and obtaining such places exists no longer. The letter of application for a place in Manchester, sent by a schoolmaster of the south, formerly cost 14*d.* or 15*d.*, or even 18*d.*; now that letter may be sent for 1*d.*; and the journey, which a few years back, from its expensiveness and tediousness, was a positive check on emigration to those great and ever-increasing fields of labour, may now be accomplished, even from the shores of Sussex, in half a day and for a few shillings.

The Committee of Council has attempted to do something to remedy this state of things; but what can it effect with only 125,000*l.* per annum in its hands, out of which it has to support its system of inspection, to assist in building schools and colleges, and to aid the teachers of the whole of Great Britain?

*We may, however, rest assured that, until we provide a better situation for our teachers, we shall never be able to improve the profession, or to renovate the schools.*

An income of at least 50*l.* per annum, the school-pence, a comfortable house, a garden, and a field for a cow, ought to be *secured* to every teacher; and until these are secured to them, we shall never be able to obtain educated men for the village schools. I know that several of the nobility are paying more than this. There are several instances, which have come under my own observation, where they are paying more than *double* this sum: but then, in these instances, gratifying as they are, there is no *security* for the con tinuance of this payment; and even if it were certain that each successive head of the house would take an equal interest in the school; yet still the position of the teacher is one of the most distressing dependence, where he is afraid, at each step, of the parents of his scholars misrepresenting him to his patron; where he is fearful at each word of giving offence; and where, consequently, his position is in the highest degree enervating and injurious to his moral character, which ought to be at least as fully developed in him as in any other citizen of the state.

But until the state will come forward and assist the Church and the dissenters, as is done in France, Holland, Germany, Switzerland, and Austria, in providing for the maintenance of the schoolmasters and schoolmistresses, things must go on as at present.

III. The want of local and public inspection.

Before I venture to offer any remarks on the necessity of inspection, let me remind my readers of the state of inspection in several of the European nations. In Holland, there are EIGHTY inspectors appointed and paid by government, who have, in reality, the management of the education of the country. In France, besides the local committees of inspection, there is one head inspector in each department; and where the number of schools is too great for one inspector to examine them sufficiently often in the year, one or two assistants are joined to him, according to the size of his department. At present, there are altogether in France 200 inspectors appointed and paid by government; and I find that the number of schools inspected and reported on by them in 1843 was 50,986. In Switzerland, there is in each canton at the seat of government a central board of inspectors, numbering generally about four or five, who have the inspection of all the primary and normal schools of the canton: and in each parish of the canton there is a school society, formed of the parish clergy or priests and several heads of families, who inspect the progress of *each individual* child in the commune and report to the central board, who in their turn report to the government. In Prussia, the clergy or priests are *ex-officio* inspectors of their respective parish schools, whilst there is also in each union a regular inspector, appointed by government, whose duty it is to visit all the primary schools of his canton several times in the year, and to report on them to a magistrate of the department within which his canton lies. This magistrate is also the general inspector of the department; he can, if he thinks it necessary, visit any of the schools or normal colleges in his department; he corresponds with the inspectors of the cantons in his department and with the parochial clergy, receives their reports, and reports himself to government on the state of education in his department. The same plan is also followed out in all the other German states; and in Bavaria, with only 4,000,000 of inhabitants, there are 286 inspectors.

Now, the very fact of this general adoption in foreign countries of the plan of a central and local inspection, is an *à priori* argument in its favour; and whoever reads the reports of the few inspectors we have yet appointed in England and Wales, will clearly understand, much better than from any thing I can say, the necessity of this encouragement and assistance to the clergy and teachers of this country. Where the religious minister is a good and zealous man, the school is certain to receive some part of his attention; but in very many cases it is not possible for him to visit it often; whilst from the trustees of the school, gentlemen engaged sometimes in the pursuit of pleasure, and sometimes in business or in the management of estates, there is often still less chance of the teacher receiving any notice, advice, or encouragement. If the teacher is a really honest man, and sincerely desirous of promoting the good of the school, he may perhaps go on tolerably well without any supervision; but how much more encouraged would even such an one feel, if he knew that there was some one to whom he could always apply for advice, and if he felt that his country was watching his exertions, and that his success was certain of meeting with reward and encouragement! France has fully comprehended this; and her government stimulates the exertions of all the teachers by the distribution, annually, of a number of silver and bronze medals to those who are the most praised by the inspectors for the management of their school classes, and for the progress of their children.

But if inspection is an encouragement and a stimulus to good and honest teachers, still more truly is it a check and restraint upon the undeserving. It may be said there is that restraint at present—that there are the religious ministers. This, in some cases, is no doubt true; but will any one deny that there are many cases where the religious ministers are forced,—by their having already far more to attend to than they have time or strength for,—wholly to neglect this additional demand upon their exertions? Will any one deny, also, that where there are lay trustees to a school, who ought to watch the progress of the schoolmaster, the duty of inspecting the school is still more frequently neglected, and that there exist at the present time numerous examples of schools possessing ample funds for the payment of the teacher and the support of the school, which, from the want of some person, whose business it is to visit and inspect them from time to time, and to inquire into the character and conduct of the teachers,—have degenerated in the most distressing manner; the teachers sometimes becoming careless, or immoral, sometimes neglecting the school altogether, or leaving it in the care of half-instructed monitors, whilst they themselves attend to other concerns; and sometimes venting their evil passions on the children,—thus diminishing the numbers of the school, and positively rendering it to the few, who remain, a miserable recollection, which they associate with the highest and most humanising principles of a Christian education. In this way many schools throughout the country have become hot-beds of immorality, rebellion, and infidelity, and, instead of promoting the progress of religion and civilisation, have been the most fruitful source of the corrupting principles now at work among the poor.

But what is the state of things in England in the *great majority* of the schools throughout the country, with the exception of the 3226 schools now open to the inspection of the Committee of Council? They receive no public inspection, and very often *no local inspection whatever*. To conduct the inspection of all the schools necessary for this country in a *tolerably* efficient manner—I mean in any manner that could be compared to the inspection the Swiss, French, German, Danish, and more particularly the Dutch schools receive—would require a force of at least 150 inspectors for England and Wales, and this force would even then be little more than one half as great, as the number of inspectors now employed by the Bavarian government. How wholly inefficient our present system of inspection is, will appear therefore, when I mention, that there are only 19 inspectors for the whole of England and Wales!

There is still another reason why an official force of inspectors ought to be supported, either by the school societies themselves, or by government, viz. the unfitness of many of the clergy to act as *sole* inspectors of the schools. I will explain myself. Is a gentleman, who has never given his attention to the practical details of school management, who has never studied the respective merits of different methods of teaching, who has never paid any attention to many of what ought to be the subjects of instruction in every school or to the minutiæ of class direction, school order, manners of master, manners of children, and all the numerous details so important to the sound progress of a school, and upon all of which the teacher has been carefully lectured in the normal colleges by able professors, who have themselves given a serious and deep attention to these matters—is, I repeat, a gentleman who has never in his life given any attention to these matters, and who may actually have a fancy for methods and plans of instruction, totally at variance with all that the teacher has been taught, and who at any rate cannot possibly have any good standard of perfection whereby to measure the progress of his school, or the excellence or faultiness of the methods pursued by the teacher—is such a gentleman the best qualified, is he at all qualified to be the *sole* inspector of a school? I say *sole*, because I willingly allow, that although other inspectors are necessary, the clergy and dissenting ministers ought undoubtedly to be *ex-officio* local inspectors of their schools; for they and they alone are the proper guardians, fosterers, and inspectors of the religious part of national education. On this ground, in Austria, Germany, France, and Switzerland, the parochial clergy and priests are always the *ex-officio* guardians and inspectors of their parochial schools.

What I wish to say is, that this inspection, *wholly indispensable as it is*, is not sufficient. We require, in addition, a body of men who, by constant attention to all the subjects of instruction and to all the minutiæ of school management, and by constant attendance at, and examination of the best normal, model, and parochial schools, should be well-versed in all that is necessary to the perfection of a school, and should thus be able —*in conjunction with* the clergy and ministers of their different districts,—to *advise* and *counsel* the teachers; encourage them to persevere when in a right course, and to check them when pursuing a wrong one; to prevent a school being ruined from want of superintendence and *surveillance;* to stimulate the teachers to renewed exertions by reporting all those who deserved honourable mention, and by thus drawing the attention of the public upon them; to acquaint government of those poor districts, wholly without school and destitute of local funds, which require its assistance, and in these different ways to guard against the possibility of any district being left to languish without the means of obtaining a sound and Christian education.

The duty of such inspectors would be to advise the teachers and religious ministers; to receive the reports of the latter on the religious and moral conduct of the schools; to act as arbitrators between the teachers and the school committees; to examine the schools, and to report to the nation on the progress of national education.

This would encourage both teachers and clergy, some

of whom in distant parts of the country, unnoticed and forgotten, are making efforts so laudable, so truly noble and so Christian, as to demand the nation's gratitude, of whom we now know little or nothing; but who ought to be held up as bright examples to stimulate others to do likewise. It is to be hoped, that if we ever do arrive at that happy time when the government, the clergy, and the dissenting ministers will aid one another in carrying out this great work, that we shall then adopt that plan, which is pursued with so much advantage in France at the present moment—I mean the awarding of medals signifying the approbation of the sovereign, and through the sovereign, of the people, to those teachers, who labour most successfully in the cause of the education of the people. Our Committee of Council might do it now in the few schools, which are open to them, and conjointly with that, they might publish a short monthly or quarterly official gazette of education, mentioning those, who have gained this recognition of a nation's gratitude, and giving the results of the examinations in the normal colleges for brevets of admission to the profession of schoolmasters, as well as all other interesting intelligence connected with the progress of education during the past month or quarter. Each inspector should be invited to send a short account of the school which he considered most deserving notice in his district, or of some one, in which some ingenious and excellent method of teaching was employed, or a short treatise on some subjec connected with school management. By these means, and especially by encouraging teachers' conferences, of which I have spoken before, the feeling of a great and united body would be encouraged among the teachers; no one would fancy he was forgotten, but each would feel that the country was interested in his individual success.

Nor is this any ideal picture of what national education in England might be, would all but unite in furthering it; for all this, and much more than this, is actually effected abroad, and with the greatest success and happiest results.

I am not aware of any foreign country which has seriously undertaken the education of its people, that has not recognised the absolute necessity of maintaining a large body of efficient and well-trained inspectors, who should act in concert with the local clergy and local authorities, and who should be at the same time a check upon, and an encouragement to the schoolmasters. Far from wishing these inspectors to be in the stead of local influence, I am only desirous of seeing them acting in unison with the clergy and dissenting ministers, aiding them to foster and promote the moral and religious progress of their several localities. The only reasons we have not long since had an effective body of these inspectors, are, that the state has not sufficiently explained what would be the special duties of those officers; that the clergy have consequently feared that the *surveillance* of their parochial education, which is one of their principal duties, would be taken out of their hands, instead of the inspectors for the Church being chosen from the clergy themselves, and being directed to act in unison with them; and that the whole country has had far too low an idea of what the education of the people ought to be, so that we have imagined any one fit to be a schoolmaster; that it did not matter what the teacher did, after he was put at the head of the school, and therefore, that he required neither checking nor encouraging in any way or by any person.

I have thus briefly sketched the present state of the means of educating the people of England.

What is the Committee of Council on Education doing to improve this state of things?

When we have scarcely one half as many schools, as we require, not one third as many teachers' colleges as are necessary, and not one third as many inspectors as we require; when many populous districts have no school, and cannot raise any thing towards building one; when most of our teachers are ignorant men or women, and are so poorly paid, that it is hopeless to persuade any well-educated man to take their places; when most of the normal colleges we do possess, are so poor, that they cannot afford to support a sufficient number of professors, or to keep the students long enough to give them an education nearly adequate to fit them for their work; when most of our schools and colleges are wretchedly provided with books, furniture, and apparatus; and when nearly half of our present school-buildings are disgracefully wretched and inefficient; all that our government is doing, is to dole out 125,000*l.* per annum to remedy the numerous and great deficiencies I have mentioned! When one considers the enormous sums, which are being expended annually, both by the governments and parishes of Western Europe, in promoting the education of the poor, and when one regards the present state of education in England, it is hardly possible to believe, that in the nineteenth century the efforts of the English government in this great work should be so miserably and absurdly inefficient. If the Committee of Council is really to remedy the consequences of our past neglect, and to supply us with even a moderately efficient system of public education, it will require funds to the amount of at least 3,000,000*l.* per annum. If it had even this amount of funds at its disposal, it could not even then, under the present system, unless local activity were very much increased, supply us with the means of public education so well, as the educational systems of the countries of Western Europe, combining as they do local and central activity, have supplied those countries.

I would not be understood to disparage in the least the very great and admirable labours of the Committee of Council. Nearly all the advancement which national education has made during the last ten years in this country, may be said to be owing to the labours of men connected with that Committee. Fifteen years ago, before the Committee of Council began to show what national education really meant, and how it was to be effected, there was not a single teachers' college in England or Wales; there were scarcely fifty teachers in either country, who were even *decently* acquainted with the subjects or methods of instruction; the schools were wretchedly arranged; most of them were *wholly* unfurnished, and without even a desk or form, unventilated, badly situated, and wretchedly built; inspection of schools was not thought of; no one knew its use or its necessity; there was not one inspector in England or Wales; any one was thought good enough to be a teacher; the idea of a previous training being necessary was ridiculed; the subjects of instruction were confined almost always to reading, writing, arithmetic, and the most meagre and injudicious Bible instruction, and the books used in the schools were ridiculously poor.

About ten years ago, my brother, Sir James P. Kay Shuttleworth, reformed the industrial school at Norwood, and accepted the situation of Secretary to the Privy Council on Education, and shortly afterwards he and Mr. Tufnell founded the first English normal college at Battersea. Since that time twelve normal colleges have been built—four others are in the course of completion—nineteen inspectors have been appointed —3226 schools have been opened to public inspection, —several thousand monitors have been trained—many schools have been furnished with parallel desks, rising one above another—many school-rooms have been well furnished with maps, books, and apparatus—many excellent school-books have been published—the subjects of instruction have been extended—many excellent school-buildings have been raised—people have begun to be ashamed of the "dame schools"—and as far as the amount of funds raised by voluntary efforts will allow, the country has, under the teaching and example of the Committee of Council, improved the means for the education of the people.

All this has been effected, be it remembered, notwithstanding the opposition of some, the lukewarmness of others, the taunts of those who sneer at education, the fears and outcries of the religious parties, and the slanders of those who wished to make the education of the people a means of increasing their own influence and power. Nothing but an enthusiastic earnestness of purpose, and inflexible impartiality, has enabled the committee to succeed thus far.

But to enable us to advance any further, we must have improved and very greatly enlarged means. We want, in short, much more money. The ridiculous insufficiency of the funds at the command of the Committee of Council is apparent, when we consider what we have to do. The normal colleges, the schools, and, in fact, all parts of the organisation, by which we are to effect the education of the people, are languishing, and losing the greater part of their efficiency from want of funds. The annual funds of the Committee of Council *would not suffice for the education of Cheshire*, but they have to be sprinkled over the whole of England, Wales, and Scotland.

Moreover, the Committee of Council does not assist those districts which most need assistance; viz.

1. Those, which have either no school or not sufficient school room, and which are too poor to raise any parts of the necessary funds themselves.

2. Those, which are too ignorant or too careless to make any effort themselves.

3. Those, which are so divided between different religious parties as to be unable to make combined effort, however, small.

Now there are vast numbers of each of these three classes of cases, and none of these are assisted at all by the Committee of Council, and yet these are the very cases which more than any others stand in need of assistance.

And even in those cases, in which the Committee might, in accordance with its constitution and regulations, render assistance, its capability of doing so is confined within very narrow limits, owing to the absurdly small funds put at its disposition, amounting as they do to only 125,000*l.* per annum.

We want a system, which would create us at least twice as many schools, as we have at present; which would enable the towns to establish large schools containing each of them ten to fourteen teachers and class-rooms, where the children might be well classified, and assist instead of hindering one another's improvement;

we want a system, which would enable us to pay our teachers so well, that we might hope to see men of ability entering the profession; which would enable us to support our normal colleges efficiently, to supply each of them with a sufficient number of professors, and to keep the students in them at least THREE years; which would enable us to inspect each school in the country several times a year, and to publish a *public* report once every year, on the progress of each teacher and school in every part of the country; *which would enable us to distribute copies of the report on each county among all the religious ministers, teachers, and magistrates of the county, in order to interest them all in the progress of the schools around them;* which would enable us to furnish every school throughout the country with desks, forms, maps, books, all necessary apparatus, and with a good play-ground and garden; and though last, not least, *which would enable us to educate* GRATUITOUSLY *the children of all those poor, who cannot afford to pay any thing for the instruction of their offspring.*

The educational systems of the nations of Western Europe have enabled those countries to realise all these great objects. We, however, are still far removed from the attainment of this end. Surely it is not impossible for us to accomplish, what nations less rich and less active than ourselves have succeeded in effecting.

The *possibility* no one doubts. The only question to be solved is, by what means is this great end to be attained?

But difficult as the solution of the question, "How hall we effect the education of the people?" undoubtedly is, it would be the extreme of folly to imagine, that there is no solution of it, *but a revolution;* and that what Germany, Holland, Norway, Sweden, Denmark, and Austria have accomplished in times of social tranquillity, cannot be undertaken here, until, as in France and Switzerland, a social earthquake has levelled the obstructions to the settlement of this question. Still, though I believe that we want in England nothing but the will, and though I am convinced that it would be easy to carry out this great work of social reformation did that will exist, I freely confess that I see no prospect of its being done, until the people accomplish it for themselves; as I see it opposed by the bigoted sectarianism of one party, by the ignorant hostility of a second, and the selfish ambition of a third, by the blind indifference of a fourth, and by the luke-warmness of even its real friends.

Let it not be thought, that I am at all desirous of superseding local efforts, or of taking the direction of the parochial schools out of the hand of local authorities; far otherwise: I only wish to see the local efforts aided, where without aid they are confessedly impotent, and a security given to the country, that some one shall provide for the wants of those localities, which cannot do anything for themselves.

Nor do I wish to interfere with the educational societies further than we now do, that is, by assisting them in every possible manner; by assisting the diocesan boards to realise their present desire to establish and support normal colleges, and by assisting the Church and the Dissenters to educate efficient teachers for their schools, and to provide an efficient system of inspection for them all. Government ought to give every possible guarantee to the different religious bodies, that it will not attempt in any way to undermine the influence, which they legitimately claim to exercise over the religious education of the people, whilst at the same time it should require sufficient guarantees, that the secular education of the people shall be properly attended to.

But whilst the church and the dissenting bodies both continue so suspicious of all government interference whatever, what can we hope to do? Without the aid of Government, I have shown that the efforts to raise sufficient funds for the education of the people have always failed and must always fail, and that on the other hand, the government will always be crippled in its efforts to promote national education, if it does not act cordially with the religious bodies, and if it attempts to carry on the work alone. I sincerely hope, then, that it will not be thought by any, that I am desirous of undermining the influence of our clergy, or that I think the education of the country can be carried on without their most cordial co-operation. I fully agree with them that the great end of all human education is to develop the religious character of mankind, and I cannot wonder, that they are suspicious of every public interference, which appears to overlook this great truth. But let them take great heed, that this suspicion is not carried too far, and that it is not expressed, when no cause for it exists; let them avoid exciting a belief, that their opposition does not proceed from this holy feeling, but that it is stimulated by the desire of raising their order, and increasing their political influence. If such a suspicion ever attaches itself to them, from that day the fall of the church will be sealed.

We stand on dangerous ground. We know not now how far the mine has been excavated. We know not how strong the enemy is; but certain it is that a spirit omnipotent for evil, a spirit of revolution, irreverence, irreligion, and recklessness, and, more dangerous than all, a spirit of unchecked, unguided, and licentious intelligence is abroad, which will be the most dangerous enemy, with which Christianity has hitherto had to cope. Remember, that it is utterly impossible in these days to stop the rapidly unfolding intellect of the people, even if it were desirable, and that *uneducated* intellect is the worst enemy to the best interests of mankind. Cheap literature, which may be had for the asking, cheap postage, cheap and rapid communication between different districts, the continually increasing interest, which the people take in political transactions; the lessons, *the practical lessons*, they are daily receiving on the effects of combination, and the wholly unfettered exercise of thought and speech in this country, have utterly precluded the possibility of their remaining stupefied, and have ensured their *intellectual* advancement beyond a doubt. Cannot we, then, see the consequence of all this? If religious teachers are not found, and that soon, for this people, where will the church be fifty years hence? Where the French church was in 1796 —overthrown by an infidel multitude. Can any one think our social condition to be compared to that of Holland? Can any one look on, for the next half century, without dismay? Are not the cause of religion, the cause of morality, the cause of social order, and the future prosperity of this country, all compromised, deeply compromised, by our present inaction?

And yet what are we doing? Behold us, in 1850, with one of the most pauperised, demoralised, and worst educated people in Europe; with the greatest accumulated masses in the world; with one of the most rapidly increasing populations in the world; behold us, in 1850 developing our productive powers, giving the most tremendous stimulus to our manufactures and our population—resolved to turn the North into one vast city—to collect there the labourers of the world, and to leave them without a religion! Not only are we fearfully careless of the best interest of our brethren, not only are we acting, as if we were ourselves convinced that our religion was a lie; but we are blind to the absolute necessities of the commonwealth. The very heathens would have laughed our policy to scorn. They all saw, that even if there were no God, it was necessary to invent one for the peace of mankind; they bound their people by religious formulas, wanting although these were of all true vitality; whilst we, in an age of the world when the intelligence of the multitude is advancing with giant strides, we stand still, saying to one another, it is impossible to do anything with our neighbours, for this party differs from one religious dogma we have started, and that party differs from another: each thus assuming for himself that perfection and that infallibility, which he scorns his neighbour for pretending to; whilst, alas! all are too ready to omit the inculcation of the weightier matters of the law—judgment, and justice, and mercy.

Moreover, the very genius of the Protestant religion requires, more than any other ever did, that its members should be educated, in order that they should be influenced by it. The different religions of the old world and the Roman Catholic religion have retained their hold upon the mind of the multitude by striking and affecting ceremonies, and by means of the senses have established their empire over the spirit of mankind. But Protestantism has thrown aside almost all, and many forms of Protestantism have thrown aside all the ceremonies, which so strongly affected the mind of the unthinking people, and which so powerfully contributed, and in many countries at the present day still so very powerfully contribute, to excite a reverential and religious feeling among the ignorant; and we boast, that ours is not a religion merely of the feelings, but peculiarly one of the understanding. But do not Protestants perceive, that in order that an intellectual religion should affect the people, it is absolutely necessary, that their intellects should be fitted for the exercise, or that the religion will lose its hold upon them and be entirely neglected? What has contributed to the spread of many of the lowest kinds of dissent in this country? Simply because they have appealed to the *feelings* of the people. And so it will be, as long as we offer an intellectual and spiritual religion to a people incapable of reflection or of thought, and who cannot take any pleasure in a service, which to them appears cold, meaningless, and formal. In this way does the English Church contribute to the increase of the Ranters, the Mormonites, and all the wild and visionary enthusiasts, who have so great a hold upon the minds of the people in North Wales and in our manufacturing and mining districts, and who know right well, that a religion, which appeals to the feelings and passions, is the only one which can have any influence over an ignorant multitude. It is impossible for the intellectual and unimaginative Protestantism of the English Church ever to affect the masses, until the masses are sufficiently educated to dispense with all need of mental excitement, which they never will be able to do, until they can think. If, then, the Protestants of England are not willing to prepare the people for the reception of our pure and spiritual religion, and as there can be no doubt that some form of religion, even although erroneous, is better for mankind than the absence of all religion whatsoever, it surely would be better for us, if we had the ceremonial religion of the Romanists, with all its faults, capable, as it would be, of affecting and influencing an unthinking multitude, than the spiritual religion of the Protestants, requiring an educated mind for its reception, when the English Protestants have seemingly resolved they will not educate the people. Much better to have a faith for the people, although it be erroneous, than to have no faith at all.

Why is it, that in Protestant countries like England and America, where nearly all the poor above thirty years of age are wholly uneducated, we find so many of the very lowest forms of the expression of religious belief, as the Mormonites, the Ranters, &c., whilst in countries like Holland, Wirtemberg, and Baden, where the people have been fitted for the reception of a higher species of Protestantism, there is hardly anything analogous to these religious extravagancies? Why is it, too, that in Romanist countries, where an objective religion is given to the people—where the uneducated are not required to accept a religion requiring an educated mind,—why is it, that in these countries there is nothing like the extravagant religious enthusiasm, or the still more lamentable atheism, which is found existing among our poor?

The reason is, that in each case the governments have wisely judged, that it was of primary importance to the people and to the state, that the people should have a faith, and where that faith has not been one, like Romanism, suited to captivate the ignorant, but one, like Protestantism, fitted only for the educated, they have wisely educated their people, so as to fit them for its reception, not in a low and degraded form, but in its highest and purest spiritual development.

I repeat that the great majority of the people in the great towns of this kingdom have no religion. They are not fitted for the reception of Protestantism, or if they are so in a few cases, it is only for the reception of a corrupted and *corrupting* phase of it; and we have taken from them the only religion capable of influencing them in their present state.

How deeply, then, does it behove us, as true Protestants, and especially as members of a church boasting, and boasting truly, to offer to the people the purest and most beautiful form of Protestantism! but a form, whose very purity and freedom from the captivating errors, which have rendered other religions more influential on the ignorant poor, more urgently requires, that the people should be educated to accept it;—how deeply does it behove us, to be tenfold more diligent than Romanist countries, to prepare the people, by means of education, for the reception of its tenets. And yet, alas! Romanist countries have far outstripped us in the eagerness with which they are promoting the education of their people. They understand the signs of the times, but we have yet to learn them. Then, and not till then, shall we understand the real necessities of the poor.

I cannot imagine anything more injurious to the clergy, more hostile to the influence they ought to possess over the people; I cannot imagine anything more certain to separate the people from them, than that it should be fancied for one moment, that they oppose government interference (after sufficient guarantees have been offered them that it is not intended to take the direction and surveillance of the moral and religious education of the people out of their hands,) merely from a vain desire to manage and direct the education of the people themselves, especially after they have given such proofs of their utter inability to raise a tithe of the funds necessary for such a purpose. They are doubtless the fit and proper guardians of the religion and the morality of the country, and they are only performing their high duty, when they oppose any measure, which may seem likely to undermine the religious and moral influence they ought to have; but let them be most careful they do not demand more. Let them take care that they do not reject the assistance of government, after having shown the country that they cannot raise one paltry half-million for the primary education of a nation of 16,000,000 souls. Far from thwarting government, it behoves them, *if* they can discern the signs of the times, to be the first to demand the co-operation of the state, and to confess their inability to carry on the education of the people without it, instead of appearing for one moment satisfied with, and still less venturing for one instant to vaunt, the miserably small progress that education has yet made.

First, then, let me again briefly state what we have to do, referring as proof of what I lay down here to the deeply interesting reports of her Majesty's inspectors.

I. We require twice as many schools as we at present possess; nor is this want confined to either towns or country, but is equally felt in each.

II. We require an annual provision for the payment not only of nearly all the teachers we at present have, but for all that we shall find it necessary to appoint for the education of our numerous and increasing population.

III. We require, as I have before shown, annual

funds for the efficient support of at least forty-one normal colleges, for the education of teachers.

IV. We require, also, an annual outlay of 70,000*l.* on the support of an efficient body of inspectors; those for the church-schools being chosen from the ranks of the clergy, with the sanction of the ecclesiastical authorities, and those for the schools of the Dissenters being chosen from among them, sufficient guarantees being at the same time given them, that no one shall be chosen, to whom they can honestly object.

First, then, how can we provide sufficient schoolrooms for the population?

The present plan both of the government and the educational societies is, to wait until some locality provides about two-thirds of the necessary funds and applies for aid, and then to furnish the other third, requiring guarantees for the proper outlay of the money, as well as the right of inspecting the progress of the school. What is the consequence? There are many districts, as the reports of the inspectors only too plainly show, where no one takes the least interest in the education of the young; so that no voluntary local efforts are ever likely to be made, and where, consequently, no assistance is ever likely to be given, and which remain at the present day wholly without schools or teachers;—there are many other districts where there is literally no one, who knows how to make an application, even if sufficient local funds could be raised, the population being wholly composed of small farmers and labourers, or of manufacturing operatives or miners;—and there are many other districts, where, although the clergy or ministers have succeeded in raising two-thirds of the funds necessary for one or two schools, they are *utterly* unable to raise more, and where several more schools are imperatively required; under this class will fall nearly all the larger towns of the kingdom, where, from the vast numbers of the poor, a great number of schools are required, and where it is utterly hopeless to raise sufficient funds from the few inhabitants of the district, who happen to understand the necessity of education. And though it may be answered, that the National Society has assisted several of these districts, even when local funds could not be raised, yet it requires no demonstration to show, how utterly incapable that society is to meet the disheartening deficiency in the manufacturing districts, with the ridiculously small funds at its disposal. Why, it would require at least a million of money to provide schools for the districts in the north, which are *now* unable or unwilling to do any thing for themselves, and are wholly without, or very deficiently provided with, school-room, for the population.

Whenever we do resolve to undertake the education of the country, it will be necessary for government so to increase its force of inspectors, as to obtain information of the exact condition of the means for education in every parish throughout the kingdom. The state of the different parishes should, then, be ranged under the following heads:—

1. Parishes, which are already supplied with sufficient school-room.
2. Parishes, which have some school-room, but require more, and are able to provide what is wanted.
3. Parishes, which have some school-room, but require more, and are unable to provide what is wanted.
4. Parishes which have no school-room, but which are able to provide sufficient.

5. Parishes which have no school-room, and are not able to provide any.

Now, as I have already shown, and as the reports of the inspectors still more clearly show, there is no hope of anything being done in very many parishes capable of great local efforts, unless government requires it of them. As several of the inspectors show, over great tracts of country, there does not at present exist a single school. It is evident, therefore, that the present voluntary system, cannot, with all our efforts, provide the country with schools, and that if we are to have them, *government must interfere and oblige each parish, as far as it is able, and assist it when unable to provide itself with sufficient school-room for its population.*

In each parish, all tenants of houses, whose rent amounts, say to at least 10*l.* per annum, might be made liable to a certain rate, to be apportioned according to the wants of the parish and the number of the householders who are liable to the rate. Each of these householders might have a vote in the election of a committee of eight or ten members, for the administration of the educational expenditure of the parish. Of this committee, the clergy and the dissenting ministers ought to be, as in all European countries, the ex-officio members.

Before this committee, when elected, the inspector for the district should lay an account of the exact state of education in the parish, showing the quantity of school-room required for the population; where the required school or schools should be situated, so as best to suit the convenience of the poor of the parish, and also how many houses for teachers should be provided. The committee might then deliberate, whether it would supply the wants of the parish by mixed schools for the different religious sects, or by separate schools for each sect, and whether it would at once provide for all the schools required, or by the imposition of separate rates in separate years. At these deliberations the clergy, the dissenting ministers, and the inspectors should be entitled to assist, the latter, by affording all necessary information as to the exact wants of the district.

I am firmly of opinion, that were the government to OBLIGE each parish to provide itself with sufficient school-room, and to leave it to the option of the several parishes, whether they would support separate or mixed schools, that there would be little difficulty. Wherever any one party was decidedly too small to establish a school for itself, it would concur in the arrangement for a mixed school. It is when government endeavours itself to decide upon it, that all parties are alarmed, and begin to suspect ulterior designs, and to fear the effects of a scheme, over which they have had no control. All that government should do, *is to oblige each parish, as far as it is able, to supply itself with sufficient school-room*, and to leave to its own decision the *manner*, in which this should be done. I am confirmed in my opinion that mixed schools would not be objected to, if the establishing of them were left to the inhabitants of the different parishes, by the experience I have had in the North, where I have frequently found schools expressly intended for the church, filled partly with the children of dissenters, who did not object in the least to their children remaining, even during the religious lessons given in the school. But whenever a power from without endeavours to force mixed schools upon a locality, then the clergy and the dissenting ministers, and many of the parents, begin to be alarmed. Of course government ought to require, when a school was established for two sects, and the schoolmaster was chosen from the most numerous sect, that the children should either attend the religious lessons given in the school, or should receive daily religious instruction from one of the ministers of their own sect.

In those cases where the committee could not agree to provide a mixed school, and where the minority was too small to support a school for themselves, the majority should be obliged and empowered to levy the rates and build the school, on condition that the minority should be allowed to send their children to the secular instruction, and remove them during the religious instruction given in the school. We should soon find, that the minority would not object to their children attending the secular instruction given at the school, and receiving their religious instruction from their own minister. Many parishes, moreover, would require *several* schools, and in these cases the committee could easily arrange, if desired, that the schools should be appropriated to the different sects, according to their respective numbers.

Where a parish was not capable of doing more than it had already done, or of making any but very inefficient efforts, government ought to be prepared to give the necessary assistance, instead of confining its grants, as at present, to those parishes alone, which are able to raise a considerable part of the necessary funds. But in the poorest parishes, where several schools were required, the householders ought to be consulted, whether they wish to have *separate* or *mixed* schools.

These parish committees might be called on to meet at certain periods, to examine the state of the school-buildings, and to provide, by the levying of a small rate on the householders, for all the repairs required for all the schools and schoolmasters' houses in the parish; and when the population was increased so much, as to require another school, for the building of another school in the parish. The inspectors of the district would inform them of the exact wants of the parish. *It would be also wise to give these parish committees the power of requiring the attendance of all the children at school between certain ages, and of enforcing that attendance, whenever they saw fit to do so.* In many districts, the parochial authorities would not object to put this regulation into force, while government will be wholly unable for some time to enforce a general regulation of this kind. The people would not object to it, if it issued from themselves, although they would call it unwarrantable interference on the part of government. And although, doubtless, very many districts would not consent to enforce such a regulation for some years to come, yet it would be a great gain to the country, if the inspectors could induce *any* of the towns or parishes to make such a regulation. But, whether they would do so or not, yet a general encouragement would be given to parents to send their children, if the inspectors reported yearly to the committees the names of those parents who neglected this duty, and urged the members of the committees to use their influence with them in inducing them to allow their children to be educated.

The mere fact of the attention of their parish being directed to their negligence would induce many parents, who are now wholly careless about it, to promote the education of their children, by sending them to the parochial schools.

Another thing which might, with great advantage, be left to the decision of these parochial committees, would be the fixing of the amount of the weekly school fees. They would be better acquainted, than any other persons, with the exact condition of the inhabitants of the parish, and with the sums they would be able to pay. A power ought, however, in all cases to be given to the clergy or dissenting ministers, in conjunction with the schoolmasters, to allow those children to attend the schools, whose parents were notably too poor to pay any part of the settled weekly fees, and in these cases, the parish committees should be required to pay the fees to the teacher out of the parochial school funds.

In all those cases where there was in a parish a national school, or a school belonging to some sect of the dissenters, and the numbers of the other sects in the parish were very small, the committee would inquire of the minister of the sect, to which the school belonged, whether he would allow the children of other religious denominations to attend the secular instruction given in the school. In very many cases, this would be done willingly, but where it was refused, the committee should, unless the numbers of the other sects were too small, be required to establish another school in the parish.

Where such permission was granted, then the parochial committee should be required to support such school, and provide all the funds necessary for its repair, for the salaries of the teachers and for the necessary apparatus, &c.

But how should the teachers for these schools, and for all the schools in the country, henceforward be chosen? In the case of all schools at present established, directed by trustees, school societies, religious congregations, or private individuals, I would, of course, leave the selection of the teachers in the hands of the persons in whom it is now vested, reserving for government, however, the right of examining by means of its inspectors the persons chosen, and the power of annulling the election, if the candidate was found upon examination to be unfitted for the exercise of his important duties. In the case of schools erected by the parochial authorities, the teachers should be always chosen, if the school was intended for only one sect, from that sect, by its school committee, and if for several sects, by the minister and members of the school committee, who belonged to the most numerous sect in the parish, subject, however, in every case to the approval of government. When we have a sufficient number of normal colleges, of course no person should be permitted to be a candidate for the situation of teacher, but one, who had been educated in such a college, and who had obtained a certificate from its director and professors of high moral character, and of satisfactory intellectual attainments.

It is very important that government should have the right of examining every candidate for the situation of a schoolmaster, and the power of rejecting him, if found upon examination unworthy of the situation. Until government is entrusted with this privilege, we shall always be liable, in the event of the trustees or managers of a school being careless, (which does and will constantly happen) to have men chosen, who not only are wholly unfitted by their want of any previous education, but who are capable of doing the greatest possible mischief to the children committed to their care, by their exceeding low moral character. I have seen men occupying the post of schoolmasters, who had been elected by the managers or trustees of the schools, and who were positively doing a great moral injury to the children in their schools, and who were unfitted in every respect for their situations.

It is monstrous, that this should be even *possible*, much more that it should be of constant occurrence. But it is the necessary consequence of leaving the selection of the teachers to men burdened with other affairs, who have not sufficient time for a truly laborious and difficult duty, and who, in the generality of cases, are wholly unfit to be judges of the capability of any one for such a post. Imagine one of our country farmers choosing a schoolmaster! The very idea is absurd. And yet, I have seen farmers performing this responsible duty in their capacity of managers of country schools, attended by nearly one hundred children, and choosing men who were unworthy to be even the monitors in the lowest classes. Government need not interfere with the rights of trustees and managers, further than to require to be satisfied of the capability of the candidates, but so far it undoubtedly ought to interfere, making it the law of the land here, as it is in Holland, Prussia, Saxony, France, Hanover, Baden, Wirtemburg, Bavaria, Switzerland, and Austria, that no one should be allowed to be henceforward chosen, as teacher of a school for the poor, until the country had been satisfied of his capability of conducting the religious and secular instruction of a school. Every teacher should be required to obtain a certificate of high moral character from the director of the normal college at which he was educated; a certificate of capability to conduct religious instruction of children from the clergyman or dissenting minister who directed the religious superintendence of the college, and a certificate of capability to conduct the secular instruction of children from the inspector of the district, in which he desired to be a teacher. By this means, followed universally abroad, we should raise the profession of teachers in the public estimation, we should secure a set of men of high character and qualifications for these important posts, and we should raise the standard of religious, moral, and secular education throughout the country.

II. We require an annual provision for the payment, not only of all the teachers we at present possess, but of all those we shall be obliged hereafter to appoint.

Each teacher ought to have a certain salary of at least 50*l.* per annum provided him, as well as a house and garden and the school-fees, which, however, as I have before mentioned, should be so limited by the parish authorities as not to prevent, any, but the very poorest parents, who were unable to pay anything, sending their children to school; and in the case of these parents, the clergy or dissenting ministers should have the power of admitting their children into the schools free of all expense, on ascertaining that their plea of poverty was a true one.

We must provide good situations for the teachers, or we shall never obtain well-educated teachers for the schools.

We should therefore be prepared to provide a salary of at least 50*l.* per annum for every teacher at present appointed to a school, on his presenting one certificate from the clergyman or dissenting minister, who directs his school, of his religious and moral character, and of his capability of directing the religious education of his school; and another from the inspector of his district of his capability to conduct the secular instruction of his school. But no salary should be paid, unless these certificates were first obtained; and in the case of any teacher appointed in future, a third certificate of character should be required to be obtained from the director of the normal college, in which the candidate was educated. Where any school is endowed, the annual income settled on the teacher should be raised, where deficient, to 50*l.* per annum, on condition that he presented the above-mentioned certificates. But even where any school is so endowed, that the income secured to the teacher amounts to at least 50*l.* per annum, the government should demand the right of inspecting the school, and of having a veto on the appointment of any teacher in future.

The reports of the inspectors prove only too plainly, that the country can have no security against the negligence or ignorance of local authorities, until government has the *surveillance*—I do not say the direction, but the mere *surveillance*—of all the primary schools in the country, and a veto on the appointment *and dismissal* of all the teachers in the country. It is what all foreign countries, where education has made any progress, have granted their government, and it is what our government must have sooner or later. Until government has this direct influence on the choice and dismissal of the teachers, the education of the country, left in the hands of careless local authorities, all engaged in other affairs, and having little time to look after the schools, will remain what it is at present —defective, unproductive of any satisfactory results, and in many cases positively hurtful and demoralising.

Of course out of our present schools there would be but few teachers who would be able to obtain the necessary certificates of character and competence; and of the few respectable teachers we have, most of them are at least temporarily provided with sufficient salaries; so that the *immediate* provision required for this purpose would be comparatively very trifling. Now there are several ways in which this annual outlay might be provided, did we but take any real interest in the education of the people. But I confess that, as far as I am able to judge, one method appears to me to offer many advantages that no other does. I have in the course of the observations I have ventured to make on the state of the English poor pointed to the way in which the out-door expenditure of the Poor-Law Unions of England and Wales has been steadily and rapidly increasing. It is needless for me to remark how very much better it would be for the poor themselves, if this relief could be *gradually* withdrawn. The evil effects of a public charity of this kind, in the stimulus it gives to improvidence and carelessness among the poor, is now too generally admitted to need any notice from me. It is however impossible, as I have before observed, to withdraw this relief suddenly. We have, by our own neglect of the poor, fostered the growth of our present pauperism; cruel therefore, in the extreme, would it be to *suddenly* withdraw the stimulant, which we have made necessary to the people. We have pauperised the people by our own ignorant sectarianism, so that we could not, in common justice, or in common humanity, deny them that relief, which we ourselves have rendered necessary.

But we can provide for the education of their children in habits of temperance and prudence, and having done this, we might then withdraw that relief, of which they would no longer stand in need. As I have before shown, the payment of the teachers at first would amount to a comparatively small sum. This sum I think the unions should be required to provide from the poor-rates. Each union should be required to *check the increase* of its expenditure in out-door relief, and to provide for the payment of such of its teachers as obtained the certificates mentioned above. The sums required for this purpose at first would be very small, and as they increased, the out-door relief might be slowly and gradually withdrawn in the same proportion; so that in fifteen years from this time, we might hope to have substituted the expenses required for the support of the teachers in places of honourable independence for a part of the present enormous expenditure on out-door relief. An auditor might be attached to each board of guardians for the purpose of managing the educational expenses of the union; and to this officer the inspector of the district might send information of the teachers whom he, in conjunction with the clergy and dissenting ministers, had deemed worthy of receiving their salaries from the union. Moreover, the unions might be required to supply the school apparatus necessary for those schools, whose teachers had obtained the necessary certificates. Of the apparatus necessary for the use of the school, the clergyman or dissenting minister, who had the direction of the school, in conjunction with the schoolmaster and inspector, might decide; and on an application forwarded by them jointly, the union might be required to furnish the necessary outlay.

This plan would not interfere with private munificence or local benevolence, but it would always provide for the failure of those supplies, and it would secure to a good schoolmaster a sufficient and independent livelihood, so that he would be satisfied with his situation and would be able to devote his undivided atten tion to his duties.

Of course, as I have said before, government should, through its inspectors, require to have a veto on the dismissal as well as on the appointment of every teacher, so as to secure a worthy teacher from all risk of losing his situation through any mere caprice on the part of the local authorities who elected him. The annual expenditure in out-door relief is now about 3,000,000*l.* per annum, and the annual expenditure of the unions in the national education, supposing they supported the normal colleges, provided the incomes of the teachers and the apparatus for the schools, would not for many years amount to more than 2,000,000*l.* per annum, and would not amount to even that sum, until many of the present race of uneducated and low-minded teachers had become superannuated or had died at their posts. If, then, government were to limit the annual expenditure of the unions on out-door relief and on education to 3,500,000*l.*, never allowing them to exceed that expenditure, it is manifest, that the retrenchment of the out-door relief would be so very gradual, as scarcely to be felt, whilst it would not be superseded by the educational expenditure for many years, as population must have considerably increased, ere we would require 3,500,000*l.* per annum for the school apparatus and for the education and support of the teachers of this country, in addition to the present endowments and to the efforts of private benevolence.

There are two reasons, which point to the adoption of a plan such as the one I have very briefly and imperfectly sketched; one is, that we have the organisation necessary to obtain the local funds already provided— an organisation, moreover, admirably suited for the purpose, since it would interest the local authorities in the progress of the education of their localities, as they would not like to feel, that they were bearing such expenses and reaping no returns; another is, that it would not only tend to check the rapidly spreading pauperism of the country—by applying a remedy to the root of the evil; but it would also enforce the *very gradual* withdrawal of that out-door relief, which very greatly contributes to the spread of that disease which is threatening the very vitals of our commonwealth. I look on the withdrawal of this demoralizing expenditure as only second in importance to the education of the people. I believe this expenditure is demoralizing the poor. I am certain, from its effects on districts, which have fallen under my own observation, that it is contributing very greatly to the pauperism, immorality, and degradation of our poor. I have seen it bestowed in the most careless and indiscriminate manner, as if it were intended to encourage to the utmost the spirit of improvidence, now, alas, so generally existing among the poor. I have known poor families (who, if they had not had this injurious benevolence to depend upon, would have provided in their prosperous days against the return of slack times,) living in a careless and profuse manner, whilst their prosperity lasted, without the least idea of providing against a return of adverse seasons, spending all their earnings in drink and good living, with no idea of providence or foresight, knowing that, however careless they were, it mattered little, as they could easily persuade the Union to assist them, if they should be overtaken by adversity. What can be worse than such a system? Can it be too strongly reprobated? Is it not offering a premium to improvidence, and a stimulant to pauperism? I can imagine no better plan of demoralizing the country, than by continuing tc dispense this false, injurious, and absurd charity in our present injudicious manner, and by confining our efforts to our present contemptible sham of national education.

III. We require, as I have before shown, annual funds for the efficient support of *at least* forty-one Normal Colleges for the education of teachers.

As I have mentioned in the last chapter, in several of the dioceses, attempts have been made to establish normal colleges, which have in great measure failed from the want of sufficient funds. Until government comes forward, and assists the bishops and the Dissenters to carry out these laudable efforts, we shall continue without any sufficient supply of teachers fitted to carry out the education of the country. However great the deficiency of these training establishments for the Church, the Dissenters are still worse provided for in this respect. As I have shown, a public provision is set apart for the support of the normal establishments in each of the European countries, of which I have so often spoken, and the benevolence of private individuals is exercised in creating endowments for the education of poor but worthy aspirants to the teacher's ranks. This is a way in which private benevolence may be very beneficially encouraged; but certainly it is not right, that institutions of such great public importance as training establishments for teachers should be left dependent on such benevolence. Government should therefore be prepared to enable each diocese to support at least one good and efficient normal college for teachers for the schools of the Church, where the pupil-teachers should receive at least *three* years' training, before they were permitted to undertake the management of a village or town school. But in addition to these, government should be prepared to provide for the support of a second normal college in the diocese of Bangor for the teachers of the schools of the Methodists in North Wales; of two others in the populous diocese of Manchester, one for the teachers of the Methodists and the other for the teachers of the Baptists and Independents; of another also in the dioceses of Lichfield and Coventry, St. David and Durham, for the education of the teachers of the schools of the Dissenters in these populous districts; of two others in the populous diocese of York, one for the Methodists, and another for the Baptists and Independents; of four in the diocese of London, two for the Church and two for the Dissenters; of two in the diocese of Exeter, one for the Church and one for the Dissenters of Devonshire and Cornwall; and of two others in the diocese of Norwich, one for the Baptists and Independents, and another for the Methodists.

All the government normal colleges should be open to members of any religious sect, who would consent to observe the rules and regulations of the institution; and if any such entered a college set apart for a religious sect different to their own, they should be permitted to be absent from the religious lessons and exercises, on condition that they received regular religious instruction from some religious minister of their own sect.

The whole number of normal colleges required for the different dioceses would then be as follows:—(See next page.)

I will suppose that forty-one colleges for teachers would suffice for 17,000,000 inhabitants. The question then arises, how shall we provide for their support? Now the expenses of the normal colleges and of the annual payment of the teachers, together with the provision of the necessary school apparatus, would not amount, probably, to more than 2,000,000*l.* per annum for our present population. I should be prepared to

*No. of Normal Colleges for the Education of Teachers, which ought to be provided for England and Wales.*

| Diocese. | No. of Normal Colleges. | For what Sect intended. |
|---|---|---|
| St. Asaph | 1 | Church. |
| Bangor | 2 | 1 Church.<br>1 Methodists. |
| Bath and Wells | 1 | Church. |
| Bristol | 1 | — |
| Canterbury | 1 | — |
| Carlisle | 1 | — |
| Chester | 1 | Church. |
| Chichester | 1 | Church. |
| St. David | 2 | 1 Church.<br>1 Congregationalists. |
| Durham | 2 | 1 Church.<br>1 Congregationalists. |
| Ely | 1 | Church. |
| Exeter | 2 | 1 Church.<br>1 Dissenters. |
| Gloucester | 1 | Church. |
| Hereford | 1 | — |
| Landaff | 1 | — |
| Litchfield and Coventry | 2 | 1 Church.<br>1 Dissenters. |
| Lincoln | 1 | Church. |
| London | 4 | 2 Church.<br>1 Methodists.<br>1 Congregationalists. |
| Manchester | 3 | 1 Church.<br>1 Methodists.<br>1 Congregationalists. |
| Norwich | 3 | 1 Church.<br>1 Methodists.<br>1 Congregationalists. |
| Oxford | 1 | Church. |
| Peterborough | 1 | — |
| Rochester | 1 | — |
| Salisbury | 1 | — |
| Winchester | 1 | — |
| Worcester | 1 | — |
| York | 3 | 1 Church.<br>1 Methodists.<br>1 Congregationalists. |
| Total | 41 | 28 for the Church.<br>13 for the Dissenters. |

throw the whole of this expenditure, together with that required for the support of the teachers, upon the unions, substituting it *gradually* for the greater part of the present expenditure of out-door relief, now given in the *encouragement of pauperism.* I would require all the Poor Law Unions, within the different dioceses, to provide the necessary sums for the building and support of the diocesan normal colleges. I would leave the normal colleges of the Church in the hands of the bishops, giving to them the appointment of the principals and professors, and only requiring for government the inspection of the colleges, and a veto on the appointment of the principals. So in like manner with the normal colleges for the Dissenters. Government should select the principals, in the case of the colleges for the Methodists, from the Methodists, and, in the case of the schools for the Congregationalists, from the most numerous of their sects in the diocese; and a requisition signed by a certain number of the ministers of the Methodists or of the Congregationalists should be able to annul the selection, which had been made by the government. In these cases also, government should, of course, require the right of inspection. I have not mentioned the normal colleges for female teachers, because I am willing to own that I see great difficulties in the way of the education of the schoolmistresses. But I think, supposing it is possible to educate efficient schoolmistresses in the same manner as we have commenced to educate the schoolmasters; I mean by selecting young girls of a religious character, and by placing them for three years in a training establishment, that a normal school for mistresses might be established in every two or three dioceses, and the support of it be thrown upon all the unions in those dioceses.

I offer these suggestions with diffidence, knowing the extreme difficulty of the subject, of which I have ventured to treat, but feeling the deep importance of doing something, instead of leaving every thing to work its own way unchecked and unguided. It is impossible to educate the people without good teachers; it is impossible to obtain these, unless we have a sufficiency of training establishments; and it is impossible for us to retain them at their posts, when we have obtained them, unless we provide certain and sufficient salaries for them. Why then do we leave all these things undone? Is it that the country is not so able to bear the expenses of an educational system as Holland or Switzerland? Is it that an educational system is not so necessary for a country like ours, where the masses of poor are so great and so rapidly increasing, as for one, where their numbers are much smaller, and the rate of their increase much slower? or is it, that we do not care for the happiness or improvement of the people, and that we cannot see the evident tendency of events, with our present demoralised masses?

IV. We require a much greater number of inspectors. I have already said so much on this head, that little more remains to be noticed. I have already shown, that we require at least 150 inspectors; and I have also shown, that it is impossible to do anything, until we have ascertained, by their agency, the actual state of education throughout the country. On this point we are at present in the profoundest ignorance. We only know *that we have not more than one-half the schools we require* for our population; but as to the exact wants of the different parishes throughout the kingdom, we know nothing. It behoves government, therefore, to examine this matter, and to increase its staff of inspectors in such a manner, as to enable it to obtain exact statistics of the state of education throughout the kingdom. The State has given the Church a veto on the appointment of the inspectors for the Church schools; it has also given the same security to the Dissenters, that no inspector shall be chosen to visit their schools, to whom they can object.

Let government only come forward and assist the ministers of religion, and let it continue to avoid any attempt to undermine their influence, or to take the entire direction of education into its own hands, and it will meet with no opposition ; but, on the contrary, it will find among them the fullest appreciation of the necessity of education, and of the importance of the State's assisting the religious teachers in giving it to the nation. But as long as the State and the religious ministers exhibit so much distrust, the one of the other, nothing can be done ; but that day will be advanced, when, after the turmoil of a fierce political strife, the people will create an educational system for themselves, and will reject the interference of the clergy altogether, having learned to associate their names with the idea of an unwillingness to advance their improvement ; and the consequence will be, that an educational system will be established void of all religion, thoroughly atheistical and revolutionary in its tendency, and which will completely overthrow all that influence, which it is most important, for the best interests of the people, that the clergy should have on the education of the nation.

Before I conclude, there is one other point, which I would shortly advert to, and that is the need of assistants for the masters. Every schoolmaster, having the care of more than fifty scholars, ought to have the assistance of *well-trained* monitors, capable of conducting the instruction of the younger children. The reports of Her Majesty's Inspectors will show this much better than anything I can say. Now we can never obtain the services of efficient monitors unless we pay them ; for if they are not paid, they will always leave the school before they are old enough to be entrusted with the care of the junior classes. Very few children remain at school after attaining the age of twelve, and it is manifest that a child of twelve years old is not capable of being of much assistance to a schoolmaster. But if we paid the monitors of the village schools about as much as they could earn, if they went to work, we should be enabled to keep them much longer, and should provide useful assistants for the schoolmaster. Here would be an ample field for the exercise of private benevolence. Private individuals should be encouraged to provide small salaries for monitors in all schools, where the number of children exceeded thirty. Moreover, another good result would ensue from this plan. We should in this way educate a number of candidates for the normal colleges, who would be admirably fitted to be trained as teachers, as their education would have all along prepared them for this life, would have accustomed them to its arduous duties, and would thus have ensured their perseverance afterwards in the exercise of the toilsome duties of a profession, to which they had been accustomed from their earliest years. So let it not be said, that in throwing the maintenance of the schoolmasters upon the country, we should take away the means for the exercise of private charity, (I have heard this absurd argument used,) for we should then leave a field open for the exercise of that charity, so vast that all the efforts of the educational societies, and of all the benevolent individuals in the country, would not suffice to supply it.

The committee of council has attempted to enable the parochial schools to educate monitors; but its efforts in this respect, as in every other, are thwarted by the small amount of funds at its disposal.

With these few and imperfect suggestions I take my leave for the present, of a subject on which I may not, perhaps, have offered valuable counsel, but in which I have long taken the profoundest interest. I hope however valueless the observations I have made may be, that they will at least lead some to reflect on the rapid unfolding of the democratic tendency of the times, and of the imperative necessity of providing beforehand for it. I would ask them to regard Europe, where nothing at all similar to our social condition exists, and to ask themselves, why it is that Prussia, Germany, France, Holland, Denmark, Sweden, Norway, Switzerland, and even Austria, have judged it absolutely necessary to consider this great question so seriously; and then I would beg them to turn their gaze on our own land, and to ask themselves, whether it can be really true, that with our social symptoms we are really so miserably provided with educational means as the reports of government would have us believe? Alas! it is only too true. Here, with our vast accumulated masses; with a population increasing by 1000 per diem; with an expenditure on abject pauperism, which in these days of our prosperity amounts to 5,000,000*l.* per annum; with a terrible deficiency in the numbers of our churches and of our clergy; with the most demoralising publications spread through the cottages of our operatives; with democratic ideas of the wildest kinds, and a knowledge of the power of union daily gaining ground among them.

—here, too, where the poor have no stake whatever in the country; where there are no small properties; where the most frightful discrepancy exists between the richer and the poorer classes; where the poor fancy they have nothing to lose and every thing to gain from a revolution; here, too, where we are stimulating the rapid increase of our population by extending and steadying the base of our commercial greatness; where the majority of the operatives have no religion; where the national religion is one utterly unfitted to attract an uneducated people; where our very freedom is a danger, unless the people are taught to use and not to abuse it;—and here, too, where the aristocracy is richer and more powerful than that of any other country in the world, the *poor are more depressed, more pauperised, more numerous in comparison to the other classes, more irreligious, and very much worse educated than the poor of any other European nation, solely excepting Russia, Turkey, South Italy, Portugal, and Spain.*

Such a state of things cannot long continue.

THE END.

www.ingramcontent.com/pod-product-compliance
Lightning Source LLC
LaVergne TN
LVHW020227110826
845151LV00003B/845

* 9 7 8 1 4 2 5 5 3 2 1 0 9 *